CHICKEN SOUP FOR THE GOLFER'S SOUL: THE 2ND ROUND

More Stories of Insight, Inspiration and Laughter on the Links

Jack Canfield
Mark Victor Hansen
Jeff Aubery
Mark Donnelly
Chrissy Donnelly

Health Communications, Inc.
Deerfield Beach, Florida

www.hci-online.com
www.chickensoup.com

We would like to acknowledge the many publishers and individuals who granted us permission to reprint the cited material. (Note: The stories that were penned anonymously, that are in the public domain, or that were written by Jack Canfield, Mark Victor Hansen, Jeff Aubery, and Mark and Chrissy Donnelly are not included in this listing.)

Who Is the Greatest Golfer? Reprinted by permission of *Christian Herald.* ©1967 Christian Herald.

The Promise Keeper, A Change of Heart, Can't Ty Him Down, and *My Course, My Rules.* Reprinted courtesy of *SPORTS ILLUSTRATED:* "The Promise Keeper" by Rick Reilly, *SPORTS ILLUSTRATED,* February 21, 2000. ©2000 Time Inc. "A Change of Heart" by Rick Reilly, *SPORTS ILLUSTRATED,* October 4, 1999, ©1999. Time Inc. "Can't Ty Him Down" by Rick Reilly, *SPORTS ILLUSTRATED,* December 17, 2001, ©2001. Time Inc. "My Course, My Rules" by Rick Reilly, *SPORTS ILLUSTRATED,* April 10, 2000, ©2000. All Rights Reserved.

The One Hundred Greatest Golf Courses. Reprinted by permission of Bruce Nash and Allan Zullo. From *Golf's Most Outrageous Quotes* by Bruce Nash and Allan Zullo. ©1995 Nash & Zullo Productions, Inc.

Daddy Tees Off. From *A Man Called Daddy,* ©1996 by Hugh O'Neill and published by Rutledge Hill Press, Nashville, Tennessee.

(Continued on page 347)

Library of Congress Cataloging-in-Publication Data

Chicken Soup for the golfer's soul, the 2nd round / [compiled by] Jack Canfield . . . [et al.].
    p.   cm.
    ISBN 1-55874-982-9 (trade paper) — ISBN 1-55874-983-7 (hardcover)
    1. Golfers—Conduct of life. 2. Golf—Moral and ethical aspects. 3. Spiritual life.
I. Canfield, Jack

GV965.C4737 2002
796.352—dc21   2002020850

Publisher: Health Communications, Inc.
              3201 S.W. 15th Street
              Deerfield Beach, FL 33442-8190

Cover design by Lisa Camp
Inside formatting by Lawna Patterson Oldfield and Dawn Von Strolley Grove

*With honor and respect, we dedicate this book
to the memory of Payne Stewart,
and to the wonderful family
for whom he cared so much.*

Contents

2. GOING FOR THE GREEN

3. SPECIAL MOMENTS

4. GOLFMANSHIP

5. GOLF LINKS A FAMILY TOGETHER

6. OUT OF THE ROUGH

7. THE NINETEENTH HOLE

Acknowledgments

As we near completion of *Chicken Soup for the Golfer's Soul: The 2nd Round*, we realize it's been a walk down memory lane, providing us an opportunity to revisit the exciting world of golf and the wonderful friends we made while working on the original *Golfer's Soul*. And as before, we received important help from many people.

First and foremost, we thank our families for all of their love and support on this project: It all begins and ends at home. We are grateful to the following people who read and scored nearly two hundred stories and helped make the final selections: Matt Adams, Fred Angelis, Diane Aubery, Pat Barmasse, Don Cummings, Chris Garman, Kelly Garman, Donald Gurley, Brad Halfon, Tom Hazard, Angela His, Mike Johnson, Shannon Karasoulas, Tom Krause, Barbara LoMonaco, Roger McGarrigle, Chris Melcher, Linda Mitchell, Terry Mitchell, Bob Neale, Jeanne Neale, David Norcross, Brien Patermo, Steve Perrin, Chad Sayban and Vickie Rayson.

Patty Aubery, thank you for always being there for us with your love, friendship and support.

Kelly Garman, thanks for making the project go so smoothly. Debbie Merkle, Paul Van Dyke and Jane

St-Martin, thanks for your help and encouragement along the way.

Heather McNamara and D'ette Corona, thanks for your input and expert editing.

Mark Victor Hansen's team: Patty Hansen, Trudy Marschall, Maria Nickless, Laurie Hartman, Michelle Adams, Tracy Smith, Dee Dee Romanello, Dawn Henshall, Lisa Williams, Kristi Knoppe, David Coleman, Laura Rush, Paula Childers, Tayna Jones, Faith Fuata and Shanna Vieryra.

Jack Canfield's team: Kathy Brennan-Thompson, Dana Drobny, Veronica Romero, Cindy Holland, Leslie Riskin, Robin Yerian, Vince Wong and Geneva Lee and the many wonderful interns.

And Jeff's team: Tom Hazard, Linda Mitchell, Shannon Karasoulas, Steve Perrin, Julie Martinez, Brien Patermo, and Diane Aubery.

Bob Carney, you remain an example of what is and always has been good about the golf industry—the people. Thanks for your support and friendship.

Julie Ware, thanks for all of your hard work in the final stages of bringing this project together.

Bret Avery, thank you for all of your help in tracking down permissions at *Golf Journal*.

The entire Health Communications team, your professionalism, dedication and teamwork are an inspiration and make all of our jobs easier.

Peter Vegso, thanks for bringing such a wonderful team together and making this possible.

Terry Burke, it's amazing to think how far we've come together since *Golfer's I*—we couldn't have done it without your insight and hard work. We also thank the entire sales and marketing team for their enthusiasm and expertise.

Christine Belleris, Lisa Drucker, Allison Janse, Susan Tobias and Kathy Grant, thanks for the expert editing.

Larissa Hise Henoch, Lisa Camp, Lawna Patterson Oldfield, Dawn Von Strolley Grove and Anthony Clausi, thanks for the excellent design work.

Kim Weiss, thanks for helping us reach all those golfers.

We also thank those who made the heartfelt effort to submit the thousands of stories, letters, poems and quotes we reviewed for possible inclusion in the book. While we weren't able to use them all, we were touched by each one. Your stories provided us with constant encouragement and reinforcement that we were in the ballpark. Thank you all!

Introduction

The smaller the ball used in the sport, the better the book.

George Plimpton

As we set to work on this heartfelt sequel to *Chicken Soup for the Golfer's Soul,* we paused for a moment and asked ourselves: *What is it about golf? What is it that separates golf from every other sport? What is it that causes its participants and fans to have an experience that is altogether different from that of other endeavors? What is it that elevates our experiences, mostly in retrospect, to something a little more transcendent than just a game played with a ball and sticks?*

A number of answers come immediately to mind. Like, golf is unique because we play it against ourselves. Or, golf is endlessly challenging because of its mostly unattainable standard of par. Or, the beautiful natural settings upon which the game is played make it a singular escape for golfers everywhere. Or, golf is something people can enjoy all of their lives, unlike, say, a Monday night softball league or a pickup game at the local gym. Or how about, golf allows us to forge and strengthen a wide range of relationships in a uniquely relaxing setting. Or maybe golf is different simply because of the countless myths and legends that surround this five-century-old endeavor.

There is certainly some truth in these and many other comparisons between golf and other sports. But they all seem, at least in our humble opinion, to fall a little short. So we delved into the encyclopedias, dictionaries and other oracle-like tomes of golf that offer up endless explanations and metaphors, and we did our best to boil them down to the essence of what it is that sets golf apart, and this is what we came up with.

Golf is a mirror. It is a 360-degree mirror that surrounds our every shot, decision and intention on the course, and reflects it back in perfect clarity. We have no teammates to hide behind, or to obscure our triumphs or failures. We have no defenders to offset our efforts and take their share of praise or criticism. We have no lines to prescribe a specific path towards the goal. We have no one to turn to after a shot and thank or blame. We have only ourselves.

We are faced with situations in every round that allow us a glimpse in this mirror, if we are willing to look. The well-hit shot out of the sand for an up-and-down par, reflecting hours of lessons, hard work and follow-through. The wedged-behind-the-tree-root character test when your partner isn't looking, giving us the opportunity to cheat not just our opponent, but more importantly, ourselves. The choice of how to react after missing that putt for an 8 on the easiest par-4 on the course. The simple joy of watching a son or daughter fall in love with the game. Or the pure exhilaration of a drive hit straight and true.

Perhaps no moment in golf's long and illustrious history better exemplifies these possibilities than the final match of the 1969 Ryder Cup. The most competitive matches in the history of the event, it all came down to the 18th hole on the final day, with Jack Nicklaus and Tony Jacklin both needing to sink their next putt for par. After Nicklaus, who was playing in his first Ryder Cup matches, holed out his four-footer, he graciously, and courageously, conceded Jacklin's two-footer to halve the round and result in the first tie in Ryder Cup history. That simple gesture embodied all that is good about golf, its reflective character and its glorious possibilities.

Jack Nicklaus, acting on behalf of all of us, looked in that mirror, and in that moment, on that illustrious day, the best of the human spirit smiled back. And in our humble estimation, that is *what it is about golf.*

Share with Us

We would love to hear your reactions to the stories in this book. Please let us know what your favorite stories were and how they affected you.

We also invite you to send us stories you would like to see published in future editions of *Chicken Soup for the Soul.* Please send submissions to: *www.chickensoup.com.*

Chicken Soup for the Soul
P.O. Box 30880
Santa Barbara, CA 93130
fax: 805-563-2945

We hope you enjoy reading this book as much as we enjoyed compiling, editing and writing it.

1

THE
FIRST TEE

*I can sum it up like this:
Thank God for the game of golf.*

Arnold Palmer

Who Is the Greatest Golfer?

For the first time in my personal golfing history I had broken 90. Because of it, I couldn't sleep. In the midnight darkness I nudged my sleeping wife, "Can you believe it?" I cried. "I'm no longer a duffer! The secret of golf is simply a matter of . . ."

". . . Of beginning your downswing with your shoulders instead of your hands," she muttered.

"How did you know?" I asked, amazed.

"Only because that's what you've been muttering all night." She felt my brow to make sure I was not delirious. "Try to get some sleep now, darling. You've got a big day coming up, remember?"

She was right. I should have been asleep hours ago. In a few hours I would play my first-round match in the club tournament against my arch golfing enemy, Steve Galloway. I chuckled into my pillow sadistically. With the secret of the game now locked in my breast, I would humble him at last.

I shut my eyes and ordered my mind to go blank, but to no avail. It insisted that I again replay each stroke of my day's round. During the first two holes my smile all but illuminated the night shadows of the room. But when I again found myself missing that twenty-inch putt on the 3rd green, my smile turned itself off. That putt had hurt. So had the four other short ones I had muffed later on. If I had sunk them instead, I would have completed my round in 84.

Nor were those missed putts the only additions to my score that should not have happened and most certainly would not happen again. If one of my drives hadn't sliced out of bounds, costing me two penalty strokes, I would have toured the links in a sizzling 82.

Or might not I have scored better still? The supposition caused me to gasp aloud, waking my wife with a start. Now that she was no longer asleep, I could find no reason for not sharing my joyous discovery.

"I had some tough breaks today, not of my own doing," I explained. A perfect pitch shot to the 9th green took an astounding hop into a bunker, and my drive on the 12th freakishly scooted beneath a bramble bush. And on the 17th hole, my caddy sneezed at the top of my backswing, all but causing me to miss the ball completely. Wouldn't you agree that because those were obviously non-recurrable accidents, I should further reduce my score by that same amount?"

"Why is it," my wife interrupted, "that a man can recall for a week every shot of his last game but can't remember for five minutes that the screen door needs fixing?"

I lay back in the pretense of sudden sleep. But my sub-conscious kept busy subtracting those three strokes from my hypothetical round of 82. On arriving at the amazing answer of 79, my body seemed to float toward the ceiling.

"Good Lord," I cried, "I'm a championship golfer!"

Every shred of evidence now pointed to my being able to par even the toughest holes on the course, and should it be my good fortune to slap in an occasional birdie—and, after all, why shouldn't I?—well, the implications were downright staggering.

Ever so carefully, so as not to cause my wife to phone a psychiatrist, I slithered from bed and stood beside it, my hand gripping an imaginary driver. For a moment I waggled it back and forth in delicious anticipation, then powerfully and smoothly I swept my body through an entire swing. Had the situation been born in reality, the ball surely would have zoomed into orbit. I drew in my stomach and threw out my chest and, in the utter darkness of the bedroom, exuded more confidence than ever before in my life.

Confidence, that was the key . . . confidence born of my new mastery of technique. How incredible to realize that in all these years I had simply conducted an endless series of tiger hunts on the golf course, violently beating the earth with my clubs, exhausting myself with my very ineptness. Not once, in fact, had I gotten past the first round of the club tournament. But tomorrow would be vastly different. Poor, unsuspecting Galloway!

At 2 A.M., I begged my mind to let me sleep. My plea was in vain. By three o'clock I had won the club championship. An hour later I captured the U.S. Open. Dawn was creeping over the windowsill before I divested myself of an armful of phantom trophies and tumbled into a canyon of sleep.

My wife and I and the Galloways sat together on the golf club terrace, watching the sun call it another day on the fickle fortunes of man. Now that my tournament match was over I wished I were alone, like Napoleon, on Elba Island. Not even on Boy Scout timber hikes had I met up with so many trees. No doubt about it. I would have scored better with an axe. What could have gone wrong to lead to all that abject, humiliating agony? My wife reached over to pat my knee. "Didn't you remember to keep your eye on the ball, sweetie?"

Her question was so ridiculous that I refused to answer. Without looking up I felt the sting of Steve Galloway's mocking glance. This time I was through with golf for good. Should I give my clubs to some deserving caddy, I wondered, or instead salvage a scrap of retribution by wrapping them around my opponent's neck?

My wife was talking again—a far too usual procedure—and I was trying not to listen. I chose instead to gaze out over the course where the evening dew already had tinted the fairways with silver and where, on either side, the terrible towering trees now slept, harmless and serene, as a moon tip rose above them into the night. It seemed impossible to believe that this gentle pastoral scene had, by daylight, proved itself such a violent battlefield.

I poured myself another drink and downed it quickly. Somehow it made me feel better. I reclined in my chair, my eyes again drawn back to the lush and quiet fairways. The course was beckoning me now like a temptress in the shadows. "Come conquer me," she seemed to whisper. "You can, you can."

I closed my eyes, but the voice refused to go away. When I refilled my glass and drank deeply from it, I began feeling surprisingly relaxed. Much the same as I had felt yesterday when I had shot my 89.

Ah, so that was it—relaxation! Not how you gripped the club or pivoted your hips or snapped your wrists, but simply how well you relaxed. No wonder Galloway had trounced me so completely. My mind had been gorged with a jumble of mechanical do's and don'ts. By taking it smooth and easy, wouldn't those technical elements fall naturally into place?

Yes, yes, I saw it clearly now. After years of huffing and puffing on the links, I caught the message at last. Silently, almost breathlessly, I started out over the vastness of the golf course, lost in wild surmise. *What*, I wondered, *should*

I wear while competing in the British Open? A touch of heather, perhaps? I could only hope I would not be so relaxed as to drop my trophy on the toe of the queen.

Pulling myself back to the present, I tried not to sound condescending as I turned to Steve Galloway. "How about a return match next Saturday?" I asked.

"But darling," my wife protested, "that's when you promised to fix the screen door."

For a moment her words buzzed near my ears like mosquitoes, then mercifully took flight when Galloway's voice chose to lead him to slaughter. "In the mood for another licking, eh?"

I only smiled in the dark. Already I was growing joyfully tense just contemplating the wonders of relaxation.

Graham Porter
Submitted by Ken and Judy Chandler

"How early are you teeing off?"

Reprinted by permission of George Crenshaw, Masters Agency.

The Promise Keeper

*He is an old man in golf at age twenty-four,
has reached his peak and can't get any better.
It's a question of how long this boy can hold
what he has.*

Sam Snead—on Jack Nicklaus, 1965

You know what the coolest thing was about Tiger
Woods's streak?

Nah, not the six straight wins, one of the top-ten feats in
modern sports history.

Not the way he almost made it seven, even after losing
his swing somewhere among the hang gliders and moon-
doggies and nude beachers at Torrey Pines Golf Club outside San Diego.

Not that during those seven tournaments he fricasseed
623 other golfers, tied one and lost to one.

Not that he earned just cab fare less than $5 million over
those seven weeks, or did enough ads to make people
actually believe he drives a Buick, or that he went from
seventeenth on the career PGA Tour money list to first.

Not that during that stretch he passed Ralph Guldahl,

Tommy Bolt, Ken Venturi, Tom Weiskopf, Fred Couples, David Duval, Paul Azinger, Mark O'Meara, Davis Love III, Phil Mickelson, Corey Pavin and Nick Price in career wins even though he still isn't old enough to rent a car in most places.

Not that he beat the nastiest sticks from all over the world while tromping through ten time zones and being herded daily through last-day-of-Saigon mobs, Watergate press conferences and lobbies full of get-a-life autograph hounds, including one at 5:50 one morning at the Torrey Pines Hilton.

Not that he had done all this when no other Tour golfer had even won four in a row since the '50s. And not that after losing at Torrey Pines to Mickelson he wasn't relieved as any sane human would be, but was genuinely pissed at what he called "finishing second" to Byron Nelson's antiquated, not-even-comparable streak of eleven in 1945 against a whole lot of Jug McSpadens in Miami Four Balls.

Not even that last Saturday night somebody actually asked, "Tiger, would you be surprised if one of these guys makes a run at you?" and Woods was trailing by six at the time.

No, the coolest thing about the Tiger Woods streak was that when he was hotter than a six-dollar pistol, in a publicity boiler, he kept a promise he'd made to a junior high school buddy three months before and let him caddie in San Diego.

Can you believe that?

Woods benched his regular caddie, Steve Williams, in favor of a gangly twenty-four-year-old childhood friend, Bryon Bell, who was trying to earn a little money for med school.

Wouldn't you have said, "Look, B, I'll catch you sometime when I'm not trying to climb Annapurna." Or, "Yo, B, can I front you the cash instead?"

"If it were me in a situation this big," said one longtime

Tour caddie, "I wouldn't have let anybody but my regular guy within a mile of that bag."

But as Tiger's mother, Tida, said on Saturday night, "My son has changed completely. He's all grown up now." It's true. He laughs more, glares less, looks you in the eye more, storms out less, breaks out in grins more, breaks shafts less, makes bogey more, triple bogey less and, maybe because of all that, has become the most thrilling athlete in the world.

He's the kind of man who risked the streak in the madness of Pebble Beach to play with his best college buddy, Jerry Chang. He's the kind of man who would put Bell, a 10-handicap Pacific Bell planning engineer, on the hottest set of tools this side of Bob Vila's—just to be true.

Of course Woods did much of the caddying himself. He double-checked every yardage B gave him. B read fewer of Tiger's putts than the guy from *The Des Moines Register*. Sometimes B would throw some grass to check the wind, and Woods would reach down and throw some, too. No offense, of course. None taken.

"I was a little worried about screwing up," said the bespectacled Bell, who's known Woods since the seventh grade and played No. 2 to him on Anaheim's Western High golf team, "but we've had a great time." Profitable, too. Figuring Woods's usual fat caddie fees, Bell made upward of $25,000, which is about half what he makes a year at Pac Bell. Med school, here we come.

Nurse, which way does this break?

Yeah, Tiger can make a driver scream in fluent titanium, or get balata up and down out of Sing Sing, or make twenty-year vets turn Maalox-white and pull over at the sight of him in their rearview mirrors, but all that's the outdoor pool-shark stuff.

What's cool now is what's *inside*.

Rick Reilly

Augusta Heaven

I started to shake with anticipation as I hung up the phone. Could it really be true that I would be playing a round of golf at the hallowed ground of Augusta National?

The generous offer had been extended by my friend, Frank Christian, a world-renowned golf course photographer and the official photographer of Augusta National for the last thirty years. Each year Augusta allows selected employees to invite two guests to play the course. Our date was to be just two weeks after the Masters.

I brought along my friend Tim Townley. Tim and I have been friends forever, but I have since found myself constantly reminding him that he will be indebted to me for just as long a period of time. Needless to say, the weeks leading up to our date seemed like an eternity. We talked every five minutes, sharing some nuance of Augusta history.

Frank Christian has a way to make people feel special and make his friends' trip to Augusta a once-in-a-lifetime experience. So it was when we arrived in Augusta.

Frank has a long-standing tradition that he invites you to partake the night before you play. You see, when the great Bobby Jones died, Frank was in charge of cleaning out Bobby's locker. In it he found a bottle of 1908 Old Rye Whiskey some three-quarters full. With permission, Frank cradled home his prize. Frank's preround ceremony consists of each member of the foursome taking a sip of whiskey from Bobby Jones's bottle. To this day, I get the chills thinking back on it.

I awoke before dawn the next morning in anticipation of the day that lay ahead. Finally the hour of our departure arrived, and we headed out to the course.

On approach, I had my first glimpse of the famed gate and the magnolia-lined drive. Just outside the gate stood a man and his young son craning their necks to get a peek inside. The young boy was attired in knickers and a tam o'shanter, just like Payne Stewart. Clearly golf was a passion the father had passed on to his son and now was being jointly shared. If I had the ability to let them inside the gates I would have, but alas, as we passed, I wished them luck in their efforts.

Everything was perfect, just the way I had always imagined it would be. Every blade of grass was perfectly cut, the gardens were brilliant and every shrub was precisely manicured. The golf course was very different than it appears on television. Namely, the course is distinguished by deep and numerous undulations and hills. Although the difficulties of the greens are well documented, I believe they are even tougher in person.

I have played St. Andrews, Royal Troon, Muirfield, Pebble Beach and many others, but Augusta National was without a doubt the best overall golfing experience I have ever enjoyed.

I have my own tradition whenever I play one of these great courses. I collect a small vial of sand from one of the bunkers and display it alongside its distinguished brethren. I pinched some sand from the famous bunker alongside the 18th of Augusta as my keepsake.

Arriving at the airport for my return home I spotted the father and son I had seen at the gate to Augusta. I asked the little boy, whose name was Max, if he had a good time in Augusta, and he gave me a reluctant "yes." His dad mentioned to me that Max was really disappointed because he could not get in the gates of Augusta National to get a souvenir. Well, here I was just fresh from a round at Augusta wearing my new Augusta shirt and my new Augusta hat, and this little boy had nothing.

At that point I took off my hat and put it on his little head. I then reached into my bag and grabbed my vial of sand from the 18th hole and explained to Max what it was and how I got it. I told Max that this would be a great start for a new collection for him.

The look on his face was absolutely priceless.

As great as my golfing experience was at Augusta National, my most memorable moment was the look on Max's face.

Jeff Aubery

The One Hundred Greatest
Golf Courses

A golfer called the Chicago Golf Club and explained that he was playing the "One Hundred Greatest Courses" and desperately needed to add the club to his list. The club was very private but reluctantly agreed to allow him to play under these special circumstances.

After the round, a member asked the man, "By the way, how many do you have left to complete the One Hundred Greatest?"

"Ninety-nine," he replied.

Bruce Nash and Allan Zullo

"You broke a hundred? So did I!"

Daddy Tees Off

All children find chaos congenial.

George F. Will

If James Joyce was right about our errors being portals of discovery, then a miniature golf course—the Poconos Putt-o-Rama—was the door to Saint Basil's Cathedral. I made a honey of a mistake there, and on the 11th hole (dogleg left, up a ramp, through an alligator to an elevated plywood green) I made one major discovery about children.

It was Rebecca's sixth birthday. The plan was to simulate the PGA championship: cake and juice and miniature golf for everybody. According to the log at Putt-o-Rama, my wife Jody paid green fees for eighteen.

Even before we teed off, there were bad omens. The kids battled over who would play with what color ball. Brenda complained that green didn't match her shorts. Julian hated yellow.

Sensing chaos, I jumped into the breach with parental authority. "Rule number one: Any dispute over the color of your golf ball," I said, choosing order over good cheer, "will result in immediate disqualification."

I looked over at Sean, who had Joey in a chokehold with the midget putter.

"Rule number two," I went on, "no player shall at any time hold his club against the trachea of another player."

"What's a traker?" Brendan asked.

"It's my neck," Joey gasped.

"Close enough," I said.

While the kids were choosing clubs, Jeffrey claimed to have won the world miniature golf championship. His twin brother, Mark, in an attempt to publicly humiliate his clone, shouted, "He's never even played miniature golf before."

Nice, I thought, *very nice.*

"Shut up, Mark. I have too played golf."

"Oh, yeah? When?"

"Uh, uh . . . I . . . I . . . ," Jeffrey stammered, paralyzed by the fact that he and the Grand Inquisitor not only had identical DNA packages but identical life histories. "I played once when you were asleep."

My heart broke for the little liar.

But before I could even say anything in his defense, Jeff lunged past me and stabbed his brother in the belly with the business end of his putter. When I stepped between them, I took a club head in the kneecap.

I should have enjoyed it more; it was the high point of my day.

On the tee at No. 1, the first foursome argued about who should tee it up first. I gaily suggested the birthday girl should have the honor and then we go in birthday order. Mark said that was unfair to kids born nine minutes after their stupid-head brother. He teed up his ball in protest. Another boy—Brian, I think—kicked it into a wishing well on the 9th fairway.

I wrapped five or six of the kids in a big old Daddy hug—or was it a threatening headlock?—and gave a quick little speech about how if there were sportsmanship we would all have a wonderful time. Absent cooperation, I went on, our memories of Becky's birthday would be full of recrimination.

"Rule number three," I had to announce a few minutes later, "no player shall help another player count his shots."

"Eleven . . . twelve . . . ," said Jill in gleeful play-by-play on Beth's first dozen strokes.

"Three," Beth chirruped as her ball clunked into the hole. There was mayhem in the air.

I did a quick count of the children. Came up one short.

"Jody, give me a count, will ya?" I yelled through the clamor to Mom.

"I make us minus one," she shouted back, apparently unconcerned since both of the kids to whom she had given birth were accounted for.

I grew frantic. There's nothing I hate more than having to tell a parent I lost a child somewhere on the front nine. "Lock the front gate," I shouted to the kid in charge.

"Hey, I don't do security, pal," he replied. "I do lessons."

I grabbed a perfectly calm little girl—Wendy, I later learned her name was—by her shoulders and said with panic in my voice, "We've got to find somebody."

"Who?" she asked.

"I don't know. Who's missing?" I answered.

"I think Jonathan's in the windmill," she said, clearly worried I was exactly the type of man her parents had warned her never to talk to.

I raced across to the windmill and found a little boy cowering inside. He was holding a rather large hunk of devil's food, which appeared to have been ripped from the birthday cake we had left in the pro shop "for later."

"Are you with the Becky O'Neill party?" I asked.

"Yes," he confessed, trying to hide the fistfuls of cake behind his back.

By the 5th hole everybody was hitting golf balls simultaneously. Orange and blue and green golf balls were whirring around Putt-o-Rama, like mesons in a particle accelerator. Becky's friend Jessica hit a shot that would have done Tom Kite proud—a low boring liner that ricocheted off Sneezy's foot into Josh's chin.

"Hey, mister, there's a liability ceiling of ten grand," said the teenage manager.

By the 10th hole, kids were actually dueling with their putters. There was dental work in the air.

The kids were no longer playing golf but some variation of hockey, pushing their balls toward the hole, a la Gretzky swooping the puck across the neutral zone. Every one of them claimed to have a hole-in-one on every hole. Believe it or not, when we got to the 11th hole—the seven-yard dogleg left through the alligator—things got worse.

Brendan, who was—may God hold him in the hollow of his hand—the only child still actually *striking* his ball, rolled a handsome putt up the ramp and cleanly into the alligator's throat. It did not, however, come out the other side.

"Becky's Dad," he said sweetly, "my ball got stuck." He actually appeared to think I could help him, that maybe a grown-up knew something a six-year-old didn't. I loved him for that.

I got on my hands and knees and peered down the reptile gullet into darkness. There was no light at the end of this tunnel. But I could see Brendan's ball stuck near the papier-mâché reptile larynx.

I stretched out on my stomach across the fairway and reached down the gator's throat. The ball, needless to say, was just out of my reach.

I stretched still more.

I grazed the ball with my fingertips, tried to poke it out the other side. No luck. I strained. I could feel the ball's dimples.

"Can you get it, Becky's Dad?" asked the only child in the world I cared about at all.

"Almost, Brendan . . . ," I croaked.

"Fore," I heard from behind the castle.

Brendan turned at the sound.

A golf ball whizzed past his knee.

And hit my temple with a fleshy clomp.

"Aaarrrgggghhhhh . . . ," I opined, rolling over on my stomach, in the process twisting my arm in the alligator's throat. When I tried to pull it free, I couldn't budge.

"Brendan," I said with fake calm in the manner of Timmy telling Lassie to go get help, "go find Becky's Mommy." I cast a fearful sidelong glance at the tiny foursome up ahead. They could sense weakness. If they knew I was helpless, they'd pounce.

Mark looked back at me, prone and pinned. He smiled a carnivorous smile. He said something to his brother, who turned to look at me but then decided to whack his brother with his putter again. I remember the sound of cast iron against anklebone.

The last thing I remember clearly is Jody arriving at my side. I remember resting my head in her lap.

What was the lesson I learned? Actually, I learned two lessons—one practical, one philosophical.

The practical parent lesson was never to give eighteen six-year-olds clubs, projectiles and large doses of sugar at the same time.

The philosophical lesson was that children are the opposite of golf. Golf is a liturgy of etiquette and manners. Golf is manicured, refined and disciplined. Golf is self-control. Children are none of those things. Children are—what's the word?—wild.

"In wildness is the preservation of the world," wrote Thoreau. He never wrote a word about minigolf.

Hugh O'Neill

"Miniature golf doesn't do much for our long game."

The Man with the Perfect Swing

You must work very hard to become a natural golfer.

Gary Player

On a warm morning at a country club near Orlando, a stocky gentleman with wispy gray hair makes his way past the crowd gathered for today's exhibition. To those who don't know better, the impish old fellow could be just another sunburned senior dreaming of bogey golf.

He wears a black turtleneck despite the heat. The left pocket of his neon-lime slacks bulges, as always, with two golf balls—never more, never fewer. All three watches on his left wrist are set to the same time.

Taking his position at the tee, he quickly lofts a few short wedge shots about 70 yards. At first the spectators seem unimpressed. Then they notice that the balls are landing on top of one another. "Every shot same as the last," chirps the golfer, as if to himself. "Same as the last."

Moving to a longer club, a 7-iron, he smoothly launches two dozen balls, which soar 150 yards and come to rest so close to each other you could cover them with a bedspread.

He then pulls out his driver and sends a hail of balls 250 yards away—all clustered on a patch of grass the size of a two-car garage.

Astonished laughter erupts from the crowd. "Perfectly straight," says the golfer in a singsong voice. "There it goes. Perfectly straight."

People who have followed Moe Norman's career are no longer surprised by his uncanny displays of accuracy. Many professionals and avid players consider the seventy-year-old Canadian a near-mythical figure. But few outside the sport have ever heard his name. Fewer still know the story of his struggle to find acceptance in the only world he understands.

One cold January morning in 1935, five-year-old Murray Norman was sledding double with a friend on an ice-packed hillside near his home in Kitchener, Ontario. Speeding downhill, the sled hurtled into the street and skidded under a passing car.

Both boys survived and ran home crying. But the car's right rear tire had rolled over Moe's head, pushing up the cheekbone on one side of his face. His parents, unable to afford medical care, could only pray he did not suffer serious brain injury.

As Moe grew older, he developed odd behavioral quirks and a repetitive, staccato speech pattern. His older brother Ron noticed that Moe seemed unusually frightened of unfamiliar situations. At night, Ron often heard his little brother sobbing in bed, devastated by some real or imagined slight.

At school Moe felt glaringly out of place among other kids. Desperate for friends and acceptance, he tried to be playful, but his efforts often backfired—pinching people too hard or bear hugging them until they pushed him away. He heaped ridicule on himself and even coined his own nickname: Moe the Schmoe.

He became known as a slow student in every subject—
except one. At math no one could touch Moe Norman. He
astounded his classmates by memorizing complicated
problems and multiplying two-digit numbers in his head
almost instantly.

When he wasn't acting the clown, Moe walled himself
off from others. Over time he plunged deeper into isola-
tion, and yet, ironically, loneliness led him to his greatest
happiness.

In the years following his accident, Moe spent hours
atop that same winter sledding hill, hacking around an old
golf ball with a rusty, wood-shafted 5-iron he found at
home. Here in the solitary and magical world of golf, he
found a reason to wake up each morning.

Kitchener, Ontario, in the 1940s was a gritty factory town
where working-class teenagers had little desire or money to
play the "sissy," upper-class game of golf. But Moe was
spellbound, often skipping meals, school and chores to
head off by himself in a field to hit balls—five hundred or
more a day. He practiced until dark, sometimes until the
blood from his hands made the club too slippery to hold.

In his early teens Moe landed a job as a caddie at a
country club—only to be fired when he hurled the clubs
of a low-tipping local mogul into some trees. Soon he gave
up caddying to concentrate on playing, honing his skills at
a nearby public golf course. He quit school in tenth grade,
and by the time he was nineteen, he knew he was blessed
with a rare talent: He could hit a golf ball wherever he
wanted it to go.

Moe left home in his early twenties, hitching rides to
compete in amateur golf tournaments all over Canada,
supporting himself with a succession of low-paying jobs.
At his first few tournaments in the late 1940s, fans didn't
know what to make of the odd little fellow with the garish,
mismatched outfits, strawlike red hair and crooked teeth.

His manner was playful, almost childlike, his self-taught technique wildly unorthodox. Legs spread wide, he stood over the ball like a slugger at the plate, clutching the club not with his fingers, as most golfers are taught to do, but tightly in his palms, wrists cocked, as if he were holding a sledgehammer.

Many spectators dismissed him as an amusing sideshow. Some giggled when he stepped up to the tee. Soon, though, Moe Norman was turning heads for reasons other than his personal style.

Recognized as a gifted player who could hit a golf ball with breathtaking precision, he quickly became a sensation on the amateur golf circuit. In one year alone he shot 61 four times, set nine course records and won seventeen out of twenty-six tournaments.

Even as his fame grew, Moe remained painfully shy and could not shake the sense that he was undeserving of the attention. Rather than bask in the spotlight, he avoided it. In 1955, after winning the Canadian Amateur Open in Calgary, Moe failed to show for the awards ceremony. Friends later found him by the nearby Elbow River, cooling his feet.

That victory qualified Moe for one of golf's most prestigious events: the Masters. When the invitation to the tournament arrived, he was only twenty-six and spending his winters setting pins in a Kitchener bowling alley. The Masters was his chance not only to represent his country but to show skeptics he wasn't just some freak on a run of beginner's luck.

But his old demons would give him no rest. Moe felt like an intruder among some of golf's bright lights. He played miserably in the first round and even worse on day two. So he fled to a nearby driving range to practice.

While hitting balls Moe noticed someone behind him. "Mind if I give you a little tip?" asked Sam Snead. The

Hall-of-Famer merely suggested a slight change in his long-iron stroke.

But for Moe it was like Moses bringing the Eleventh Commandment down from the mountaintop.

Determined to put Snead's advice to good use, Moe stayed on the range until dark, hitting balls by the hundreds. His hands became raw and blistered. The next day, unable to hold a club, he withdrew from the Masters, humiliated.

But Moe climbed right back up the ladder to win the Canadian Amateur again a year later. A string of victories followed. In time, he had won so many tournaments and collected so many televisions, wristwatches and other prizes that he began selling off those he didn't want.

When the Royal Canadian Golf Association charged him with accepting donations for travel expenses, which was against regulations for amateurs, Moe decided to turn professional. His first move as a pro was to enter, and win, the Ontario Open.

As a newcomer to professional golf, Moe approached the game with the same impish lightheartedness of his amateur years. When people laughed, he played along by acting the clown. An extremely fast player, he'd set up and make his shot in about three seconds, then sometimes stretch out on the fairway and pretend to doze until the other players caught up.

Fans loved the show, but some of his fellow competitors on the U.S. PGA Tour did not. At the Los Angeles Open in 1959, a small group of players cornered Moe in the locker room. "Stop goofing off," they told him, demanding that he improve his technique as well as his wardrobe.

Friends say a shadow fell across Moe that day. Some believe the episode shattered his self-confidence and persuaded him to back out of the American tour, never to return. More than anything, Moe had wanted to be accepted by the players he so admired. But he was unlike the others, and now he was being punished for it.

The laughter suddenly seemed barbed and personal. No longer could he shrug it off when some jerk in the galleries mimicked his high-pitched voice or hitched up his waistline to mock Moe's too-short trousers.

Because Moe never dueled the likes of Americans Jack Nicklaus or Arnold Palmer, he achieved little recognition beyond Canada. At home, though, his success was staggering. On the Canadian PGA Tour and in smaller events in Florida, Moe won fifty-four tournaments and set thirty-three course records. While most world-class golfers count their lifetime holes-in-one on a few fingers, Moe has scored at least seventeen.

Despite his fame and the passing years, Moe was continually buffeted by the mood swings that tormented him in childhood. Even among friends he could be curt, sometimes embarrassingly rude.

At other times he was charming, lovable Moe, bear hugging friends and tossing golf balls to children like candy— the happy-go-lucky clown from his amateur days.

Through the 1960s and '70s, Moe racked up one tournament victory after another. But in the early 1980s his enthusiasm for competition began to wane. His winnings dwindled, and he slipped into depression. Not being wealthy, he seemed to care very little for money, lending thousands to aspiring golfers and never bothering to collect.

Broke and all but forgotten, he drifted from shabby apartments and boardinghouses to cut-rate roadside motels, often sleeping in his car. Had it not been for the generosity of friends—and a stroke of good luck—he might have faded entirely into obscurity.

Moe has never had a telephone, a credit card or owned a house. Few people know where he might be living on any given day, and he seldom talks to strangers. Little wonder it took Jack Kuykendall two years to track him down.

Kuykendall, founder of a company called Natural Golf Corp., finally caught up with him in Titusville, Florida. He told Moe that, trained in physics, he had worked for years to develop the perfect golf swing—only to discover that an old-timer from Canada had been using the same technique for forty years. He had to meet this man.

Moe agreed to demonstrate his swing at clinics sponsored by Natural Golf Corp. Word spread quickly through the golfing grapevine, and before long, sports magazines were trumpeting the mysterious genius with the killer swing.

Among those following Moe's story was Wally Uihlein, president of the golf-ball company Titleist and FootJoy Worldwide. Hoping to preserve one of golf's treasures, Uihlein announced in 1995 that his company was awarding Norman five thousand dollars a month for the rest of his life. Stunned, Moe asked what he had to do to earn the money. "Nothing," said Uihlein. "You've already done it."

Two weeks later, Moe Norman was elected to the Canadian Golf Hall of Fame. Even today, however, he remains largely unknown outside his native country except among true disciples of the game. For them, Moe is golf's greatest unsung hero, the enigmatic loner once described by golfer Lee Trevino as "the best ball-striker I ever saw come down the pike." Many agree with Jack Kuykendall—had someone given Moe a hand forty years ago, "we would know his name like we know Babe Ruth's."

In the parking lot of a Florida country club, Moe Norman is leaning into his gray Cadillac, fumbling through a pile of motivational tapes. He seems nervous and rushed, but as he slides behind the wheel, he pauses to reflect on his life, his family and his obsession.

Moe never had a real mentor or a trusted advisor. "Today's kids," he says, "are driven right up to the country club. Nice golf shoes, twenty-dollar gloves, nice pants. 'Have a nice day, Son.' I cry when I hear that. Oooh, if I'd ever heard that when I was growing up . . ."

He squints into the sun and cocks his head. "Everyone wanted me to be happy their way," he says. "But I did it my way. Now, every night I sit in the corner of my room in the dark before I go to bed and say, 'My life belongs to me. My life belongs to me.'"

With that, he shuts the door and rolls down the window just a crack. Asked where he's going, Moe brightens instantly, and a look of delight spreads across his face.

"Gone to hit balls," he says, pulling away. "Hit balls."

It is, and forever will be, the highlight of his day.

Bruce Selcraig

Common Ground

Growing up in Egypt, I never had a chance to play golf or even come close to being on a course, even though Egypt was (as a golfer once told me) "a big sand trap." Now, courses are sprouting everywhere in Egyptian resorts.

Golf is too much of an individualistic and disciplined game for someone who, for most of his life, played the undisciplined game of football (soccer), which is full of improvizations and creativity.

Golf is a sport found in a culture of abundance, where players usually bring their own balls, bags, shoes, umbrellas, raincoats, hats, carts, clubs and caddies. For years I subscribed to the notion that golf is an elitist game, where men with ugly pants go to strike business deals on the course away from women and minorities.

When I went to the course for the first time I found, to my surprise, mostly younger baby boomers with nice pants. And the only thing they cared to strike was the ball. The only business they talked about was the business of controlling this small ball and keeping it straight on the fairway.

I was alone and leery as a first-time golfer, equipped with only my golf bag and a few trips to the driving range, mostly wondering about the rules and the etiquette of this enigmatic game.

First, they lined me up at the clubhouse with three other men I had never met before. Very few sports do that. They asked if I could fill out a foursome. I wondered for a second if this had something to do with my handicap.

On the 1st hole, we were just men getting to know each other for the first time. On the 5th hole, we became associates. Once we strode off the 9th hole, we became drinking buddies (nonalcoholic, please). Golf is one of the few sports that you can play and drink at the same time—if you don't count bowling.

By the time we got to the 18th hole, we had become friends who had just spent more than half of the day away from work, families and wives. We were cut off from any sign of civilization, bonding together, surrounded by the primitive nature of the course.

What a refreshing experience and a wonderful treat for me as an Arab-American, surrounded by people who looked at me as one of them. I wasn't looked at as a hyphenated American, to be interrogated about Middle East affairs and asked to explain Saddam Hussein's complicated self-destructive behavior.

I was not asked to help find Osama bin Laden. All that was asked of me was to find the ball. The only jihad we had was to fight the course terrain and stay on the fairway. With this camaraderie, we were cut off from our ethnic roots, bias and prejudice. We were merely men against the course. We had transcended our race, color and ethnicity. The only color we saw was the color green. On the course, no cultural sensitivity or diversity training is required. I was just another golfer. Bad golfer I may be, but never a bad Arab.

The concentration and the exotic exhilaration of smashing this small ball onto the fairway overwhelmed our own stereotyping, racism and ethnocentricity. We were liberated men, free of all the societal burdens of accomplishing big tasks in life.

For Arab-Americans, our energy has been consumed for years by the long debate over the fate of a piece of divine real estate thousands of miles away that we can't do anything about. On the course, the only piece of divine real estate was the green before us. This game was our reality, and I was the only one who could do anything about it.

Golf anyone?

Ahmed Tharwat Abdelaal

Fore Play

It's a gloriously sunny day in Miami, and I'm standing in a semicircle of maybe five hundred people on a carpet of lush, sweet-smelling, green-glinting grass, the kind that makes you want to get naked and roll around on your back like a dog.

But the people around me are not doing that. They're silent and solemn, like a church congregation, except that a lot of them are smoking cigars. They're staring intently at some tiny figures way off in the distance. I'm staring, too, but I can't quite make out what the figures are doing. Suddenly the crowd murmurs, and five hundred heads jerk skyward in unison. I still can't see anything. The crowd holds its breath, waiting, waiting, and then suddenly . . . *plop* . . . a little white ball falls from the sky, lands in the middle of the semicircle and starts rolling. Immediately the crowd members are shouting at it angrily.

"Bite!" they shout, spewing saliva and cigar flecks. "BITE!!" This is how they tell the ball they want it to stop rolling.

The ball, apparently fearing for its life, stops. The crowd members applaud and cheer wildly. They're acting as though the arrival of this ball is the highlight of their lives.

Which maybe it is. These are, after all, golf fans. And this ball was personally hit by—prepare to experience a heart seizure—*Jack Nicklaus.*

This exciting moment in sports occurred at the Doral-Ryder Open golf tournament, an event on the professional golf tour, wherein the top golfers from all over the world gather together to see who can take the longest amount of time to actually hit the ball.

I don't know about you, but when I play golf—which I have done a total of three times in my life—I don't waste a lot of time. I just grab a club, stride briskly to the ball, take a hearty swing, then check to see if the ball has moved from its original location. If it hasn't, I take another hearty swing, repeating this process as necessary until the ball is gone, which is my cue to get out another ball, because I know from harsh experience that I will never in a million years find the first one. I keep this up until there are no balls left, which is my cue to locate the part of the golfing facility where they sell beer. In other words, I play an exciting, nonstop-action brand of golf that would be ideal for spectators, except for the fact that most of them would be killed within minutes.

Your professional golfer, on the other hand, does not even *think* about hitting a ball until he has conducted a complete geological and meteorological survey of the situation—circling the ball warily, as though it were a terrorist device, checking it out from every possible angle; squatting and squinting; checking the wind; taking soil samples; analyzing satellite photographs; testing the area for traces of O. J. Simpson's DNA, etc. Your professional golfer takes longer to line up a six-foot putt than the Toyota Corporation takes to turn raw iron ore into a Corolla.

I know that it may sound boring to watch grown men squat for minutes on end, but when you see a pro tournament in person—when you're actually watching these world-class golfers line up their shots—it is in fact *unbelievably* boring. At least it was for me. I would rank it, as a spectator sport, with transmission repair.

"HIT THE BALL, ALREADY!" is what I wanted to shout at Jack Nicklaus, but I did not, because the crowd would have turned on me, and my lifeless body would have been found later buried in a sand trap, covered with cigar burns. Because these fans worship the golfers, and they seem to be truly fascinated by the squatting and squinting process. The more time that passed with virtually nothing happening, the more excited the golf fans became, until finally, when Jack got ready to take the extreme step of actually hitting the ball, everybody was nearly crazy with anticipation, although nobody was making a peep, because putting is an extremely difficult and highly technical activity that—unlike, for example, brain surgery—must be performed in absolute silence.

And so, amid an atmosphere of tension comparable to that of a space shuttle launch, Jack finally bent over the ball, drew back his putter and gently tapped the ball.

"GET IN THE HOLE!" the crowd screamed at the ball. "GET IN THE HOLE!"

The ball, of course, did not go in the hole. Your world-class golfers miss a surprising number of short putts. Too much squatting, if you ask me.

"NO!" shouted the crowd, when the ball stopped, maybe an inch from the hole. Some men seemed to be near tears; some were cursing openly. These people were *furious* at the ball. They did not blame Jack. Jack worked *hard* to line up this putt, and here this idiot ball *let him down*.

But Jack was magnanimous. He tapped the ball in, and the fans applauded wildly, as well they should have, because it is not every day that you see a person cause a little ball to roll six feet.

Dave Barry

Ladies, Is Golf for You?

Our minds need relaxation, and give way
Unless we mix with work a little play.

Moliére

I took up the game of golf eight years ago when I was at the age of . . . never mind. I became so addicted to the game, I didn't have time to do the laundry anymore. Soon after, my husband had a plaque made for me that says "Martha Stewart Used to Live Here." Sometimes I'd have to stop on my way home after a round of golf to buy him a pair of underwear for work the next day. He has two drawers full of BVDs. God forbid, but if he's ever in an accident, not only will he be wearing clean underwear, most likely it'll be brand-new.

Golf is great, but I can still remember what a frustrating experience it can be for the beginner. For the first three months, I wondered if golf was my punishment for the time I sneaked into Sister Mary Margaret's bedroom to see if she really had a poster of Bob Dylan hanging over her bed. That was the rumor around school. I cried so much as a beginning golfer, my husband suggested I have my hormone level checked. He couldn't believe it was just golf doing it. But I persevered and things became better, and so now I would like to share some tips and ideas that can make a woman's initial foray into golf a little smoother.

Whatever your reasons for taking up the game, whether it's to avoid listening to your son practice the French horn or to get away from your mother-in-law, ask yourself a few questions to see if this game is really your bag. You may be athletic, but there's more than skill involved here.

Temperament, for instance. If you have a hair-trigger kind of temper, occasionally coupled with a bad case of anxiety, a club in your hands that particular day can be dangerous. I once saw a woman do quite a number on the 150-yard marker, a pretty shrub in bloom, with her 7-iron just because her favorite pink ball went into the lake.

Vanity. Particularly in the summer. If you worry about your hair flopping on humid days, your foundation running until your face looks like it's melting, or your mascara making black tracks down your cheeks, stay at home and make pot holders.

Prudery. If you're the kind of person easily offended by less-than-ladylike words, forget it.

But before you spend a fortune on clubs and figure out six months later that what you really want to do is skydive, I suggest you borrow most, if not all, the essentials first. You'll need clubs (up to fourteen, eight of which look exactly alike, but in a few years you'll be able to tell the difference), a bag, shoes (the ones with plastic spikes for traction), balls, tees, a towel and a ball marker (a quarter will do, but don't forget to pick it up when you leave the green).

If your friends don't have a spare set of clubs to loan out, you can find used clubs at garage sales or pawn shops at reasonable prices. Buy something cheap for now. At this point, equipment doesn't matter much since you have no idea what you're doing.

Eventually, if you stick with the game, you'll find your-self buying a new driver all the time. Every time you hear about another that can help you hit the ball ten more yards, you'll go and buy it. I've noticed that no matter who the manufacturer is or what the club material, it's always "an extra ten yards." You'd think, out of all the clubmakers, one company would have an engineer smart enough to come up with a club that'll give us fifty extra yards and get it over with for a while.

I love drivers. They're all so different. They come in per-simmon, graphite, titanium, with bubbles, without bubbles, large heads, extra-large heads, stiff and extra-stiff shafts—you name it.

Now once you have your equipment, you need an instructor. But ladies: Do not let your husband teach you. When was the last time you listened to him anyway? What makes you think you're going to start now? Sooner or later even his voice will start grating on your nerves. Trust me, it won't work. Find yourself a real pro. My guess is that the person who said sex is one of the main sources of disagreements between couples didn't teach his wife the game of golf.

One more piece of advice: While you're still a beginner, don't play in events for couples if the format is that of alternate shot. Heaven help if your shot lands directly behind a tree, on top of a root or in a bunker in a "fried egg" lie and now he has to play it. That's an argument waiting to happen. And it will happen.

Another thought to keep in mind for the sake of keep-ing peace at home: If you ever hit a hole-in-one, never mention it again after the day it happens. I've had two, and he hasn't even one. I love my husband too much to upset him, so I don't talk about them in his presence. But my plaques hang in the den, one on each side of the tele-vision, where he can see them every night. I also have a vanity license plate, 2-HOLS-N-1—and he washes my car every Saturday.

Golf's like fishing: There's always the one that got away. In golf there's always the putt that didn't fall. But there's more to golf than making good shots. Fun moments that don't have anything to do with the game can happen on the course. There was the time when my husband uncharacteristically threw his sand wedge after shanking a short chip. The grip hit the cart path first, propelling the club into a 360-degree rotation and directly into the golf bag. Eventually, you'll have your own stories to tell, and you'll remember them years from now.

Above all else, have fun, even on those days when you feel you should have stayed home making those pot holders instead of going to the course, accomplishing nothing more than achieving that dreaded tan line that makes your feet look like you're wearing bobby socks with high heels in your finest evening gown.

Golf can be played long after you start collecting your first Social Security check. When you reach that age, you can start making cute ball markers and tee holders to give your friends at Christmas. By the way, did you know the Senior Tour has players in their seventies? Ladies don't have a Senior Tour. They won't admit when they turn fifty. It's a woman thing.

Deisy Flood

Like Father, Like Son

Like many fathers and sons, Bob and Dave like to play an occasional round of golf together when they can find the time. Nothing serious: Ten bucks a hole; bonuses for birdies and "polies" (approach shots that come to rest within a flagstick-length of the hole); optional presses whenever you're steamed—pretty much the same kind of convivial game fathers and sons enjoy in every part of America. The competition is fun, sure. But it's the being together that really matters. Because of career commitments and travel and all the other complications of being two working stiffs, they don't have a chance to see each other as much as they like. Even though they're in the same line of work, both master practitioners of the same profession, Bob and Dave's paths cross with depressing rarity. Like so many fathers and sons in our increasingly turbocharged world, they communicate mostly electronically, over the phone or—and this is one of the benefits of doing what they do—the television.

So when these two fellows do come together on the links, every moment counts.

When they arrive at the golf course, filled with the same kind of heightened anticipation most dads and sons feel before they're about to display their game to the most important male in their life, the conversation usually goes something like this:

Dad: "How many strokes am I getting today?"

Son, scoffing: "None."

Dad: "All right, fine. What tees do you want me to play?"

Son, indicating the back markers: "The same as me, of course."

Dad, pleading: "You may not be aware of this, Son. But the old guys? We don't play these tees. We start a little closer to the hole."

Son, resting his hand on Dad's shoulder: "You got your freakin' name on your bag, don't you? Quit your crying, and play some golf."

These days, Bob, who is one of the longest hitters you've ever seen for a guy in his fifties, is about fifteen yards shorter than his son off the tee. But as old Pops likes to remind his precocious kid, the game of golf is not merely a driving distance contest. And every now and then he proves it to young Dave. "There are days I make him dig into the wallet," Bob says proudly. "And, man, he's as tight as can be. It kills him!"

Bob laughs heartily. "It doesn't happen all the time. I'm not ashamed to admit it: He's definitely got the best of me these days. But you know what?" he says, smiling contentedly. "It's pretty cool to be able to compete with the number-two player in the world. And to know he's your son."

Bob and David Duval are both touring professional golfers. They both crisscross the United States in search of birdies and the monster paychecks that accompany them. They are both winners on their respective Tours.

And they are father and son.

Fathers try to teach their sons well, and watch with

pride and contentment as their boys blossom into the men Dad hoped they would be.

Fathers serve as role models for their blooming off-spring, idealized examples of the fully realized adult man young sons hope to become. Fathers show the way, and sons try earnestly to follow.

Sons try to make their fathers proud. Sons try to learn their fathers' lessons well. Sons hope to live up to their fathers' guiding example.

Which is all to say that Bob Duval, professional golfer, Senior Tour champion, and, yes, father, is in the peculiar and enviable position of having a son who has become the man his old dad hoped he would. And then much more.

David Duval, PGA Tour superstar, is one of the most famous golfers on the planet, a stylish, enigmatic athlete who has at times been capable of dominating his sport more completely than anyone but Tiger Woods.

Bob Duval has finished in the magic Top-31 his last three campaigns on the Senior Tour.

David Duval earns multimillions in both prize money and product endorsements. He travels the country in a private jet. He cannot go anywhere near a golf course without being mobbed by autograph-seeking fans.

Bob Duval earns a healthy six-figure income. He flies commercially. Only friends and family members recognize him.

David Duval is Bob's son. But that's not how the world sees it.

"No, David used to be Bob's kid," Bob Duval tells me, chuckling at the thought. "Now I'm definitely David's dad." He thinks for a moment.

"Everything has sort of flipped around," Bob Duval says. "The father has become the son."

We're sitting on the back deck of Bob's Jacksonville Beach home. With Buddy, Bob's faithful dog patrolling for lizards and the ocean crashing into the shore just a wedge away, it's a perfect afternoon to reflect on what it means to be a dad. And not just any old dad—though dads of any sort are cherished by their sons—but a member of the Senior Tour dad, and the father of a PGA Tour superstar dad. "I remember when it happened," Bob recalls. "It was David's first time being in contention down the stretch as a pro on the PGA Tour—and my first cigarette in several years! I was so nervous. He was battling with Peter Jacobsen at Pebble Beach. I remember having an overwhelming sense of pride—and it just got bigger when the phone didn't stop ringing for two hours, even after he finished second. At that point, in the eyes of a lot of people, he stopped being my kid and I became 'David's Dad.'"

Bob Duval doesn't say this with even the faintest trace of bitterness or remorse. He says it like a proud papa.

"I mean, my son chose the same path, the same business, as old dad. I couldn't be prouder. I don't think any dad could be prouder," Bob Duval says, smiling.

As if on cue, the phone rings. It's David, who lives a little ways down the road, in Ponte Vedra. Wants to know what time they're meeting this afternoon, for a round of golf. And if they've got a tee time arranged.

For some reason this thought amuses me immensely: David and Bob Duval showing up at a nearby golf course, wondering if, perhaps if it wasn't too much trouble of course, if they might, you know, hop on to the 1st tee? And then I realize: Today they're just a father and son looking to have an impromptu round of golf together.

And that's pretty sweet.

Michael Konik

The Dying Light

I line up the six-foot putt. All is quiet, save for a few people talking quietly in the distance. Slowly, I take the putter back and stroke the ball. For a split-second, the ball rolls toward the hole, then slides decidedly off to the right, like a car exiting a freeway long before its destination.

"Maybe you'd like to try something else," says the young salesman, watching from beside the artificial-turf putting green.

For an instant, our eyes meet. I am standing in one of the West Coast's largest golf shops, and a young man twenty-five years my junior is telling me—behind his veneer of entrepreneurial etiquette—that I cannot putt.

After thirty-two years of golf frustration, it's time, I've decided, to face the reality that I can no longer blame my ineptness on my irons or woods. Instead, I've decided to blame it on my putter. So here I am shopping for a new one. After nine years, I am kissing my Northwestern Tour model good-bye for a younger, sleeker model.

I feel so cheap; alas, I am a desperate man. At forty-five, my golf game is going through a midlife crisis. And so emerges a belief, a hope, a desperate clinging to the idea that I can somehow buy my way back to respectability.

Long a believer that the swing, not the equipment, makes the golfer, I've scoffed at friends who plunk down hundreds of dollars to find "new and improved" clubs to help them once again hit the drives of their youth. I've chided them for seeing some pro win a tournament, then rushing out to buy the replica of the putter he used; after Jack Nicklaus's stunning Masters win in 1986, who can forget that rush on putters whose heads were roughly the size of bricks? The golfer makes the club, I've long insisted—not the other way around.

But in recent years, my game has gone so far south that even my putter talks with a twang. Blame it on a schedule where golf now makes only a rare guest appearance. After months of not playing, I usually prepare for a round like I prepare for a yearly dental checkup: by flossing the night before—i.e., hitting a bucket of balls—and hoping I can fool the hygienist. Of course, it never works—in the dental chair or on the golf course.

Blame it on a number of other excuses; the bottom line is that some sales kid who didn't even start shaving until after the invention of the Big Bertha driver is now trying to help save my golf game.

I look up at the kid with one of those don't-you-think-I-know-what-I-need looks on my face, then put my pride on a leash. "Sure, let's try something else."

"If you'd like, you can go out on our real putting green and test them," says the young salesman.

The kid is nice—he's only trying to help, after all—but something about this situation just doesn't seem right. I take three putters, a couple of balls, and start walking toward the outdoor putting green.

"Uh, I'll need you to leave your driver's license," he says.

"I'll only be, like, two hundred feet away," I say.

"Store policy."

You gotta be kidding. What's he think I'm going to do—take three putters and a couple of Titleists and hop the first plane to Mexico?

"Seriously?" I say, thinking that my slight balking will probably waive the mandate.

"Sorry."

I look at the young man incredulously and say the only thing that's left to say.

"But I'm your *father*. Doesn't that count for something?"

"Sorry, store policy."

I pull out my driver's license and hand it to the kid who I once taught to drive. The kid I once taught to play golf. The kid who I haven't beaten on a golf course since he was a sophomore in high school.

I love this kid. I'm proud that, at age twenty, he's found himself a job that he likes and is good at. I think it's wonderful that he has developed into a near-scratch golfer who has shot 69, won back-to-back men's club championships, and posted an 84 at night, using a glow-in-the-dark ball.

But deep inside I have this tiny dream: to beat him just one last time, at anything: golf, home-run derby, or h-o-r-s-e on the backyard hoop. Like Nicklaus coming back to win the Masters at age forty-seven, I'd like one last hurrah to remind the world I'm still around.

It's not a vindictive thing at all. It's just a little pride thing. Not a chest-beating thing, but Pride Lite. Father-son pride. It's wanting to be the hero one last time. It's wanting to still be considered significant, like when you give your son a bit of advice about life itself and he tries it and it works and you think: I'm still needed. I still matter.

And one more thing: Weird as this may sound, fathers want their son's approval. In Ryan's journal, I wrote this about the first time we played golf together as a team. He was sixteen:

Going to the 18th, the two teams were all even. I nailed a 152-yard 7-iron to within two feet of the cup, sunk the putt for birdie and we won! But I was so nervous standing over that putt, more nervous than you'll ever know. (Until now.) Why? Because I wanted so badly to prove to you that I wasn't just this hacker of a dad. That I could pull through. That I could produce under pressure. Because I want you to be the same kind of guy, whether the venue is golf, marriage, work, whatever. I want you to pull through when you need to. Withstand the pressure.

"Do you wanna try one of these putters?" he asks, snapping me back to reality. "This is like the putter you bought me when I beat you for the first time."

I remember the day. He was fifteen. I shot 88. He shot 86. Though I'd done all I could to prevent it, I was glad he'd won, proud to have been outdueled by my own son. I wrote a mock newspaper article—"Ryan stuns Dad for first win!"—and made good on a promise to buy him the putter of his choice.

Since then, it's been his show. I've watched proudly from the edges of the fairway and learned what it must be like for a kid to grow up with high-achieving parents, because whenever I play now, people expect me to be good because Ryan is. And I'm not.

Not long after Ryan won his second men's club championship at a Eugene public course, I teed up my opening drive at the same place and promptly hit it out of bounds. It was like Einstein's father flunking Algebra I.

"So," said the starter, "you're Ryan Welch's father, huh?" As if he really wanted to say, "So much for that axiom about the acorn not falling far from the tree, huh?"

For the most part, I've accepted this role reversal. Twice now, Ryan has had me caddie for him in tournaments

that brought together all the winners of club championships from around the state. And I've considered it one
of the highest honors a father could be accorded: to be
able to carry on my back the clubs of a son I used to carry
in my arms.

But deep down, the instinct quietly gnaws at me to
prove myself—to nobody else but myself.

Bob Welch

The Doctor and the Lawyer

Thinking instead of acting is the number-one disease in golf.

Sam Snead

For several years a lawyer and a doctor had regularly played golf together. They were evenly matched, and there was a keen sense of rivalry.

Then one spring, the lawyer's game suddenly improved so much that the doctor was losing regularly. The doctor's efforts to improve his own game were unsuccessful, but finally he came up with an idea. At a bookstore he picked out three how-to-play-golf texts and sent them to the lawyer for a birthday present.

It wasn't long before they were evenly matched again.

More of . . . The Best of Bits & Pieces

"So let's get this straight.
You carefully handed him the putter?"

Reprinted by permission of David Harbaugh. Originally appeared in Golf Digest.

The View from the Tee

*Golf is so popular simply because it is the best
game in the world at which to be bad.*

A. A. Milne

Among my current jobs is that of starter, five days a week,
at New Jersey's Pitman Country Club, a good place for the
golfer who wants a chance to break whatever is his or her
goal—120 perhaps, but usually 100—because there's a little
less trouble than there is at Pine Valley or Pinehurst No. 2.

Pitman is a "forgiving" course. You can probably shoot a
lower number there than Pebble Beach. If you hit a banana
slice or a duck hook, you won't always wind up in the Pine
Barrens.

Being a starter is great fun. I get to work on my suntan,
kibitz with customers, listen to a zillion excuses, shuffle
three hundred players on a busy day, sweep out carts,
learn hyphenated words, eat chili dogs and, best of all, see
some of the worst golf shots since Mary Queen of Scots
missed a tap-in.

Of course, Pitman golfers do not have the market
cornered on bad shots off the 1st tee, even though it

sometimes seems a prerequisite for playing there.

My own most memorable 1st-tee shot was at Waynesboro (Pennsylvania) Country Club, when I was a fourteen-year-old freshman making his varsity debut. The ball came off the toe of my driver and found the forehead of my coach, who was standing fifteen feet away in what he thought mistakenly was a safe spot.

He was knocked cold and taken away in an ambulance, but he was not killed. The K-28 was surgically removed, and the ball's dimples reportedly are still visible between his eyes.

Memorable 1st-tee shot No. 2 was at Ron Jaworski's Eagle's Nest several Good Fridays ago in a foursome that included Jaws. A huge gallery surrounded the tee, eager to see how far an NFL quarterback could actually hit a golf ball.

When I took my first practice swings of the year I knew I was in trouble. I felt disoriented, as if I were on roller skates. I thought of different ways I could get out of the inevitable: "Jaws, I think I'm having a heart attack, you go on without me."

Then I heard a whisper: "That's Bob Shryock. He's not a quarterback, but they say he can hit it pretty far."

Thus inspired, I took a clumsy swing and missed, although the wind generated by the clubhead speed blew the ball off the tee. It didn't go far, but it went straight.

The embarrassed crowd gasped collectively. Someone told me he thought the shot had been staged for "America's Funniest Home Videos." I reloaded and dribbled one to the right, spectators scattering for their lives. The ball bounced against the door to the bar. I should have gone in and stayed.

Such experiences enable me to identify with the golfers at Pitman, whose excuses have kept me entertained over the years:

"Second time I've played in my life."

"First time I've played since October."

"I had open-heart surgery Tuesday."

"My wife died Monday, and I buried her this morning."

Recognizing that making an excuse on the 1st tee is strictly a defensive maneuver designed to extract shots from a playing partner, I have been as impressed by these justifications as by the subsequent shots. Or, in many cases, nonshots.

A 220-pound athletic-looking twenty-year-old takes mighty practice swings, then misses the ball three times in a row. On the fourth he dribbles one off the tee and pronounces himself ready.

Another who will not make the PGA Tour studies the ball endlessly, swings and misses. He then flexes his shoulders as if to say, "I swung at that before I was loose."

Another fans the club and pretends it was a practice swing. This golfer never looks back. He prays no one noticed. He is asking himself, *Why me, God?* His partners don't say a word, fearing he will bury his club in their heads. He then fires a twenty-five-yard wormburner to the right.

Another whiffs and looks angrily at the starter: "No wonder; we've had to wait forty-five minutes."

Lindy Ingram, once a tough football player, took a mighty rip the other morning at Pitman and did a 360-degree turn. While the ball skittered off the tee, Lindy went careening to the turf as though he'd been shot. The grass was wet and Lindy had forgotten to change from his dress shoes.

At Pitman, Lucky Lindy blends right in.

Bob Shryock

Sunday Drivers

Ninety percent of putts that are short don't go in.

Yogi Berra

We have to make a lot of choices in life. Do I want the Big Mac or the Whopper for lunch? Will I sit in the recliner or lay on the couch to watch the game? Should I get up at 6 A.M. on Sunday morning and head off to the golf course for our weekly Duffer Tournament, or should I put on my Amazon outfit and finally mow the lawn enough so that we can see out of the windows again?

As luck would have it, the mower was somewhere in the yard, and even after a full two-minute search I couldn't find it. I took this as a sign. I was sure my wife would agree, but being a gentleman, I didn't wake her to ask.

The sun was already coming up when I arrived at the golf course, so by the time I parked and rummaged through the trunk until I found both golf shoes and a pair of socks that weren't too stiff, the West Coast Duffers were already at the 1st tee, choosing up. Twelve guys and serious bragging rights on the line. The conversation went something like this. . . .

Skip: "Okay. Me and John take on Jim and Pete; Rich and Willie, you're up against Vern and Tommy; Ernie, you and Joe-Joe play Bobby and Big Mike. We're giving two strokes on the front nine, even on the back."

Big Mike: "I don't wanna be with Bobby. . . . He has gas."

Bobby: "I told you that was a medical thing."

Rich: "Since when has frijoles been a disease?"

I rummaged through my bag and found two golf balls, both dented and covered with tree marks. "Anyone got any extra balata balls?" I asked.

Jim: "What? The squirrels ain't happy with your range balls anymore?"

"I think I sliced all my range balls right back into the range the last time we played." I searched the bag again.

Joe-Joe: "I think it should be me and Big Mike. We haven't played together since July."

Big Mike: "That's okay with me, but my back's out a little, so I'll need to shoot from the white tees for it to be fair."

Jim: "Yeah, right. And what about my wrist? I've got carpal tunnel syndrome."

John: "The way you were tossing 'em back last night, it's a wonder you ain't got carpal head syndrome."

Tommy: "How 'bout Pete and me?"

Pete: "No way, Tommy. Ever since you got that Pennzoil cap, you're a psycho with a golf cart."

Tommy: "Well, if you could hit the ball in the same direction twice in a row, we could drive slower and still finish before the moon comes out."

Luckily I found a few balls. I also found half a Snickers bar stuck to my divot tool. "Anyone got any extra tees?" I asked, gnawing on the Snickers. Big Mike threw me half a dozen of his wife's pink tees. They matched my left sock perfectly.

Skip: "Pete, how 'bout you and Vern?"

Pete: "Okay, but Vern's a lefty, and this is a righties' course, so we'll need a couple of strokes."

Vern: "Sounds fair to me. We'll take on Skip and Ernie."

John: "I thought I was with Skip."

Big Mike: "You've been really hot lately, John, you gotta be with Rich."

Rich: "What's that supposed to mean, you shanker? Your handicap is higher than your annual salary."

Skip: "Willie, you and Jim?"

Willie: "I guess so, but no eating in the cart, Jim. The last time, it took me ten minutes to get all the french fries out of my spikes."

Skip: "So. We got John and Rich. You guys are with me and Ernie. That leaves Jim and Willie up with Joe-Joe and Big Mike, and Pete and Vern with Bobby and Tommy. Any other problems?"

"I need a ball marker," I said. Ten ball markers hit me in the head.

Pete: "We got a right-hander's wind going today, too. Vern's gonna need a stroke or two for that."

Tommy: "Why doesn't the poor guy just have an operation and become a normal player?"

Vern: "I'll show you who's normal, Buddy. Let's make the odds straight up."

Pete: "Oh, swell. Who do I make the check out to?"

Jim: "Make a check out to Ernie so he can afford to buy his own stuff next week."

"Hey, you guys. It's not my fault. This isn't my regular bag," I said defensively.

Willie: "No kidding. You borrowed it from me three months ago."

"Oh yeah. I think mine is in the yard somewhere near the mower."

The loudspeaker announced that we were up on the 1st tee.

Skip: "Okay, then we're all set. Now . . . who's gonna go first?"

An awkward pause ensued as we all looked at each other.

Tommy: "I'm not going first. It's bad luck."

Willie: "I went first last week."

Vern: "Lefties should never go first."

Rich: "I call last."

Jim: "I already called it."

Rich: "No, you didn't."

Jim: "Did too."

Rich: "Did not."

Next week. The lawn. I promise.

Ernie Witham

Andrew is fooled for a second weekend in a row.

Confessions of a Hooker

Bob Hope has a beautiful short game. Unfortunately, it's off the tee.

Jimmy Demaret

I've been addicted to golf for a long time, although it's not true that on my first round they strapped my bag on the back of a dinosaur. I hardly ever travel without my clubs. The beauty of golf is that you can play it long after you have to give up other sports.

I still get upset over a bad shot, though, just like anyone else. But it's silly to let the game get to you.

When I miss a shot I think what a beautiful day it is. Then I take a deep breath. I have to. That's what gives me the strength to break the club.

But isn't golf a wonderful game? I like the story of the old-timer who could still hit the ball pretty well but couldn't see where it went. One day the pro told him, "Charlie, I've got just the partner for you. Tom's about your age and he's got eyes like a hawk."

On the 1st tee Charlie hit his drive, turned to Tom and asked, "Did you see it?"

Tom: "Yes."

Charlie: "Where did it go?"

Tom: "I forget."

One of my most enduring friendships, on and off the course, was with Bing Crosby. I first met Bing in 1932 in New York City when we were both in vaudeville. Between shows we'd go over to a driving range under the Fifty-ninth Street Bridge and hit golf balls. He had the slowest backswing I've ever seen. While he was taking the club back, you could fit him for a tailored suit.

When I was playing with Crosby years later, he said, "I'll give you a stroke on this hole if you'll give me a free throw." It sounded like a good deal to me—until we arrived on the green and he picked up my ball and threw it in a lake.

I've had the pleasure of golfing with many presidents. I always enjoy playing with a president. The only problem is that there are so many Secret Service men around there's not much chance to cheat.

Ronald Reagan once broke 100—pretty good for a man on horseback. John Kennedy could have been an outstanding player, bad back and all.

My old friend Chris Dunphy, greens committee chairman of the Seminole Club in North Palm Beach, Florida, told me about the time he invited President Kennedy to play. On the 1st hole, Kennedy floated a nice approach shot about three feet from the pin. He glanced over at Chris, looking for a conceded putt. Chris just stared at the sky.

"You're going to give me this, aren't you?" Kennedy asked.

"Make a pass at it," Dunphy replied. "A putt like this builds character."

"Okay," the president sighed. "But let's keep moving. After we finish, I've got an appointment with the Director of Internal Revenue."

"The putt's good," Dunphy said hastily.

By the time Dwight Eisenhower was elected president in 1952, his devotion to golf was legendary. In fact, there was a rumor that the new dollar bill would have Ben Hogan's picture on it.

Ike was a golfer to warm every weekender's heart, playing with gusto and determination. He fumed over his bad shots and exulted over his good ones, scrapping for every dollar on the line.

I played with Ike at the Burning Tree Club, near Washington, against General Omar Bradley and Senator Stuart Symington. On the 1st tee we discussed wagers. "Well," Ike said with that infectious smile, "I just loaned Bolivia $2 million. I'll play for a dollar nassau." (That's a bet placed on the outcome of each nine holes.) I played terribly, and we lost.

The next day I teamed with Senator Prescott Bush against Eisenhower and Bradley. I was back on my game and shot 75. I beat Ike for four dollars, and I'll never forget his sour look when he pulled out his money clip and grumbled, "Why didn't you play this well yesterday?"

When Ike and Bradley were directing Allied troops in Europe during World War II, Winston Churchill could never understand their devotion to golf. Or mine. I was there doing shows for American servicemen when he saw me take a swing. He snickered and remarked, "Never before has anyone swung so hard for so little."

One of the things I'm proudest of is the Bob Hope Chrysler Classic, held each January in Palm Springs, California. A popular event on the PGA Tour, it has raised more than $35 million for the Eisenhower Medical Center and other charities in the area. Gerald Ford usually had the largest gallery of the tournament. I call him "the man who made golf a contact sport" because of his erratic drives off the tee. You don't know what fear is until you hear Ford behind you shouting "Fore!" . . . and you're still in the locker room. Ford is easy to spot on the course. He drives the cart with the red cross painted on top.

Looking down the road, I can see only good things for golf. It's growing all the time. New tournaments and new players are mixing in with established events and the older stars to create additional excitement.

And how about the women pros, who have gone from playing for lunch money to more than $40 million annually? That's terrific! I can remember the day when the women's purse was a purse. I really enjoy playing with them, but how can I keep my head down when there's so much to watch?

No matter how you look at it, the game of golf has never been in better shape.

Bob Hope with Dwayne Netland

2

GOING FOR
THE GREEN

*If it doesn't matter if you win or lose, but how
you play the game, why do they keep score?*

Charley Boswell
Professional blind golfer

A Mate's Memory of Payne's
Open Victory at Pinehurst

It's great to win, but it's also great fun just to be in the thick of any truly well and hard-fought contest against opponents you respect, whatever the outcome.

Jack Nicklaus

Although Payne and I rarely talked during a round, he always wanted me to be there as often as possible, and he claimed to know exactly where I was on the course at all times.

"Aren't you supposed to be concentrating on your golf?" I'd tease.

"I am, but I always know where you are," he said.

The U.S. Open crowds at Pinehurst were so huge by Saturday that I knew I wouldn't be able to see Payne's shots. I told him, "I think I'm going to watch the round on television today. I'll be there, though, when you get done."

I stayed glued to the television most of the afternoon. I rarely played golf—tennis is more my game—but I had watched Payne play for twenty years, so I knew his game well. As I watched, I noticed that Payne was moving his head ever so slightly on his putts, forward and upward, as though he were trying to watch the ball go into the hole. I watched helplessly as one putt after another failed to drop. "Oh, Payne!" I cried aloud to the television screen. "Keep your head down!" He ended up shooting a 72, his worst round of the championship. Though he was still one stroke ahead of Phil Mickelson, it wasn't a comfortable lead to sleep on.

After his round, I headed to the golf course. "I'm going to go hit some balls," he said.

"Okay, I'll go with you," I said. "You need to spend some time on the putting green, too." Payne nodded in agreement. "You need to keep your head down," I continued quietly.

Payne looked surprised.

"Really?"

"You're trying to watch the ball go in, rather than keeping your head down."

After hitting balls, he spent forty-five minutes working on the practice green. He forced himself to keep his head still and not look up until the ball was well away from the putter. He got to the point where he was putting with his eyes closed and hitting the center of the cup on almost every stroke.

Later, we returned to the home we were renting. Because our daughter, Chelsea, was at a basketball camp, we couldn't talk to her, but Payne called our son, Aaron, at his friend's home.

"Aaron, I'm leading the U.S. Open again!" Payne said.

Aaron, ten, was unimpressed. "That's great, Dad," he replied. "Guess what! Conner got a long-board skateboard!"

Payne laughed. Unwittingly, our kids had a marvelous way of keeping Payne's feet on the ground, and he loved them all the more for it.

With the television blaring Sunday morning, and Payne on his cell phone, I went to take a shower. When I came out of the bedroom, I was shocked to see that Payne's eyes were puffy. He looked as if he had been crying.

"Luv'ie, what's wrong?" I asked. Payne wiped his eyes with his knuckle and motioned toward the television. "NBC just ran a Father's Day segment," he said. "It was about my dad and me." Payne had been unaware that NBC had planned to broadcast a segment concerning Bill Stewart—Payne's dad, who had died of cancer in 1985—and his influence upon Payne's life and career. Payne had been tuning in to watch the early tournament coverage. As he watched the video of himself and his dad, tears flooded his eyes.

Rather than being disconcerted, Payne drew strength from the piece, inspiring him to want to play his best Father's Day round ever.

Eventually the time came to head to the course. Because of the damp, chilly weather, Payne had donned a rain jacket, but when Payne began to warm up, he felt the sleeves of the rain jacket tugging at his arms. The sleeves were restricting Payne's long, fluid swing, yet because of the weather, he needed the warmth the raingear provided.

"Get me a pair of scissors, Mike," Payne asked his caddie, Mike Hicks. Mike found a pair in the golf shop, and Payne proceeded to cut the sleeves off the jacket, trimming the garment so that it covered his shoulders and about three inches down his arms. Although Payne was known for his sartorial splendor on the golf course, he was not concerned about appearances today. All that mattered was playing his best.

After the ups and downs of a final round, Phil Mickelson approached the green on the final hole facing a twenty-foot birdie putt. If Phil made it, Payne would have to make his fifteen-footer to force a playoff. For a moment, it looked as though Phil's putt was in, but then it rolled off and stopped a few inches to the right of the hole.

Now it was Payne's turn. He slowly went through his pre-putt routine, crouching low, eyeing every undulation in the putting surface, lining up the putt. Finally, he stood, pulled the putter back evenly, and brought it forward firmly but smoothly, aiming just to the left inside edge of the cup. The blade connected with the ball, sending it toward the hole. Payne did not move his head.

From my vantage point, I couldn't see the hole. I saw Payne's ball rolling as if in slow motion, bumping over the spike marks, each one a potential land mine that could knock the ball off course. On line, curving slightly, bending; the ball seemed suspended in time, the logo turning over and over, still rolling . . . and then, suddenly, the ball disappeared.

The huge crowd at Pinehurst exploded. It was one of the loudest—and best—responses that I'd ever heard. Payne picked his ball out of the cup, kissed it and slid it into his pocket. This was one ball he would want to keep.

On the side of the green, I pushed to the front of the crowd gathered inside the roped-off area where the players exit the green. Roger Maltbie, the NBC announcer and an old friend of Payne's and mine, spotted me and we hugged. We were both too choked up to speak, and the crowd noise was so loud, it's doubtful that we could have heard each other anyhow. But it didn't matter. Words were unnecessary. Awash in an incredible sense of relief, tears of joy seemed the only appropriate response.

Payne was walking toward me. Because of the throng, he didn't see me at first, and nearly walked right past.

He pulled me close, and we embraced on the green. With my head buried in his shoulder, I heard him say in my ear, "I did it. I kept my head down. All day . . . all day, I did it. I kept my head down."

Through my tears, I said, "I know you did, and I'm so proud of you!"

Many people were amazed at how Payne handled losing the 1998 U.S. Open and winning the 1999 Open with equal measures of grace. Members of the media and some of his fellow competitors were intrigued. Something was different about Payne Stewart. Oh, sure, he was still Payne—spontaneous, outspoken, extremely confident and always wearing his emotions on his sleeve. He still loved a good party, and he'd still tell you what he thought about a subject if you asked him—or even if you didn't. He still worked hard, played hard and loved passionately. Yet people who knew Payne well recognized that he had changed somehow for the better, if that were possible. He possessed a deeper, unusual sense of peace . . . a peace that hadn't always been there.

Tracey Stewart
with Ken Abraham

[EDITORS' NOTE: *Oct. 25, 1999—A runaway Learjet partly owned by golfing great Payne Stewart crashed in Edmunds County, South Dakota. Payne Stewart perished in the accident.*]

The Journey Before "the Putt"

Golf is the hardest game in the world. There's no way you can ever get it. Just when you think you do, the game jumps up and puts you in your place.

Ben Crenshaw

A bizarre putt at qualifying school symbolizes Joe Daley's road to the PGA Tour.

On the fourth day of Q school, with two rounds to play, Joe Daley was 16 under par and moving with the leaders. "Cruisin' along," he says.

His 17th hole that day was a 158-yard par-3 into the wind. When his playing partner's 8-iron shot dropped on the green's front edge, Daley went up a club. "I wanted to hit a smooth 7, but I came over it and pulled it into the water," he says.

From the drop area, 72 yards away, he put a sand-wedge shot 18 feet behind the hole.

His first putt rolled four feet past. The putt coming back was simple. He thought, *Left center.*

The Journey

It was her birthday, in the spring of 1991, and the Atlantic Ocean moved over her feet, for after dinner they walked on the Virginia beach. Joe Daley had the ring in a box hidden in his sock.

"Come over here," he said to Carol, and he handed her the ring, and she said, "What does this mean?"

He said, "What do you mean, 'What does this mean'?"

She waited.

"Oh," he said, "I have to say it?"

She waited.

"Carol, will you marry me?"

"Yes."

He said, "But you do know, don't you, what I want to do?"

"Yes."

He wanted to chase the dream.

She wanted to chase it with him.

And what a dream at what a time. Some men his age had already given it up. He was thirty. He had been a wholesale credit manager since graduation from Old Dominion University in Norfolk, Virginia. He played golf, as he had in school, and now and then friends would remind him he could really play, as during a pro-am when he watched PGA Tour players.

"They'd ask, 'Why aren't you out here with these guys?'" Daley said.

So the newlyweds hit the road. They went to Florida, where she worked as a teacher and he worked on his game, moonlighting as a banquet waiter to help pay the bills. Slowly they saved fifty-five hundred dollars; they tried not to spend it quickly. "A big night out," Carol says, "was pizza once a week."

The Putt

If you're a professional golfer forty years old, as Joe Daley was on that day in December, you've knocked in tens of thousands of four-footers. Still, four days into Q school, you grind on those putts, because if you miss them you can be a dreamer, lover, husband and banquet waiter, but you cannot be a professional golfer.

Loft Center

For years Daley carried with him a putting-practice gizmo, a cup liner that reduced the regulation hole opening by an inch. Heaven only knows how many hours on how many putting greens in how many countries he stood hunched over putts just like this four-footer.

Of 169 players in the final-stage field, 36 would qualify for the 2001 PGA Tour. The next 51 would go to the Buy.com Tour that, nice as it is—and it's maybe the third-best tour in the world—is the minor leagues.

It's the Dakota Dunes Open.

It's the dream deferred.

Daley had played well all week at La Quinta's PGA West Jack Nicklaus courses, starting with a 65. Now, a four-footer. Left center.

The Journey

Crisscrossing North America for two years and more, Joe Daley, six-foot-three and 159 pounds, folded himself into a tiny Nissan 200SX and drove 200,000 miles. The Canadian tour in 1992. Florida mini-tour events in '93.

Chile, South Africa, Bermuda, Jamaica in '94 and '95. "It's not nine-to-five, forty-eight weeks a year," Daley says. "I had that for ten years. I know what that's about. We could have that now. We could have the two jobs, the stability, the house. But this is a lot more fun and a lot more reward- ing. It's the unknown. It's an adventure."

Says Carol: "My friends in teaching, when I told them I was going to Florida with Joe, said, 'What are you doing with your life?' Well, now they're still teaching, and I've been all over the world."

Twice he qualified for the PGA Tour, first in '96 and again two years later, but failed to play well enough long enough to stay. "Such commotion out there," he says. "So many people, so much happening." One journalist described Daley in those years as "a kid in a candy store," changing equipment, playing too many pro-ams, listening to too much well-intentioned advice.

Daley saw Tiger Woods make the first hole-in-one of his pro career. He shared a first-round lead with Greg Norman (a headline began, "Norman, unknown Joe Daley . . ."). He tied for sixth in the B.C. Open. In two years in the big leagues, Daley earned $138,379. He came to a harsh realiza- tion: "My swing needed work, big-time. I'd developed movement that I didn't need. It looked like Jim Furyk's."

While working with an Old Dominion teammate, John Hulbert, to reshape his swing, Daley lost even his Buy.com card. He already was an old man on a young man's journey. Asked by Toronto sportswriter John Gordon if he thought his time had come and gone, Daley said, "There's no quit in Joe Daley."

He made nine straight Buy.com cuts in 2000, had five top-five finishes and, with $151,233, finished twenty-third on the money list, good enough to earn a spot in the final PGA Tour Qualifying School.

The Putt

He needed to hit the four-foot putt firmly, left center. He hit it just that way on just that line. It was in. It disappeared.

Some images are processed by the brain so quickly that even as we move our eyes away, even before we can say what that image is, we realize we've seen something. Reflexively, our eyes leaving the image snap back to it. We want to know what that something is. Joe Daley saw something and looked again and knew what it was and had no idea how it could be his ball. But there it was, perched on the near edge, as if it had stopped there.

That couldn't be. He'd seen it roll over that very spot and disappear. It hadn't caught the lip and spun out. It fell over the front edge of the cup and into the darkness.

He'd made the putt. Hadn't he? Well, no.

"It came back out towards me," he says. He glared at the thing. He hurled his cap to the ground. "It was the damndest thing I had ever seen," Daley told reporters that day.

His ball had bounced out of the hole after hitting the top edge of the cup liner. By rule, the liner is to be set at least an inch beneath the green surface. In Daley's case, the liner sat crookedly in the hole, probably jerked away with the flagstick.

"I asked a tour official about it, but he said there was nothing he could do about it," Daley says. So he made a triple-bogey 6, one stroke lost to bad luck. He played the last thirty-seven holes 1 under par. Doing that good work under such pressure, the lost stroke couldn't hurt him that much.

Could it?

The Journey

It could. Thirty-six players at 417 or better qualified for the 2001 PGA Tour. Joe Daley shot 418. He'd rather have shot 417, but he's a grown-up and he knows things happen.

"It's the journey that matters, not one putt. Hey, on that same hole the last day, I made a thirty-foot downhiller with a foot-and-a-half break," he says. "I'm a lucky man. I'm doing what I want to do, my wife is traveling with me and we're having fun. That one putt is just a bump in the road."

Again this summer, then, Joe and Carol Daley will be on the Buy.com road, and if history suggests the future, there'll come a day when they're in the middle of nowhere, cruisin' along, and they'll answer to a voice that says . . .

Sky diving?

After Daley missed a Buy.com cut in 1999, he and his wife were en route from North Carolina to Virginia. "I thought we needed a diversion," Carol says. "So we stopped at a friend's who said, 'I know, how about I take you skydiving?'"

She'd been fly-fishing in Idaho, hiking in Colorado, dancing in Morocco, all with her dreamer who didn't know what to say on that Virginia beach. Now she has thrown herself from a plane and lived to laugh about it.

"Who knows," she says, "what's going to be next?"

Dave Kindred

Bag drop.

Arnie's Army

*Arnold Palmer is the biggest crowd pleaser since
the invention of the portable sanitary facility.*

Bob Hope

Arnie faced a near impossible shot, at least in the eyes of
mere mortals. Two hundred yards separated his ball and
Memorial Park's 4th hole. His ball rested on a crushed-shell
maintenance path in the pocket of trees bordering the left
side of the fairway, while the overhanging limb from a
nearby oak tree restricted his powerful swing. Numerous
swales in the fairway complicated his approach to the
green, if he chose a low punch-and-run shot, and the
canopy of tree foliage made a high-lofted shot unrealistic.

I had never seen or heard of Arnold Daniel Palmer in the
spring of 1958. You see, I was just nine years old, a sandlot
golfer since the age of seven, and totally unaware of the
world of golf outside my own little world. Golf to me was
still plastic golf balls, holes dug in the backyard and small
tree branches with rags attached for flagsticks.

My father, God bless him, had decided today was the
day to expose me to the masters of the fairways, and he

drove us nearly an hour so that we could see the 1958 Houston Open. He, too, was anxious to see the man who had just won the Masters, and by the look of it, so was the entire golfing population of Houston.

A huge gallery surrounded Palmer and lined the fairways four deep. Around the green, they were six and seven deep, some using periscopes or stools, anything for a better vantage point to view their new hero. Arnie seemed unperturbed by the masses and more concerned with his very difficult shot. He took several practice swings in an effort to see just how much of a swing he could take without striking the tree limb. With each swing, his club struck the limb with a loud thump. The gallery muttered among themselves, assuming the worst. "What's he gonna do?" asked one man. "I don't know. Surely he'll just chip out," said the other. Apparently, neither man had ever witnessed Arnold Palmer in action.

Arnie took a drag from his cigarette and tossed it to the ground. He stared into his bag, then to the hole, trying to imagine which club would produce the shot he desperately needed. The crowd, which had been buzzing, fell silent. My father lifted me to his broad shoulders, and we both peered over the dozens of heads straining to see what would happen next.

Palmer took out a 3-iron and addressed the ball. His feet scratched at the shale like a mad bull, trying to get his footing. One more practice swing and he was ready. You could hear a pin drop.

Whack! Almost instantaneously, shouts of approval and applause rose from those lucky enough to be nearest Arnie. The rest of us could see nothing, only crane our heads in the direction of the distant green—hoping to catch a glimpse of the ball streaking toward its target.

What happened next was probably more thrilling than if I had hit the shot myself. I never did see the ball, but what I heard sent chills down my spine. The thousands that lined the fairway and green let us know just how the shot was progressing. As the ball danced toward the green, the shouts and applause grew in intensity until, finally, a prolonged roar came that seemed to last forever. The enormous pines and oak trees inhabiting Houston's Memorial Park echoed the thunderous applause tenfold across the fairways to the other spectators on the golf course. They seemed to trumpet the arrival of a new legend in the making—King Arnold.

When the crowd raced ahead of us toward the green, we could finally see where Arnie's ball finished—six inches from the cup! The arrow from Cupid's bow had been thrust deep into my heart! I can still see the smile and the joy on my father's face, as we shared a truly magical moment together—father and son. From that very moment, I knew I wanted to be a professional golfer.

I was to see Arnie many more times in my youth. Whenever he competed in the Houston area, I was there with my golfing buddies, sometimes carrying signs that said "Go Arnie!" and cheering at the top of my lungs. Eighteen years after my experience at Memorial Park, I fulfilled the dream he instilled in me as a nine-year-old and qualified to play on the PGA Tour. I can honestly say that, had it not been for the man we idolize today, I might never have achieved the dream of becoming a professional golfer.

But it wasn't just Arnie's instant inspiration that got me there. It was also my wonderful father who made sure that I played and worked hard on my game. He plodded every step of that arduous journey with me—encouraging me, challenging me, and most of all, loving me. In my heart and soul, he will always be "The King."

Bill Pelham

Two Dreams Realized

One of the most poignant moments in Masters history came in 1992, when Fred Couples won the tournament—his first major championship.

After he signed his scorecard, tournament officials brought him to the CBS studio in Butler Cabin, where he would be interviewed by Jim Nantz and awarded the Green Jacket by the 1991 winner, Ian Woosnam.

What made the moment so special was that Nantz and Couples had been through this many times before in mock interviews. As suitemates at University of Houston, Nantz—who dreamed of covering the Masters for CBS—would "interview" Couples—who dreamed of winning the Masters one day.

After CBS went off the air, Couples and Nantz embraced, both with tears in their eyes.

"The thing that is so amazing is that all those years ago, we always knew it was going to be the Masters that Fred would win," Nantz said.

Don Wade

A Bright Light

Success in this game depends less on strength of body than strength of mind and character.

Arnold Palmer

It took a ravaging form of cancer to beat Heather Farr, the professional who died in 1993 at the age of twenty-eight.

Even against great odds, she was unaccustomed to defeat. Heather, the underdog, had always prevailed. Too short and too small, they said; couldn't hit it far enough.

But Heather, who barely topped five feet, ignored the common yardsticks. Tee shots had nothing to do with the size of her heart. In that, she was a giant.

At the age of eleven, she brought Lee Trevino home to dinner. At sixteen, when told that the first step to the Curtis Cup was winning the Girls' Junior, she won it the following week. At twenty, she refused all offers of sponsorship on the LPGA Tour. She had money to get to the first tournament and that, of course, would be enough.

From her first junior tee shot to her last professional putt, Heather Farr won ten state titles, a host of junior events, a couple of national championships and a million hearts.

"I don't think anyone ever loved the game more than Heather did," said Sharon Farr, her mother.

Heather was five when she first joined her father on his weekend rounds in Phoenix, Arizona. Equipped with coffee and a blanket, they lined up at 3 A.M. for a tee time at Papago Golf Course. For three years she simply tagged along, then begged, "Let me hit it! Let me hit it!"

Heather was nine when she announced that she had entered a tournament. On that momentous day, she headed for the 1st tee while her mother waited in the coffee shop, chatting with another mother.

A few hours later, Heather returned in the company of a small, tow-headed boy who addressed Mrs. Farr's companion. "Mom, you won't believe what happened to me," said the boy. "I got hit in the stomach by a golf ball. What's worse, it was hit by a girl!"

"I told him not to walk out in front of me when it was my turn to hit," Heather explained. "Finally, the only way I could play was to ignore him and go ahead and hit the ball. He turned around, and it hit him right in the stomach."

The boy, future U.S. Amateur champion Billy Mayfair, jerked up his shirt to reveal the dimpled imprint of a ball. "And this is how hard she hit it," he announced.

Despite the mishap, Heather's lifelong love of competition had begun.

"We had no idea what her capabilities or limitations were," Sharon said. "Only she knew that. We didn't know which courses she liked to play, so we told her to make her own schedule and we'd do our best to get her there."

Heather learned in victory, one memorable day winning a junior event in Phoenix in the morning and a Tucson tournament in the afternoon. And she learned the bitter lessons of defeat. Leading the ten-and-under division of the Junior World Championship, she was alarmed by the size of the gallery and five-putted the final green to finish fourth. It was simply a mistake, she said, one she would not repeat.

She lost so many balls that she was forced to borrow one on the final hole of the Orange Blossom Classic. The youngest, smallest player in the tournament, she suffered the added humiliation of finishing dead last.

"We were leaving the tournament, and Heather stood in front of the scoreboard for a long time while we waited for her," her mother remembered. "When she turned around she said, 'I'll tell you one thing—I'm never going to be last again.' And she never was."

At home in Phoenix, Heather signed up for a weight-training program at a local gym. She may have been smaller than the other players, but she could get stronger.

By this time, she was also under the tutelage of U.S. and British Open champion Lee Trevino. At the age of ten, with typical bravado, she had taken a newspaper clipping about herself to the Phoenix Open and asked the pros to sign it. Only Trevino paid serious attention to the tiny girl in tennis shoes, stopping to read the entire article, then offering encouragement.

That summer, Heather wrote a letter. "Dear Mr. Trevino, When you're in town next time, why don't you come over for dinner?"

At the next Phoenix Open, Trevino spotted her. "You wrote me that letter, didn't you?" he said. Trevino turned to Heather's mother and laughed, "That little sneak put her picture in it. Well, when's dinner?"

"Heather told him to pick a night," Sharon recalled, "and, bless his heart, he showed up when he said he would, walked into the house, grabbed a beer out of the refrigerator, and became just one of the family."

Over the years, Heather and Trevino visited often. He taught her shots, amazed at her ability to soak up his instruction.

"They had this wonderful, warm friendship," Sharon said. "He even taught her how to work on her clubs and change the grips, telling her to never let anyone do anything to her clubs if she didn't know what they were doing. When he gave her a 4½-wood, he said, 'Heather, you're going to do a lot of damage with this.' And she did."

One extraordinary winter day, Trevino telephoned, urging Heather to come to Dallas to play at Royal Oaks Country Club, a tight, tree-lined layout where he liked to practice.

"But Dallas is having an ice storm," Heather protested. "We can't play Royal Oaks."

"Come on down. We'll work it out," Trevino said.

Heather made the short flight to Dallas. In the bitter cold on a deserted Royal Oaks fairway, Trevino pulled out a pocket knife, cut out a square of sod, pulled it back from the bare dirt, and built a bonfire. Warmed by the fire, the great professional and the little girl laughed and talked, hitting golf balls to their hearts' content.

Little Heather was on her way to big things. At sixteen, she shared medalist honors in the 1981 U.S. Women's Amateur. She wasn't long, but she could smack a fairway wood closer to the hole than most players could hit a wedge. Thanks to Trevino, she had a great short game. Best of all, she believed in herself.

"Heather had a walk of confidence like nobody I've ever seen in my life," said Tom Meeks, a USGA official and longtime friend. "She walked like she knew exactly what she was trying to do and how she was going to do it. There wasn't any question in her mind that every time she went out to play she was going to have a successful round."

In 1982, she attended the Curtis Cup Match on her way to the U.S. Girls' Junior. Enthralled, she asked an official how to win a spot on the team. "Winning the Girls' Junior next week would be a good start," the official kindly replied.

Heather said only, "Okay." She may as well have said, "Done."

After that win, Heather finished as low amateur in the U.S. Women's Open the following summer. A berth on the 1984 Curtis Cup team was hers.

Her travel diary from that trip to Great Britain is the only written record Heather left behind. In rounded, youthful script, she recorded what she considered to be the greatest adventure of her life.

At Golf House, "P. J. Boatwright tells us not to be polite but to win as big as we can.

"June 3—Toured the R&A club. Actually got to see the whole thing! The upper balcony has the most awesome view . . . then ate lunch at the St. Rule Club. Glenna Collett Vare sat three people away.

" . . . At dinner, received our Curtis Cup pins. Something so small means SO much."

Of a practice round at Muirfield, site of the match, she wrote, "The afternoon was so clear. Looking out over Muirfield was such an unbelievable experience. The course was out there waiting for us."

Perhaps exhaustion kept her from writing much about her opening foursomes match. She wrote simply that it was an exciting match that her team won, 1-up.

"Yes, Heather was full of beans and ready to play," said Tish Preuss, the 1984 Curtis Cup captain. "A little cocky, but that's good; that's just the way she was. She was happy-go-lucky. She knew she could play, and she proved it."

Preuss recalled that her team had only a one-point lead going into the final round.

"And on the 1st tee, Heather said, 'Don't worry about me, Captain. I'll win my point.'" She did, of course.

Judy Bell, former Curtis Cup team captain, saw Heather play many times. "Every inch of her was positive," said Bell. "Her golf swing was traditional, orthodox. She worked hard. She worked on her mechanics, but she had the extra stuff to go with it. She had this fiber.

"That whole team was a real enthusiastic bunch," Bell continued. "She just took to it. She had never played in Scotland in her life, but pretty soon she was wearing a tam. Those were the best of her golf days."

The U.S. team won the Curtis Cup match, and Heather cried at the closing ceremonies when Preuss quoted from Bob Ward:

"I wish you joy in all your days;

"I wish you sadness so that you may better measure joy."

Heather then flew to Rapid City, South Dakota, and won the Women's Amateur Public Links. Still happy and carefree, she joined Meeks and others on a victory ride down the rapids. Giggling in ecstasy, she floated down a creek on a huge inner tube. When the creek wound through the golf course and under a bridge, USGA committee members bombarded the new champion with water-filled balloons.

The best of her golf days, yes.

She turned professional and at twenty was the youngest player to emerge from the 1986 LPGA Qualifying School. With her little bankroll, she hit the tour. Heather was once again meeting her agenda. Life was so sweet and bright that she thought every month was May, never guessing that it was really November.

Heather Farr had a great short game and she could hit a driver from the fairway, pure and true. She had a small body, a great heart and a million friends. She had a short life, granted. But how it did shine.

Rhonda Glenn

Golf's Ace with Heart

It was another tournament town, another cardboard hotel room, another evening spent staring at the too-blue, too-orange television images atop the Formica-covered bureau. Juan "Chi Chi" Rodriquez, vying for the lead at the 1967 Texas Open in San Antonio, was practicing putts on the carpet and thinking about the birdies that slipped away that afternoon.

The drone of the evening news suddenly riveted his attention: a reporter was interviewing a distraught woman whose home in Illinois had been destroyed by a tornado. All she had left were the clothes she wore. Rodriguez was so moved that he made a pact with himself. If he bagged the trophy the following day, he would send the tornado relief fund five thousand dollars. The next day he won—and so did the tornado victims.

Across the country, dozens of people have benefited from the compassion of this pencil-thin Puerto Rican golf pro. While some professional athletes spend their spare time doing beer commercials, Rodriguez checks up on things like incurable diseases, child abuse and world hunger.

Everybody on tour knows about his big heart, even the caddies. After each of his eight tournament wins, he has staged a lavish dinner party for them. "Chi Chi makes us feel we really count," says veteran tour caddie Richard Holzer.

Rodriguez's benevolence has perhaps detracted from his golf game. For a man who once outdrove Jack Nicklaus by one hundred yards and is regarded by Ken Venturi as one of golf's finest shotmakers, there should be more than eight titles, and his career earnings should have soared beyond $1 million. But Rodriguez's mind was on other things.

"He'll never be as great a golfer as he is a human being," asserts pro Bill Kratzert. "Sometimes he worries more about what's happening in Asia than what's happening on the course. During practice he talks incessantly about poverty overseas."

At age forty-six in 1979, Rodriguez continued to play the PGA Tour nonstop while other pros his age were retiring. Although he hadn't won an event in three years, he zealously pursued a comeback. The reason: He planned to give his next winner's check to Mother Teresa for her leper colony in India.

Rodriguez came from a background riddled with the kind of despair he empathizes with today. He knows the feeling of a stomach aching with emptiness. Remembering is one of the things Chi Chi does best.

Rio Piedras is a poverty-scarred village just outside San Juan, Puerto Rico. Chickens and naked toddlers and skeletal dogs mingle around shacks alongside dirt roads where Chi Chi Rodriguez grew up.

One of six children, Chi Chi labored in the sugar-cane plantations with his father, from whom he learned sensitivity, goodness and hope. "My dad worked fourteen hours a day, every day of his life." Rodriguez recalls. "He would come home dead-tired and hungry, but if he saw a kid walk by with a big belly—the sign of malnutrition—

he'd give him his rice and beans. He did that so often I was concerned he wasn't getting enough to eat, but he always told me that God would supply him with strength."

Little time was available for recreation, but occasionally Chi Chi and his older brother would push each other down the highway in a cart. One day they crested a hill, rolled to the bottom—and discovered golf: "We saw this very green grass and men hitting tiny white balls with shiny steel sticks. I figured the guys who carried the bags for the players made money. It looked easier than being a waterboy at the plantation."

Rodriguez was only seven, but he marched across the stately fairways of Berwind Country Club and asked about a job lugging "those bags." The caddiemaster told him he was too small and suggested he start as a forecaddie, the person who marks the position of a player's ball and searches for errant golf balls. Chi Chi eagerly accepted.

Along the way he invented his own version of golf. For a club he attached a pipe to a guava limb, and for a ball he shaped a tin can into a sphere; then he dug a few holes to "play." Soon he could drive fifty to one hundred yards. All those swipes with guava limbs developed tremendous hand action, eventually making the 135-pound Rodriguez one of golf's longest hitters.

Caddies were prohibited from playing Berwind, but sometimes, just before nightfall, Chi Chi would sneak onto the turf with borrowed clubs and play eighteen holes in forty-five minutes. On occasion, he was trailed by an irate greenskeeper, who took potshots at him with a revolver. "I'd hit and run," Rodriguez remembers. (He is still one of pro golf's fastest players.) When he was only twelve, Chi Chi scored an astonishing 67 and knew golf was his future.

At the entrance of Berwind was an old Banyan tree that provided a perch for Rodriguez between shifts. There he watched the Cadillacs drive by and dreamed of the day he would be rich and waving to throngs of fans.

Rodriguez enlisted in the army at nineteen, making a name for himself in military golf tournaments during his two-year stint. After his discharge, he worked for a year as an aide at a psychiatric hospital in San Juan. He fed and bathed patients, played dominoes with them, calmed them when they became violent. The job was menial, paying eighty dollars a month, but Chi Chi calls it "the most rewarding work I've ever had. I was *giving*, and there's nothing more enjoyable than that."

He hadn't forgotten his dream, however, and he found the key to it in 1957, when the Dorado Beach Resort opened. Among its amenities was Puerto Rico's first pro-caliber golf course. Chi Chi headed there with a bundle of clippings about his army golf triumphs. Ed Dudley, the pro at the new course, was bringing a man from the states to assist him, but he grudgingly agreed that he and Chi Chi could play a game.

Rodriguez was so nervous that he shot an 89. "Mr. Dudley, I played awful today," he said, "but if you help me, I could become one of the best golfers in the world." Dudley looked off in the distance, then said, "Okay, you've got a job." And for the next three years Chi Chi worked for Dudley and Pete Cooper. Both men nurtured his potential, coaching him several hours a day.

When he was twenty-five, Rodriguez joined the Tour. From the start he made a comfortable income, and soon he was taking home trophies. He was a pacesetter when it came to injecting the bland pro-golf caravan with humor. "Americans are so hard-working," he explains, "and half of them don't enjoy their work. So I try to give them something to smile about when they come out to watch us."

As a successful golf pro, Rodriguez bought the big, shiny car he'd dreamed about in the Banyan tree, and a sprawling villa at Dorado Beach, too. But before he indulged in these trappings, he sent his brother through law school and bought homes for his mother and other family members. "This is the first house house we've had," says Iwalani, Chi Chi's Hawaiian-born wife. "Until three years ago, we lived out of suitcases. When he'd give away money to strangers, I'd think, 'We don't even have a place to call our own yet!'" Says Chi Chi, "When someone hurts, I hurt. It's tough being poor, and it's so easy to say, 'Well, I made it, so can everybody.' That just isn't true. Thousands of people don't have a chance."

Young people are more and more the focus of the golfer's generosity. The Chi Chi Rodriguez Youth Foundation, a nonprofit organization based in Clearwater, Florida, draws most of his charitable energies. Established to help troubled or abused youngsters, the foundation provides a program designed as a springboard into the free-enterprise system that also includes intensive academic tutoring and lots of golf instruction. They go on field trips to see how various businesses are run and to museums and sports events.

"Basically, these kids have been defeated all their lives," says Chi Chi. "So we're introducing them to challenges and positive competition, showing them that they can succeed."

During the 1979 J.C. Penney Golf Classic in Tampa, Florida, Rodriguez became interested in the project. Some youngsters from a juvenile detention center approached him for autographs. "The next thing I knew," recalls Bill Hayes, the counselor accompanying them, "Chi Chi was offering to come out and do a golf clinic. He arrived a few days later and hit balls over the prison walls. Afterward, he sat in the cells talking with the kids and ate dinner with them." That's when Hayes outlined to Rodriguez the plans for the Youth Foundation. Today 450 youngsters are enrolled.

Meanwhile, back home, Chi Chi's kind touch is felt by

the Children's Hospital of Puerto Rico, which his annual tournament—the Chi Chi Rodriguez International Festival of Golf—continues to benefit.

But it's not just the sweeping gestures Chi Chi is known for. "If someone is hurting," points out Bill Braddock, a longtime friend, "Chi Chi's going to try to help. It wouldn't surprise me at all if he gave up golf and started making house calls."

Jolee Edmondson

[EDITORS' NOTE: *Ranked fourth on the Senior Tour's all-time victory list, Chi Chi continues to devote his energies to his youth foundation, which currently serves over five hundred kids.*]

A Change of Heart

From somewhere in that sky, deliriously clogged with corks and hats and shirts and roar and glee came the best thing of all: a pair of dark, wraparound, screw-you sunglasses. That's how you knew that everything about American golf had changed.

What's weird was that up until Sunday it looked as if nothing had. The U.S. Ryder Cup team arrived in Boston with all the emotion of wilted arugula. No team spirit. No camaraderie. Just the same old story: twelve players, twelve Lears.

David Duval had called the Ryder Cup "another exhibition." Four players had wanted pay for play. At the opening ceremony, Tiger Woods chomped gum through "The Star-Spangled Banner" behind black sunglasses. The Americans got hate mail. They were heckled. Duval played part of a Thursday practice round by himself, prompting one fan to holler, "Hey, David, playing with all your friends?"

Well, just about. Coming in, Duval had about as many Tour pals as five-putts. Being shy, bookish and having dinner every night with the Marriott room-service guy doesn't help.

The European players, meanwhile, were breaking all of Bela Karolyi's hug records. They read each other's putts, kissed each other's wives, walked down fairways linked at the elbow.

But then an impossible, preposterous, wonderful thing began to happen. The twelve American CEOs in spikes started melting a little. They started acting like *people.* Better, they started becoming teammates. Maybe it was the team haircuts that registered 13 on the Stimpmeter. Maybe it was what Duval said when everybody was just about to leave a meeting on Thursday night. "You might have read I don't want to be here," he said through teary eyes. "I do. I am *passionate* about winning this." Maybe it was the way their captain, Ben Crenshaw, kept looking at them with those aching blue eyes and saying how much he admired them, even after they'd gone out and laid the worst opening-day egg for the United States in Ryder Cup history. Whatever it was, Crenshaw found a Super Glue.

Even though the United States was down 10–6 after two days, even though no team had ever come back from three points to win on the final day, forget four, the unheard-of notion of American togetherness started to spread like a sappy chain letter. In a Saturday night meeting, every player spoke and every player cried. "Every night I go to bed with a smile on my face," Woods said. "And every morning I wake up with a smile on my face, because I can't wait to come to the team room and be with my friends." His speech stunned and then touched his teammates.

Crazier still, the Americans went out the next morning and played as if they cared for each other. A guy would thump some outmatched Swede or a lost Frenchman and sprint off to find a teammate in trouble. Duval punched out Jesper Parnevik 5 and 4, then raced rabidly around the 14th green, pumping the crowd to ecstasy with his fists, exhorting the thousands lining the par-5 fairway to chant, "U! S! A!" Yes, *David Duval.*

Behind him, Justin Leonard trudged along the 10th fairway—three holes down to José María Olazábal, needing at least a tie for the United States to win the Cup—crying. Just then, teammate Davis Love III sidled up to him and said, "You can tell me to leave if you want, but I want you to know something: You can do this."

Leonard promptly lost 10 and after halving 11 was four down with seven holes to play. Still Love stayed with him. Suddenly, all heaven broke loose. Leonard started making a beanpot full of putts, winning four of the next five holes and then burying a forty-five-foot bomb at 17 that won the Cup and sent the Yanks into a fit of boorish, shameful and ridiculously emotional behavior. Wasn't it great?

"I've been around these guys for a long time," said Crenshaw's wife, Julie. "This week, they changed."

Apparently, when it suddenly hits you that one of the greatest thrills in golf doesn't necessarily come with an appearance fee, you lose yourself. When the national anthem was played at the closing ceremony, Woods chewed no gum, wore no sunglasses and put his hand over his heart. At one point in the post-putt pandemonium, family man Tom Lehman ripped off his shirt and flung it to the crowd. Fluff and Tiger, divorcees, embraced as if filming a Kodak ad.

High above them, from a champagne-soaked balcony overlooking thousands of joy-drunks, Duval, newly baptized, ripped off those hideous face-hiding sunglasses, reared back and heaved them into all those yesterdays.

Rick Reilly

Golf Nuts

Let's talk about golf nuts.

I'll start with the runny little sixty-eight-year-old com-
batant who always insists on playing from the gold tees.

He says you can't really see a golf course unless you
play it from the tips.

He finds something terribly intriguing, as opposed to
insane, about a seventy-two-hundred-yard golf course,
particularly if it's infested with water, waste, sand, bulk-
heads, trees, moguls, deep rough, violent wind, severe
pins and slick greens.

He would never improve a lie. He is greatly offended at
the mere suggestion of a mulligan.

He loves playing a par-5 hole with driver, 3-wood, 5-
wood, 7-wood, sand blast, pitch, chip, and four putts.

He is enthralled by a long, brutal par-4 hole that he can
attack with driver, lateral, spoon, unplayable, 5-iron,
boundary, 9-iron, cart path, pitch, and three putts.

He is fascinated with a killer par-3 hole that he can bring
to its knees with driver, water, 5-wood, bulkhead, wedge,
chip, and three putts.

One day he hopes to break 126.

"How did you play today, dear?" his wife asks.

"Great. I had a putt for a par and three chips at birdies."

Next, I give you the tireless gentleman who calls me every year or so to bring me up to date on the progress he's making in trying to play all of America's famous courses.

He has been at this for about twenty-five years, I guess.

In all of the phone calls over the past quarter of a century, he has asked me the same question.

Can I suggest anything that will help him get on Pine Valley, Augusta National, Merion, Seminole, Cypress Point, Oakmont, Los Angeles Country Club, Bel Air, Shinnecock Hills, Colonial, Winged Foot, Chicago Golf, Brook Hollow or Olympic?

I used to say, "Crawl over the fence and don't play the 1st hole or the 18th."

Now I say, "Steal a hundred million dollars from your company and put a hyphen in your name."

I give you this retired fellow I've stumbled upon who plays six times a week and makes all of his own clubs. They are rather crude-looking things, but he makes them in his workshop.

Although golf is obviously his life, he has been pleased to inform me that he has never attended a tournament, doesn't watch golf on television, doesn't read golf books, doesn't read golf magazines and doesn't even read the sports pages of the newspapers.

One day he asked what I did for a living. I said I was a writer.

"What do you mean?" he said, looking at me as if he had just heard of the most bizarre profession imaginable.

I said, "Well, among other things, I write articles for a golf magazine."

He looked at me for a long moment, and then he said, "Why?"

I excused myself hurriedly and went home and reported to my wife that I thought I had just met the mysterious sniper who fires at motorists from a freeway overpass.

Also in my neighborhood is this elderly man who only plays on weekends but spends the rest of the time hunting golf balls.

He's always out there during the week, creeping through the trees or poking around at the edge of lagoons.

It is rumored that he has over ten thousand golf balls in his garage, where he keeps them neatly arranged on shelves.

More than one person has told me I must visit this man's garage—his collection of golf balls is astounding.

"It's on my list," I say nicely.

As amazing as anyone I've heard about lately is the dentist. He is said to be a lifelong fan of Arnold Palmer. He is said to be such a fan of Arnold's, it borders on mental illness.

I don't know if it's true—I can only hope—but the dentist is purported to carry in his pocket a ball marker made from the gold that was extracted from Arnold's teeth.

This might not make him the biggest Arnold Palmer fan in the world, however.

There was a journalist in Great Britain whose unbounding hero worship of Palmer became a legend. He was never satisfied, one hears, with autographs, scrapbooks, photos, paintings or articles about Arnold.

One day he got the inspired idea to begin collecting the divots Palmer would take out of fairways in England and Scotland. Eventually, the entire lawn of his home near London was made out of Arnold Palmer divots.

Actually, if I were to follow through on a thought I had the other day, I think I could be exempt on the Golf Nut Tour myself.

You see, I have this habit of knocking balls into the woods when they betray me. I might add that it doesn't take much for me to feel betrayed. A four-foot putt that curls out, a pulled 7-wood that winds up in a bunker, a chip shot that races across the green and into the frog hair, a tee shot that defies its stern warning and seeks out the forest.

I've been leaving these balls in the woods, but I've come up with a better idea. A small cemetery in my yard. It could be fenced in by a variety of broken shafts. Call me the Mortician.

In this cemetery I will bury all of the golf balls that betray me, because if they can betray me once, they will certainly betray me again. Planted into the earth, however, they will have nothing to do but rot in eternal hell forever.

Never again will they be able to bring unwarranted grief and anguish to some innocent golfer, like myself, who never meant them any harm whatsoever.

It's what they deserve, I say. All I've ever asked of them is a simple string of bogeys.

Dan Jenkins

Drive and Determination

The more I practice, the luckier I get.

Gary Player

I have to admit that I have never played golf. In fact, the only golf course that I have ever been on ended with me trying to hit the ball into a clown's mouth. That's why it is so strange that the game of golf had such an impact on my life.

I was nineteen years old and had just started dating a young man that I had met at work. We seemed to have a chemistry together and both shared a love of competition. A lot of our time with each other was spent bowling or playing arcade games like pinball or Pac Man. Being a '70s kind of girl, I was determined to prove my capabilities and be an equal and worthy opponent. As it turned out, our skills were fairly evenly matched. We were both thoroughly enjoying our playful competitions.

One day, he came to my house dressed casually as always. Searching for something different to do he asked, "Have you ever been to a driving range?" I thought, *My God! A driving range? What does he want to do now, race cars?* He explained that he was talking about driving golf balls, not cars. Well, I had never tried it before, but surely it must be simple. After all, if I can hurl a fourteen-pound ball fifty feet down a lane and knock down ten sticklike pins at the far end, how difficult could it be to swing a club and hit a tiny ball perched right at my feet? I was confident that this little activity would not damage my athletic image, so off we went to the driving range.

We arrived at Bill's Golfland & Family Fun Park—a virtual megaplex of batting cages, arcades, go carts, mini-golf and, of course, our chosen destination, the driving range. After selecting our clubs, buying our balls and several embarrassing moments of scrambling to gather the bouncing balls that I spilled out of the top of the bucket, we were ready to start.

After brief instructions from my date, I then set out to prove my abilities. The first five or ten swings I took were either total misses or full-force collisions between my club and the rubber mat on the tee. I received more instruction from my teacher.

"Keep your eye on the ball."

"Bring the club back slowly."

Okay, there were a few more useless attempts and then . . . CONTACT! The ball took air and landed just shy of the fifty-yard marker, but it was a start! Over the next hour or so, it didn't get much better than that. Balls trickled off of their mount and rolled into the grass in front of my station. Several fell off of their tee, in a delayed reaction, caused by the wind from my swing passing its target. I admit it was pathetic, definitely not the piece of cake that I had imagined.

Each time that I turned to pick up a new ball from my bucket, I would catch the sight of onlookers (a crowd was beginning to gather) wearing Titleist caps and Spalding sun visors. There were heads shaking and eyes rolling.

Occasionally, I would hear a comment like, "Your feet are too far apart," or, "Bend your knees." I felt the pressure mounting. An audience formed behind me. To each side of me, a row of fellow golfers quested after swing perfection. In front of me, golf balls were flying through the air and landing at the 200-, 250- and even the 300-yard markers. At my feet the tiny white ball, which I thought would pose no challenge whatsoever, had grown fangs and horns. The sphere was sneering up at me, as if to say, "I showed you."

Snap out of it! I thought. *You have a brain; IT does not.* After all, the ball is just a lifeless piece of rubber that I command where to go. I felt a rush of determination come over me. I took a deep breath and repeated all of the directions to myself.

"Feet shoulder-width apart."

"Knees slightly bent."

"Bring the club back slowly."

"Keep your eye on the ball."

"Smooth and steady swing."

"Finish with your hands towards the target."

With an air of confidence, I approached the ball. I carefully acted out each mental step-by-step instruction. Before I knew it, I found myself following through with my swing with absolute perfection. My concentration was broken by the sound of *whack*. I raised my head to see the ball soaring through the air. I actually lost it in the sun's glare for a while, before it fell to earth somewhere around the 300-yard marker!

"Yes!" It was perfect! I jumped. I screamed. I rejoiced at my success.

I arrogantly turned to my date, "Did you see that? I knew I could do it!"

The laughter of my companion quickly dampened my celebration. He pointed to my tee, where my ball was still perched, tauntingly sticking its tongue out at me. The incredible 300-yard drive that I was claiming credit for actually belonged to the golfer on my left (who, by the way, was also laughing). The audience that had gathered began to chuckle, as did the range attendant. After taking several bows and curtsies, I quietly and humbly returned to my futile attempts at hitting a golf ball.

Needless to say, I never made it to the LPGA. The man who was my date that day became my husband and the father of my children. My determination, his patience and an ability to laugh at life, the very characteristics that we showed each other that day during the driving range episode, are qualities that have been the basis for a long, happy, strong and successful marriage. We occasionally return to the driving range with our two teenage sons. But now, when we go, it's not to prove anything or to compete with each other. It's strictly for the fun of it.

Darlene Daniels Eisenhuth

The Boys of Summer

On the last afternoon of the last major of the century, the players meet at the golf club at three. One drives up in his Volvo, two are dropped off by a mom on her way to the grocery store, the fourth rides his bike to the course. Quickly, it's decided that Mike and the Old Guy will play Rob and Ritchie in a four-ball match.

A tee is tossed in the air. Ritchie and Rob are up first. Ritchie is sixteen, a rising junior player with blond peach fuzz on his chin. He works part-time at Burger King but is thinking about quitting because it will interfere with his golf team practice, which begins tomorrow. He sets up and casually slugs a drive about 230 yards out to the first cut of rough. The Old Guy congratulates him and he grins, almost sheepishly, and says, "That's nothing. Wait till you see Rob and Mike."

Rob, fifteen, wears baggy gray cargo pants, unlaced Foot-Joys and braces on his teeth. His hero is Davis Love III. His stance seems unusually wide, but it must get results because in twenty-five state golf association junior tournaments, he's won six times and this year has finished no less than second or third in every event in which he's played. Last year, a three-putt cost Rob the state junior title.

Rob slams a beautiful drive 270 yards to the heart of the fairway.

"Whoa," thinks the Old Guy, idly massaging an elbow that's sore from planting crab-trees that morning. "These guys are good."

Mike is up next. He is almost two years younger and fifty pounds lighter, but he's Rob's best golf buddy. They met three years ago qualifying for the club junior championship and have been nearly inseparable ever since. You see them constantly talking game, shooting the breeze and making birdies.

Neither has a girlfriend but they do have golf, and for probably the last splendid summer of their lives neither even works a part-time job—though Mike allows that he mows a few lawns and umpires Little League games now and then to pick up movie money. His favorite all-time flick is *Shawshank Redemption*, and he seems a bit disappointed when you admit you haven't seen it.

Mike takes dead aim with his strong grip and beat-up War Bird driver. His battered Foot-Joy shoes look ancient—they turn out to be only four months old. His artfully faded Nike shirt is buttoned neatly to the top, David Duval style, and his khakis seem to hang on his slight frame the way clothes cling to a wire coat-hanger. In a driving rainstorm he might weigh ninety-eight pounds wringing wet. "Hey," he protests when you innocently mention this fact, "I'm exactly one hundred—a triple-digit guy." Mike is a freshman who will start his high school playing career tomorrow following in the footsteps of his older brother Pat, a rising senior. According to Rob, Mike is pound for pound probably the longest driver in the entire club. He also has an ace and several eagles on his resume. He coolly tees up and hurls all three digits into a shot that send his Maxfli SX Tour arching toward his best friend's ball, prompting Rob to turn and glare at him. "You better not outdrive me," he warns Mike, finally displaying some impressive mouth hardware that shows he's pleased.

The Old Guy hits his ball respectably and breathes a sigh of relief, watching the Boys of Summer shoulder their bags and bolt down the fairway. Mike and Rob walk together, bags slung low, talking sand wedges and Smashing Pumpkins, like young guns late for the shoot-out. The Old Guy almost has to lope in order to keep up with them and for a moment tries to remember what it feels like to be that young and that limber and so deeply drawn to chasing a game with your best friend.

Among American boys, golf is booming. According to the USGA, a record 4,508 competitors showed up at sixty-one sectional qualifying sites for this year's U.S. Junior Amateur Championship at York, Pennsylvania, which was won in August by seventeen-year-old Hunter Mahan of McKinney, Texas. For the seventh year in a row, the field of entries grew substantially—this year by a whopping 12 percent, a surge many attribute directly to the influence of Tiger Woods. Golf is not about greatness; it's about good-ness—good shots, good friends, good times.

However, Tiger is popular with these particular north-ern Boys of Summer. "No question, the way he holds a lead, he'll win the PGA," Mike sagely asserts three hours before the verdict of the PGA Championship is formally recorded. "But you gotta like that Weir guy, the Canadian. He's a ballstriker. Solid . . ." So are Love and Justin Leonard and half a dozen others who, at this moment, seem as remote as rock stars.

To quote Mike, who whistles softly when he walks and cleans his grooves with the exactitude of a gum surgeon as he waits to hit, "Fame is kinda cool." But fathers and friendship probably have more to do with why Rob and Mike and Ritchie are so hopelessly smitten with the game and never seem to go home from the club except to take meals and sleep a bit.

Rob toddled onto his father Jim's homemade putting green at age four, and by ten he was being dropped off at a local nine-holer where he could play all he wanted till dark for a few bucks. Then a cousin gave him eleven hours of videotapes that included the swings of golf's greatest players, and he took a few free lessons from a pro at a driving range. That was sufficient to kill his basketball dreams.

A year later; he entered his first state junior event, shot 103 and realized he'd have to practice much more if he wanted to compete. This summer, he fell only a couple strokes shy of qualifying for the National Juniors at Essex County Club near Boston. He has three more years of eligibility and no shortage of golf dreams—hopes of a collegiate career "somewhere down south" and maybe the PGA Tour.

Mike's tale is different only in shades of ambition. Both his father and grandfather caddied and played the game, so it seemed only logical for him to at least "give golf a shot." He was a promising team player in soccer and basketball until his dad, a golf-loving forester named Kevin, began taking him to a local par-3 course.

Quickly, reading books and watching players on television, Mike essentially taught himself to play and graduated to the muni and finally the golf club. Now he has a deft putting touch that would impress Dave Pelz and talks of eventually studying medicine and "finding some kind of job—I don't care what—in the golf world."

He displays his surgical touch chipping in for birdie at a critical moment in the match on two consecutive holes, slicing Rob's and Ritchie's lead over him and the Old Guy to one with two to play. "He always does this," says Ritchie, rolling his eyes and then explaining that he followed Mike into golf primarily because they were school pals and promptly got hooked himself.

On the 17th hole, amused by the engaging teen banter about the Frenchman's Folly and the upcoming Ryder Cup selections, the Old Guy finally contributes a birdie putt to the cause and the match is suddenly all square with one to play. The players fall silent, adjusting grips and grinding thoughts. Faraway Medinah, at this moment, holds no more magic than this tiny scene of high drama played out on an almost empty northern golf course where autumn seems imminent. Mike's tee ball catches the hazard and the Old Guy scrambles for par but it isn't good enough—both Rob and Ritchie close with birdies to win.

They shake hands and the Old Guy thanks them for allowing him to tag along, noticing as he does that the northern thistle is in bloom and the goldenrod is almost over—a sure sign, as locals say, that first frost is just six weeks away.

For the record, the Boys of Summer have real last names—*Rob McDonough, Mike Doran* and *Ritchie Thibeault.* You may hear a lot about them someday. Or nary a peep again. In a way, it doesn't matter. These guys are eternal, with their homemade swings and small-town dreams. The reason the game keeps going.

After a five-minute pause for Rob to phone home, the Boys decide to go another loop before darkness catches them. They shoulder their bags, wave politely, speed off on Softspikes worn to nubs. Six weeks till first frost, thinks the Old Guy, rubbing his sore elbow and shaking his head as he heads for the Volvo.

Summer ends far too soon. Not to mention youth.

James Dodson

A Hole in "How Many"?

I try to use a method I call the positive-negative approach. I positively identify the negatives and work from there.

Bob Murphy

Two golfers were on the green of the 3rd hole at Bethpage Golf Course, when all of a sudden a golf ball came from nowhere and rolled right up to the cup. One of the golfers said, "Let's put the ball in the cup and give the guy a hole-in-one."

All of a sudden a golfer came out of the woods and said, "Did any of you see a golf ball around here?"

One of the golfers on the green said, "Yes, it landed right in the cup."

"Good," said the man who hit the "hole-in-one," "that gives me a 13 for this hole."

Steven Schockett

Can't Ty Him Down

From Maine to Maui, parents dropped their spoons into their oat bran last week when they read the headline HIGH SCHOOL JUNIOR QUALIFIES FOR PGA TOUR. To my wife Linda and me, it was like reading CARROT TOP ON MARS PROBE.

See, we happen to *know* a high school junior, our son Kel. Rumor has it he lives in our house. In fact, that may have been Kel who just headed off to school with a Pop-Tart trapped in each armpit, a Pepsi spilling out of one hand, a toothbrush in the other, hat worn sideways, jeans big enough to lose Charles Barkley in and shoes with laces that have never been introduced. It was very difficult to picture him heading off to, say, win the Masters.

Yet seventeen-year-old Ty Tryon of Orlando became a regular on the PGA Tour in January 2002. To us, it seemed unthinkable, like naming Britney Spears Federal Reserve chairman. Naturally, we *had* to talk to Ty's parents.

But Bill and Georgia Tryon say their high school junior is pretty much like ours—big mop of hair, standard-issue pimples, eats more than the Marines, skinny as a two-iron, size 13 boats and loves Taco Bell, his headphones and girls, in that order. Like Kel, Ty has gotten tickets, one for speeding and one for playing his stereo so loud it rattled Gap windows—two malls over. The folks at the Bob Hope Classic are going to love that.

Like our son, Ty has a girlfriend (except that his is an Elite agency model), homework (except that his aunt tutors him wherever he is) and neighbors to annoy (except that his include 'N Sync's Justin Timberlake, two doors down). The big difference is that Bill's kid drives the ball an *average* of 309 yards laser-straight, shot 66 on the final day of Q school to earn his Tour card and stands to make more money by his 18th birthday than the gross national product of Uzbekistan.

"I just look at it like a job," says Ty. "A lot of my friends work at Publix. I'll be working on the Tour." Except that instead of $6.50 an hour, Ty will make $1 million next year in endorsements alone. Wait till his buddies hear that. *We need a cleanup on Aisle 11.*

You figure if Ty wins a tournament, he can get, say, Fred Couples to buy him a six-pack? You think he'll try to burn courtesy-car rubber down Magnolia Lane? How's he going to play Tiger in one of those night matches if it runs past Ty's curfew?

Golf better not expect this kid to carry himself like Davis Love III. If Ty's anything like our son, he'll try to ride one lap around on the baggage carousel, turn his dirty underwear inside out and declare it clean, and leave lit bags of dog poop in front of Nick Faldo's room before knocking and running. *Room service, can you send up that real squiggly kind of Kraft Mac & Cheese?*

How's he going to get his homework done? *Please excuse Ty from school last week. He was in Los Angeles winning the Nissan Open.*

Actually, either Bill, a mortgage lender; Georgia, the mother of four; or Ty's grandfather Bill Sr., an insurance man, will travel with him at all times. They'll all be yelling at him to turn off the PlayStation 2 and go to bed, just the way they do at home. "Ty will get school credit for having a job," says Georgia. *Teacher: Ty, I had to give you a B in golf. Next time, try to bring your A game.*

Still, the Tryons' ears have been scorched for letting Ty turn pro, even by friends like Tour players John Cook and Scott Hoch. "I think it's a joke," says Hoch. "I know Ty. It's a terrible decision."

The Tryons, however, didn't see any other choice. "In my opinion, it would have bordered on child abuse if we hadn't let him," says Bill. "That's how badly he wanted to do this—and he's good enough to do this. Look, he's our son. We're going to work with him to help him in his chosen career. If that means not making him play at some charade of a golf college for two years to make everybody else feel better, so be it."

I asked our Kel if he would ever want to leave high school with a year and a half left, to live the glamorous and lucrative life of a touring golf pro. He happened to be eating a turkey, cheese, bacon, Hershey's syrup and Ruffles BBQ potato chip sandwich at the time.

"Ngh chnc," he mumbled.

"Because you feel like high school and college are priceless years you can never have back?" I asked.

"Ngh," he said. "Id nvr wr thos gky glf clths."

Rick Reilly

Uecker Jr.'s Golf Dream
Goes to the Front Row

Two years ago, Bob Uecker Jr. was an upwardly mobile lawyer with a nice home, a loving wife and infant daughter and all the benefits of an upper-middle-class existence.

He was living the American dream. But it wasn't his dream. So he chucked it all to tilt at windmills with a pitching wedge. Imagine what his wife thought when Uecker approached her in the fall of 1996 and said, "Cathy, what would you think if I quit my job and tried to become a professional golfer?"

Considering Uecker was your average, thirty-three-year-old weekend hacker who had only once broken 80, she probably wondered if he had been hit in the head by a stray Titleist.

"Obviously, there were a lot of things we had to iron out," he says. "But once we got the details ironed out, she was very, very supportive."

The seed was planted when Uecker attended the 1996 Greater Milwaukee Open.

He wondered how good he would be at golf if he committed to the game 100 percent.

His father-in-law knew Dennis Tiziani, the respected Madison teacher who works with PGA golfer Steve Stricker, and facilitated a meeting.

"Dennis said, as far as mechanics go, anybody can learn to swing a golf club," Uecker says. "Now, whether you can actually play the game and be successful at tournament golf, that's a whole different question. He said the only way to find out was to quit my job and try to play golf full time.

"As long as I wasn't committing financial suicide and as long as my wife was totally behind it, he said he'd help me."

Uecker also had to get the blessing of his father, the Milwaukee Brewers broadcaster and celebrity of the same name.

"Dad said he wanted to check my medication," Uecker says, chuckling. "Once he realized I was serious about what I was doing, he supported me 100 percent."

Uecker Jr. worked with Tiziani for several months, then moved to Tampa in the winter of 1996 to 1997, where he continued to revamp his swing under Brian Mogg, an instructor at the Leadbetter School of Golf.

At first, the progress was dramatic. In one year, Uecker's handicap dropped from 14 to 7. He returned to Wisconsin and entered a handful of amateur tournaments, with no success. He spent the winter in Scottsdale, Arizona, working with instructor Mike LaBauve.

Soon Uecker's handicap dropped to 3. He finished sixtieth in the State Amateur, shooting 76-81-88-76.

The difference between finishing sixtieth in the State Amateur and making it as a pro is huge. But as long as Uecker continues to make progress, he sees no reason to give up on his dream.

"Half the fun of what I'm doing is enjoying the journey to where I'm going," he says. "It would have driven me crazy sitting around ten, fifteen years from now and saying, I shoulda, coulda, woulda."

As far as how he's making ends meet, Uecker will say only that he receives help from family members. He hasn't imposed a timetable on himself.

"I'm still not at the level I need to be at, but Dennis always reminds me that I'm in a marathon," he says.

This fall, Uecker plans to sell his house in Menomonee Falls, move permanently to the Phoenix area and turn professional.

"Believe me," he says with a grin, "this is as crazy to me as it is to you."

Crazy or not, give him an "A" for effort.

Gary D'Amato

Take Your Best Shot

It was a warm summer day and my friend had invited me over to his house. He lived close to the local golf club and I was always eager to visit, because we spent most of our time playing in the woods near the golf course or on the course itself. We had our very own hideaway in the woods, and from this hideaway you could see, in the far distance, a flagged hole on the course.

On this specific day, my friend and I were relaxing on the green of the course, just enjoying the quietness of the day, with the sun on our faces, and without a care in the world, when suddenly a golf ball came out of nowhere and landed right in front of us. We both looked at each other and laughed. Our first instinct, as typical seven-year-olds, was to toss the ball back and forth to each other while running around, not giving too much though, to who owned the ball.

We played around with this golf ball, running with it and throwing it. When we approached the hole, we realized it was getting late, so we did what any normal seven-year-old would do: We put the ball in the flagged hole and started to leave. Then we heard voices. Fearful it was the owners of the ball, we panicked and ran to the woods before being seen. From there we watched and waited, hoping they would not be too angry we moved their ball.

We watched the men scanning the horizon and peering into the grass and we heard them wondering aloud where in the world the ball could have gone. Almost ready to give up their search, they checked the flagged hole. What we saw then was quite a sight: These two grown men hugged each other and screamed and then they jumped up and down again and again. We soon understood why. Both men were screaming with excitement that one of them got a hole-in-one on the hardest hole on the course.

Their excitement made it hard for my friend and myself to confess to our intrusion, so we left it alone and went home. While we realized we had done something wrong, we convinced ourselves it was harmless and someone sure was happy because of it. So we decided to leave well enough alone and forget it. After all, it was just two local men out for a round of golf. Until . . .

I will never forget the feeling that came over me when I saw the local newspaper the next morning. It was a big front-page article, with a huge picture of a beaming man, smiling from ear to ear, holding his golf club.

It was a face I knew well, because I had assisted him in his famous shot!

The headline read: "Local man honored for his best shot."

Until that moment, I didn't realize the importance of moving that ball had until I saw the front page of the paper. Seeing that golfer's face on the front page of that paper brought back the excitement that we witnessed the day before. Reading to what extent placing that ball in that hole made on his life was a bittersweet moment.

This man, just an average guy, became a legend around the club because of that shot, and he was recognized for his talent as a golfer. He was presented with awards for making the hardest shot look so easy, and he was the first one to ever make a hole-in-one on that hole. This man was clearly so happy, and I know to this day that he will never forget that magical moment and the glory it brought him.

I guess things happen for reasons, and for some reason, we were meant to put that ball in that hole that day. We were innocent children playing with a ball, never realizing the power of our actions and how they can affect so many lives. Just a little golf ball being put into a little hole changed the life of one man. To this day, people remember the golfer's name and his "best shot." When we reminisce over our long-kept secret of that summer day, many years ago, my friend and I still look at each other and laugh.

Ann Birmingham

In Search of the Perfect Pro-Am

I would rather play Hamlet with no rehearsal than golf on television.

Jack Lemmon

The perennial pro-am player is in many ways a strange animal, and definitely not an endangered species.

It has always amazed me, for instance, how many stiff and staid captains of industry are prepared, even eager, to make fools of themselves in public on the golf course, a situation they would never allow to occur anywhere else. Men of dignity and business acumen when sailing through the corridors of power with a flock of underlings and yes-men in their wake become semiparalytic when overcome by 1st-tee nerves. Yet they will fall over each other in a furious dogfight behind the scenes to ensure a featured pairing alongside Jack Nicklaus rather than some unknown rookie, although they are fully aware of the almost certain consequences. Five thousand people will be clustered around the 1st tee to watch Nicklaus crunch the ball, while the rookie will probably start in total obscurity from the 10th tee in the company of his current girlfriend, either toting the bag or pulling the trolley, and a couple of close friends. Of course any chance of our hero hitting even a halfway decent first drive evaporates under Nicklaus's baleful glare, while those five thousand spectators, many of them incompetent golfers themselves, will chuckle and rub their hands with gleeful sadism as our man dribbles his ball along the ground, just reaching the ladies' tee. Naturally he could have taken the pressure off himself and played an enjoyable, uncluttered game alongside the rookie in question.

But as a perennially masochistic pro-am player myself these past thirty-odd years, I know only too well that, deep down in my heart, for reasons that defy logic, playing in pleasant obscurity is not what I crave. If I am going to suffer a round that will take the best part of six hours to complete, I want to rub shoulders with the best, and later show off the mandatory photograph of our illustrious group, duly mounted, to my children and grandchildren. I'll probably tell them how well I played, for good measure!

A pro-am will not necessarily be a pleasant experience, even if you happen to play the best golf of your life. A thankfully small minority of famous professional golfers have gained well-deserved notoriety for their scornful disdain of their amateur hacker partners, on whom their very living really depends. This shortsighted, brainless bunch is very much outnumbered by those who are only too aware of the value of pro-ams as a powerful public relations exercise.

I have since become a friend, admirer and commentating colleague of Tom Weiskopf. But this most magnificently elegant of world-class players did not earn his nickname "Terrible Tom" for nothing. In early 1968 I was the pro-am guest of the long-defunct National Airlines at their tournament at the Country Club of Miami to inaugurate their service between that city, their home base, and London. I arrived several days in advance and worked diligently on my game, then played to a respectable 5 handicap. Poor Tom came down from the snows of Ohio, having just completed a compulsory period of army reserve training. His game was very short of its awesome best. And for eight glorious holes I outplayed him into the greens, constantly hitting my second shot or tee shots much closer to the hole. Imagine my chagrin when, on the 8th green—with my ball five feet from the hole and on Tom's line but his ball twenty feet farther away—he hissed: "Putt your *** ball and get out of the *** way." I promptly three-putted, quickly fell apart, and did not speak to Weiskopf for five futile years, having written about the incident in the *Financial Times* and *Golf World* magazine (UK). To Tom's eternal credit he apologized by inviting me to his intimate dinner party at the Marine Hotel, Troon, to celebrate his Open Championship victory of 1973—a memorable evening indeed—and we have laughed about the incident several times since.

Two more types of perennial pro-am players continually amaze me. The first jealously guards a low handicap although his first swing tells his professional partner he has no earthly chance of playing to it or even anywhere near it. As one world-class professional golfer told me recently, "Before the end of the round, as his game becomes more and more unglued, this type of player will always look you squarely in the eye and say, 'I can honestly tell you this is the worst round I've played in ten years,' or something to that effect. Can you imagine how many times he has to tell that story, and how many times I've heard it before?" The vanity of this type of amateur golfer is obviously monumental.

But I infinitely prefer his sadly deluded type to the cheat, or in American parlance "sandbagger," who checks in with a 16 handicap, and from his very first practice swing shows his professional he is unlikely to drop more than half a dozen strokes to par. He rarely, if ever, does so. Of course some high-handicap golfers enjoy magical days in the sun, and they are very often professionals at another sport, who are not mortally afraid and totally unhinged by playing in front of sizeable crowds, and who possess obvious ability at all ball games—natural athletes. To me nothing is more enjoyable than being in the company of an obvious hacker who is playing way over his head and basking in the consequent euphoric glow. Goodness knows, such euphoria is destined to be very short-lived.

I well remember being paired with Charles Heidseck in a long-gone American Express French Open pro-am. This elegant purveyor of fine champagne took his pro-am debut so seriously he went into a health farm for two weeks, did not touch a drop of his company's product and took a lesson every other day. Hardly surprisingly Heidseck played well below his handicap in the company of an Irish professional who shall be nameless because he shot 86 in that pro-am and had the courage to return that score rather than tear up his card. The elegant Frenchman obviously drew inspiration from his partner's travail!

Going from the sublime to the ridiculous, several years later I played in the Heritage Classic pro-am at wonderful Harbour Town Links on Hilton Head Island. When we set out in early afternoon a score of 22 under par (par is 71) had already been posted, and I remarked to my partner that going out was hardly worthwhile in the face of such insurmountable odds.

To my astonishment one of my amateur partners replied, "Nonsense! We'll beat that score. You'll see." Five and a half hours later we brought in a score of 23-under-par 48, and I fully understood why my partner had been so confident. Off an 18 handicap he had scored 75 off his own ball. Our professional, Lou Graham, the 1973 U.S. Open Champion and a true Southern gentleman from Tennessee, was so angry that he gave our sandbagger a stern lecture. And all we amateurs won was a box of a dozen golf balls!

My own pro-am experiences have embraced farce, tragedy, comedy and, on very few occasions, the ecstasy of victory.

My first "major" pro-am appearance was in the old, long-forgotten Bowmaker tournament at Sunningdale, England, in the company of the late, great Bobby Locke. I arrived hours ahead of my starting time, ever the neurotic, asked the caddie master for assistance, and was told my caddie was known as "One-Tooth Jock." A giant, malodorous Scotsman in a too-long military greatcoat, cloth cap and laced-up boots emerged from the caddie shed, the solitary fang in his upper jaw hanging over his lower lip. We made for the practice tee, where I flailed away for what seemed like an age with no comment, just an inscrutable stare from my companion. And then I made my fatal mistake.

"Do you need lunch before we go at 12:52?" I asked Jock.

"Yessir," he answered with his first display of transparent enthusiasm. I handed him a five-pound note, took my putter and four golf balls, and told him to meet me on the 1st tee at 12:45 by the clubhouse clock.

Needless to say, despite several appeals over the public address system, Jock failed to appear. My confusion was complete. Eventually the legendary Arthur Lees, Sunningdale's professional at the time, sent out a brand-new set of clubs and accessories and, totally embarrassed, we set out. We were walking up the hill from the 7th tee when I first heard the raucous strains of "Glasgow Belongs to Me," a famous Scottish ditty, and Jock heaved over the horizon towards us, stumbling dangerously, my bag of clubs slung across his chest.

"Where the hell have you been?" I asked One-Tooth.

"Well, sir," he grinned frighteningly through a haze of Scotch whiskey fumes. "I set off with this group, sir. And after we had gone seven holes and nobody had asked me for a club, I realized I was with the wrong foursome, and came looking for you. . . ."

The best pro-am partner I ever had, bar none, was Gary Player. In the 1974 La Manga Campo de Golf resort's pro-am played over seventy-two holes, the owner of that splendid southern Spanish facility, American entrepreneur Greg Peters, conceived the idea that the professionals should not record their individual score, but rather record that of their team's best ball. It was a praiseworthy attempt to foster cameraderie between professionals and amateurs, and with the exuberant South African it worked like a charm. Each team played with a different professional every day, and we drew Player for the vital third round in 1974 or, as Gary calls it, "moving day." So determined was Player to make the three of us play to the summit of our capabilities, he mostly ran from amateur to amateur to coach us on every shot. I don't remember what phenomenally low total we posted as a team that marvelous day—I think it was 19-under-par 53—but it helped us to spread-eagle the field, and we won the event going away by seven shots with a record aggregate. And Player was the professional winner, hardly surprisingly.

The euphoria I experienced that magical day alongside the great Gary Player is unlikely to be repeated. But I keep on trying and hoping. And I suppose that is what pro-ams are all about. They bring out the Walter Mitty in all of us hackers.

Ben Wright

READER/CUSTOMER CARE SURVEY

CB3

We care about your opinions. Please take a moment to fill out this Reader Survey card and mail it back to us.
As a special **"thank you"** we'll send you exciting news about interesting books and a valuable **Gift Certificate.**

Please PRINT using ALL CAPS

First Name [   ] MI. [ ] Last Name [   ]

Address [   ]

City [   ] ST [ ] Zip [   ]

Phone # ([   ]) [   ] — [   ]   Fax # ([   ]) [   ] — [   ]

Email [   ]

(1) Gender:
____ Female   ____ Male

(2) Age:
1) ____ 12 or under   40-59
2) ____ 13-19   60+
3) ____ 20-39

(3) Marital Status
____ Married
____ Single
____ Divorced/Widowed

(4) Did you receive this book as a gift?
____ Yes   ____ No

(5) How many Chicken Soup books have you bought or read?
____ 1   ____ 2-4   ____ 5+

(6) How did you find out about this book?
Please fill in ONE.
1) ____ Recommendation
2) ____ Store Display
3) ____ Bestseller List
4) ____ Online
5) ____ Advertisement
6) ____ Catalog/Mailing
7) ____ Interview/Review (TV, Radio, Print)

(7) Where do you usually buy books?
Please fill in your top TWO choices.
1) ____ Bookstore
2) ____ Religious Bookstore
3) ____ Online
4) ____ Book Club/Mail Order
5) ____ Price Club (Costco, Sam's Club, etc.)
6) ____ Retail Store (Target, Wal-mart, etc.)

(9) What subjects do you enjoy reading about most? Rank only **FIVE**. *Use 1 for your favorite, 2 for second favorite, etc.*

	1	2	3	4	5
1) Parenting/Family	O	O	O	O	O
2) Relationships	O	O	O	O	O
3) Recovery/Addictions	O	O	O	O	O
4) Health/Nutrition	O	O	O	O	O
5) Christianity	O	O	O	O	O
6) Spirituality/Inspiration	O	O	O	O	O
7) Business Self-Help	O	O	O	O	O
8) Teen Issues	O	O	O	O	O
9) Sports	O	O	O	O	O

(14) What attracts you most to a book?
(Please rank 1-4 in order of preference.)

	1	2	3	4
14) Title	O	O	O	O
15) Cover Design	O	O	O	O
16) Author	O	O	O	O
17) Content	O	O	O	O

TAPE IN MIDDLE; DO NOT STAPLE

BUSINESS REPLY MAIL

FIRST-CLASS MAIL PERMIT NO 45 DEERFIELD BEACH, FL

POSTAGE WILL BE PAID BY ADDRESSEE

CHICKEN SOUP FOR GOLFERS 2
HEALTH COMMUNICATIONS, INC.
3201 SW 15TH STREET
DEERFIELD BEACH FL 33442-9875

||.||...||.||..|.|.|.|..|.|.|.|||.|..|.||..|.|.|..|.|.|.||.|

FOLD HERE

Comments:

Do you have your own Chicken Soup story that you would like to send us? Please submit separately to: Chicken Soup for the Soul, P.O. Box 30880, Santa Barbara, CA 93130

3

SPECIAL MOMENTS

Don't hurry. Don't worry. You're only here for a short visit. So don't forget to stop and smell the roses.

Walter Hagen

The Spirit of Harvey Penick

My father says to me, "Respect everybody, and your life, it will be perfect." Then, even if you are poor on the outside, on the inside you are rich.

Costantino Rocca

It's funny how circumstances sometimes transpire to lead us in unexpected directions. This tale recounts the chain of events that led me to the legendary Harvey Penick and the subsequent effects that encounter had on my life.

I was visiting an uncle I had not seen in many years, a golfer's kinship sort of thing. Uncle Norman introduced me to the game of golf, starting as his caddie. A miserable experience, thanks to weather and other circumstances; I hated the game, and I didn't take it up in earnest until the age of thirty-five. Immediately, the golf bug bit me. During this visit, I picked up a book lying on the kitchen counter, Harvey Penick's Little Green Book, *If You're a Golfer, You're My Friend.* The book so impressed me, I read it cover to cover that night and decided to meet Mr. Penick. Now was as good a time as any.

From South Florida, I drove the following week to Austin, Texas. After checking into a motel on a Sunday night, I looked up his phone number and anxiously placed the call. I knew that Penick was old and frail, but I was shocked to learn his current condition. Helen Penick informed me that her dear husband was "released from the hospital that very day and he was not expected to make it." It was even more surprising that she said to call in the morning and if he felt up to it, "Mr. Penick would be happy to see you." I was given directions to the house and instructed to call around 10 A.M.

My emotions surged. At first, I felt sorry for myself. I had driven fifteen hundred miles, and I expected that effort would get me the audience I came for. I began to feel guilty, knowing how selfish that was. Saying a prayer, for Mr. Penick and myself, I retired early.

Arising at the crack of dawn the next morning, I restlessly waited for 10 o'clock to arrive. Precisely at 10, I began dialing, and for what seemed an eternity, I heard busy signals. The worst crossed my mind. *Was he even sicker? Did he die?* Paranoid that I am, I even thought that the phone was intentionally left off the hook to discourage my calling. At 11, I drove to the house.

Following precise directions, I arrived at the Penick home, situated in a beautiful part of town. Worried about coming before calling, I sheepishly knocked on the door. When a nurse answered, I asked for Mrs. Penick. She was out shopping, but the nurse asked if I would like to visit with Mr. Penick. After traveling such a long distance I was aching to say yes, but I declined. "I think I'd better wait to see if it's okay with Mrs. Penick first." The next several hours were awe-inspiring and would change the course of my personal and professional life.

Outside, in this pristine setting, I became aware of changes, faint at first, in my sensory perceptions. The colors of the flowers were distinctive and bright. A gentle breeze blowing, the air was crisp and clear. Rich, pleasant aromas abounded. I heard several birds and could distinguish the differences in each of their songs. My body tingling all over, I was captivated by a heightened sense of awareness, actually feeling a part of nature. For a cold, calculating, bottom-line guy like me, this experience was a first.

I remember seeing a squirrel on the opposite side of the street. I closed my eyes, believing the squirrel would come closer, and to my delight he did. Closing my eyes again, I knew he would come right beside me. Well, nobody's perfect. This trancelike state lasted for what seemed an eternity, yet in reality was only thirty minutes or so. Mrs. Penick arrived and asked me to come in.

The bedroom resembled a hospital ward with tubes and machines everywhere. Mr. Penick was glad that I had come, eager to talk golf and share his wisdom. His love for the game was obvious, and talking about golf seemed to lift his spirits. A glow enveloped him as he shared with me a lifetime of teaching, people and stories. He asked about my personal life, my game, and how he might help me. What we discussed is almost irrelevant, for I knew that I was in the presence of greatness.

His son Tinsley stopped by the house, and our session continued. From his deathbed—he would pass away the following week—Mr. Penick was giving me a golf lesson. Incredibly perceptive, from our conversation, he could detect my flaws. After a few hours, I could see how tired he had become, so I excused myself to see if I should go. Though Mr. Penick wanted to continue, Tinsley felt it was time for rest. I thanked them all and left. How remarkable this family is. At a time when most people would only think of themselves and their troubles, they welcomed me into their home as if I was a lifelong friend. I made a conscious decision to live my life and play the game of golf according to a higher principle, Harvey Penick's way. Meeting him altered my life.

To make a long story short, that encounter led to my writing *The Secrets to the Game of Golf & Life,* for which Tinsley agreed to write the foreword. I still get goose bumps every time I read it. Among other thoughts in his foreword, Tinsley wrote that his father and I became "kindred spirits and soul brothers" and that "Leonard has brought that special feeling to the pages of his new book." I am now firmly entrenched in the golf community, as a writer and consultant. Meeting Harvey Penick helped me to become a better golfer, but more importantly, a better person. I look at both golf and life from a different perspective, more aware and more appreciative.

Leonard Finkel

The Passing of the Mantle

If you think Tiger Woods was under a lot of pressure when he won the 1997 Masters, or when he won three U.S. Amateurs, or when he outgunned Sergio Garcia to win the 1999 PGA Championship, just consider the pressure he felt at the PGA Tour's 1997 Awards Dinner.

He was awarded the Arnold Palmer Award by the Great Man himself, and as he approached the podium, Palmer stopped Woods in his tracks—and sent a chill through the audience.

"Wait right there," Palmer said, motioning to Woods to pause. "I have something to say. You have an enormous responsibility. When I think of when I started playing this Tour so long ago and how much it's changed, it is amazing. I think we should be thankful, but we should also be careful. Remember how we got here and the guys who helped get us here. You guys are playing for so much money. Always remember that you have an obligation to protect the integrity and traditions of the game. It is important. When I see bad conduct, it truly disturbs me."

Then he signaled for Woods to come stand next to him.

"It's all right here," he said, placing his hands on Woods's shoulders. "The responsibility is all on your shoulders. Protect the game. It's beautiful."

Don Wade

Through the Footsteps of Time

The men crouched behind low stone walls. Musket fire pierced the air above their heads, seeking randomly the warm flesh of the unlucky one who happened in its path. Worse yet were the sorry souls cut down by cannon fire, the evil spheres that succeeded in the demise of multiple patriots with every blast.

It is hard to imagine the angst, the fear and the nobility of the brave soldiers who squared off on this rocky slope.

I was flooded with emotion as I strode down the majestic fairways of the Carnegie Abbey Course in Portsmouth, Rhode Island. On a perfect New England spring day, I was playing golf with new friends Don, Patrick and Bill. We had just hit our drives on the tight, slightly dogleg left, par-4 6th hole. I was struck by a sight of a Colonial-era graveyard surrounded by massive stones, stones that for hundreds of years had silently stood as sentries to the confines of its occupants. While the inscriptions were moving, I found it even more fascinating that this noble sight must have sat in near obscurity for two centuries before its liberation from the scrub brush by the artistic stroke of the golf course architect.

Describing my emotions to Bill, he was quick to note that

directly beneath us, less than twenty yards off the tee, was the final resting place for forty former slaves who had lived and farmed the property during part of its long history.

Approaching our drives, I turned to Manny, my caddie, to express my reverence for this special place, when Manny informed me that far more was to come. On cue, Bill explained that this beautiful, rolling property on Narragansett Bay was the location of numerous confrontations during the American Revolution. Specifically, the hole we were playing was the very sight of the "Battle of Bloody Run," where estimates are that five hundred to two thousand men had lost their lives and were buried beneath the ground we strode.

I stood for a minute in awe, consumed by the thought that a place that was now so beautiful could have been the sight of such violence.

I can never remember feeling on a golf course the way I did that day. Part of me felt out of place, as if I was violating this land that still belonged to the hearts, sounds and emotions of its past. Another part of me felt a true reverence, a sense of common union with this spot and an appreciation for the people who had been there before me.

That's when it hit me.

How wonderful, how fantastic is this game of golf that by using this land as the canvas upon which a beautiful and challenging golf course would unfold, this distinguished land would be freed from its past and from the obscure pages of history. I will admit that I did not know a thing at that time about the "Battle of Bloody Run," much less the actual spot where the battle took place.

Now, thanks to Carnegie Abbey, the efforts and the sacrifices of these brave men would not be lost to obscurity, but would be remembered and forever celebrated because of numerous historical markings and environmental sensitivity.

I love the game of golf, not only for its dignity and camaraderie, but because every now and then the game becomes a vehicle to explore and appreciate something deeper, as on this day, a garden memorial to people who gave so much so that we may enjoy the moment.

Matt Adams

Dr. Scholl's Caddy

I spent many a Saturday and Sunday in my father's 1946 Chevy parked in the lot at the Ridgewood Country Club in New Jersey. My father would earn extra money as a caddy, and he would always tell me not to wander too far from the car. The pro at the time was George Jacobus who was also president of the PGA at one time. In the thirties he hired a young pro named Byron Nelson as his assistant. My dad showed him to me one day and said, "Make sure you are near the car if you see Mr. Jacobus around."

Well, after a few Saturdays and Sundays, I had my timing down to a T. I could run to the woods to watch the members play and shag some balls for fifty cents. All in all, I felt I wouldn't be seen away from post. I had an old 5-iron, and when I would see Mr. Jacobus pull away in his car, I would run over to the practice fairway and try my luck. I tried not to make divots because then I would have to waste too much time replacing them.

Once I began to make contact, the ball would sail so far that I was afraid to retrieve it. The members who I shagged for usually parted with a few old balls and kept me in supply. I stashed my old 5-iron and the balls in the rough off the practice fairway so if I was seen walking around, at least I was empty-handed. I soon noticed that every golfer wore the nicest shoes I had ever seen, just like the pros in the magazines and on the television. I worked extra hard that summer shagging balls and even washing some of the members' cars in the lot. The caddymaster took a liking to me and supplied the soap, pail and towels.

One day as I was sneaking toward my cache of club and balls, I noticed Mr. Jacobus leaving the clubhouse. I ducked behind a huge Buick that would have stopped an artillery shell and was sure I was not seen. As I watched his car round the bend I grabbed my 5-iron, chucked the balls onto the fairway and ran over to practice. For sure he had gone home—it was almost 5 o'clock. My dad should almost be done with his second round. As I approached the balls, my sneakers slipped as I was taking the biggest swing I could muster for a ten-year-old and landed on the seat of my pants. I didn't have a chance to get up when I heard a voice behind me say, "Son, I'd say that was a little overswing." It was Mr. Jacobus and was I ever speechless. "You need two good things to hit that ball, Son," he said. "A better swing and a pair of golf shoes."

I guess he knew how hard I was working to earn a pair of my own, and he took me into the locker room and told the attendant to find me a pair in the pile of old golf shoes slated to be tossed out by the members. After a few minutes of trying on shoe after shoe, the attendant came out with the neatest pair in the pile. Black-and-white wing tips. I saw Sam Snead and Arnold Palmer wearing them. The attendant said, "Try these on." I remember him saying over and over, "These are Dr. Scholl's, these are Dr. Scholl's, this is a great shoe."

They fit like a glove, and the attendant polished them and buffed them and even replaced a few spikes. After all, Mr. Jacobus put him on the case, and he was up to the task. My dad returned after his caddying and couldn't believe his eyes. He asked me where I got the shoes, and I told him the truth. "Some rich doctor was throwing them away, and Mr. Jacobus gave them to me." He had to pull over to the side of the road on the way home when I asked, "Hey, Dad, did you ever caddy for Dr. Scholls?"

Dennis Oricchio

Father's Day Arrives During Christmas

A few days before Christmas I got a Father's Day card from my dad, who passed away nearly three years ago. It arrived while my son and I were at the Palo Verde Golf Course in Phoenix. Palo Verde is a compact little course on Fifteenth Avenue north of Bethany Home Road. We started going there shortly after my mother died in 1997. My father was staying for a time in Phoenix, and his doctors told him he should try to get some exercise. He hadn't been well. Specialists described his condition as coronary artery disease. We knew it simply as a broken heart.

My boy and I own nine battered old golf clubs between us. My father had left his set back in Pittsburgh. So we only utilized Palo Verde's driving range. We'd bring along a few lawn chairs, and my dad and I would sit and talk while Sam teed off, hacking at each golf ball like a power hitter chasing a slider in the dirt.

"Why don't you teach him to swing the right way?" I asked my dad.

"As long as he's having a good time and hitting the ball, that is the right way," he answered.

He had been retired from the steel mill for fifteen years by then. When I was growing up, he coached baseball and bowled on a team from the mill's tin plate department. Only in retirement did he and his friends discover golf. It got so they'd go out several times a week in the summer.

Every once in a while during our trips to Palo Verde, my father would get up from his chair and hit a few balls. Years of practice had given him a fluid stroke. He'd send a tee shot arching high into the darkness beyond the range's big lights.

"That ball's going to outer space," my boy said one night. "Maybe all the way to Grandma."

When my father returned to Pennsylvania, he kept a photograph of himself and Sam in a homemade frame in his basement workshop. After he died, Sam and I took the picture home with us. We keep it in our golf bag and take it out each time we go to the driving range at Palo Verde, so my dad can watch us hit balls and evaluate our unorthodox swings.

The last time we were there over the holiday vacation, the frame my father made for the picture came apart and the photograph slipped out. While fixing it, I saw that the matting board on which the photograph had been mounted was actually an old greeting card. I had sent it to my dad years ago on Father's Day. This Christmas, he sent it back.

During my father's final days, my brother and I kept the conversation light. We knew he was dying. He knew he was dying. He had a stroke and couldn't speak, so we said and did things to try to make him smile. To make ourselves smile. It was all a blur, and afterward a part of you wonders if your true feelings came through. Then you get this gift, this greeting card addressed to your dad in your handwriting that you don't even recall having sent.

A person can be more sentimental in a card than in conversation. At least it was that way in our family. I wrote in the card about how I never doubted that my father would do anything for me and ended by saying that as a dad, "You're a helluva hard act to follow." The card is back in its frame now. Back in the golf bag.

When I was a kid, the first thing friends asked when we returned to school from Christmas vacation was, "What did you get?" It was a happy, hopeful way to start the new year.

This Christmas, among other things, I got a Father's Day card from my old man.

E. J. Montini

You May Be a Winner

My friend Tony gave a golf trip to his son one Christmas. And Tony's son gave a golf trip to his uncle. And the uncle gave a golf trip to Tony. As these gifts were revealed, one by one, over the course of Christmas morning, Tony's mother-in-law's astonishment grew. "I can't believe you all gave each other a vacation to the same place! And on the same weekend!"

Not all non-golfers are as easy to fool as Tony's mother-in-law was. A gambit like that would never work with my wife, for example, because she knows (and is appalled) that my brother and I long ago agreed to simplify our lives by never giving each other anything for any reason. Tony's wife wasn't fooled, either, but she said nothing, because the men of the family had (astutely) expressed their selfishness in a form that seemed to endorse a deeply cherished belief held by the women of the family: that major holidays are important occasions for loving, commitment and renewal, and so forth. The men got what they wanted by pretending to play the game by the women's rules.

Anyway, Tony's success at Christmas got me to thinking, and I'm pretty sure I've come up with an even better idea. My idea is so good, in fact, that I'm going to share it with you.

Here's what I've done. I've started a company called the International Golf Sweepstakes Foundation, Inc., of which I am the sole employee. Let's say that you and three buddies want to take a ten-day golf trip to Ireland, but you know that your wives would never in a million years let you go. You contact me by e-mail, and I send you an entry form for a contest in which the grand prize happens to be an all-expenses-paid ten-day golf trip to Ireland for four. You fill out the form and ask your wife to sign her name on the line marked "witness."

"What's this?" she asks.

"Oh, just some dumb animal-rights thing they made us contribute to at work."

Your wife happily signs, you send the form back to me with a check for five hundred dollars (my fee), and you never again mention the contest to your wife. Three or four months later, a fat, official-looking FedEx package arrives at your house. You open it in the presence of your wife, appear puzzled for a moment, then begin hooting, "Remember that dumb contest? I actually won!" you shout.

Non-playing wives view all golf trips as wasteful extravagances, but they can't help thinking of contest winnings as money in the bank. To fail to cash in a prize already won would be like throwing jewelry out in the trash, so of course you'll get to go—especially if you promptly offer to give your wife some sort of compensating goodie, like a new kitchen. You'll have to make all your travel arrangements yourself—and conceal your credit card charges as you do—because that's not part of what my foundation does, at least for the time being. All I do is get you out the door. The rest is up to you.

David Owen

My Course, My Rules

Did you hear about the guy in Chattanooga who won a Big Game lottery jackpot worth $60 million and went out and bought himself a golf course?

Damn right.

All my life I've wanted my own golf course. I dream of calling the starter and asking, "Any way you can squeeze me in for a round?" and having him answer, "All we got left is 6 A.M. until 7 P.M. Will that work?"

If I felt like playing 27, I could. If I felt like playing 54, I could. If I felt like playing from the 14th tee into the deep-fat fryer, stark naked on a unicycle, I could. Overnight, I guarantee you, my handicap would drop to a four. That's because I would turn par into a radio station, say, 103.5.

Not that there wouldn't be rules. Oh, there would be rules at Chop Acres.

- No collared shirts. They all look like an explosion at the Dutch Boy plant anyway. No kilties, either. And none of those ridiculous screw-you sunglasses.
- No men's locker room. That's what the trunk of your car's for, right? Or can't you get through your day

without Vitalis, Bay Rum and Old Tom Morris's comb soaking in blue formaldehyde?

- No tee times for women. No tee times for kids. No tee times for men. If you can play in less than three-and-a-half hours, get out there. If not, we've saved the midnight-to-2 A.M. window for you.
- Come to think of it, all you *get* is three-and-a-half hours. After that, the carts run out of juice and the caddies hop the fence—with your Pings over their shoulders.
- No mulligans, breakfast balls, Clintons or hit-till-you're-happys. You don't have to prove to us you can smother-blade a driver twice in a row. We believe you. Besides, the first hole is a twenty-three-yard, downhill par-3 from an elevated tee to a huge funnel green. We love seeing people make holes-in-one. We also love drinking free.
- No practice swings. We've seen your practice swing. It's slow, graceful and bears absolutely no resemblance to the hideous chop you end up using, so why bother?
- No cell phones, either. There's a $10 fine for incoming calls, $25 for outgoing. One thing we don't need on our backswing is you discussing the freaking Acme account.
- Take a caddie or a cart, but we think you'll like the caddies. They get a $20 bonus if they get you home in three hours, and they usually do. That's partly because they have you hitting from the women's tees.
- Mandatory betting. What do you think this is, the Walla Walla First Presbyterian Four-ball? As our head pro, Two Down, likes to say, "If you're not betting, you're just going on a very long walk in very ugly pants." And if you get a little upside down in your

wagers, don't worry. Two Down gives fast and friendly auto appraisals.

- No duck-hooking into the adjacent fairway just to stop the beverage-cart girl. One comes with every foursome.
- No plumb-bobbing without a Ph.D. in physics. Like anybody knows how to do it anyway. If a caddie sees you plumb-bobbing, he'll confiscate your putter and make modern art out of it.
- No pacing off yardage. Does it really matter whether you're 230 or 231 yards from the hole? That's still three seven-irons and a canoe for you.
- No out-of-bounds. White stakes are for albino vampires. If you can find your ball, hit it. If you can't find it, hit it from where you think you would've found it. If you can't decide where you would've found it, return to the cart, reach into the glove box, pull out the complimentary copy of *Quilting for Fun and Profit* and begin reading.
- If it's within the leather, it's good. If it's within the Bertha, it's good. If it's something that a Bruneian slave would give the Sultan, it's good.

After the round, come on in for All You Can Pour Night. The hot-tub massages are free, the cigars are smuggled, and the mook who answers the phone never heard of you.

Oh, and if you don't feel up to driving home, stay the night next door at Courtyard by Hooters.

You might as well.

Two Down will have sold your car.

Rick Reilly

The Greatest Shot of My Life

*Pressure is playing for ten dollars when you
don't have a dime in your pocket.*

Lee Trevino

Like most guys I know, I was introduced to the game of
golf by my father. My dad was a pretty good golfer when
he was younger (5 handicap). When my sisters and I came
along, he couldn't play as much as he'd like, but he still
stayed in touch with the game.

In the early sixties, dad bought a bar in Portage Lakes, a
nice series of recreational lakes in Ohio. My dad was in his
fifties by this time and still liked to play the game. The
problem was that after practically giving up the game, he
would still take sucker bets from the younger guys who
frequented his tavern. One guy bet Dad one hundred dollars that he could give Dad five and use only three clubs.
Dad lost one hundred dollars. Another guy bet Dad fifty
dollars that he could throw out his worst two holes, and
once again Dad lost.

I felt bad for Pop because he was such a nice guy, and
although these guys spent lots of money at Dad's tavern,

at the age of twelve, I felt people thought Dad was a joke around the golf course and everyone was making fun of him.

Several days later, Jimmy Ray Textur, a young "hot shot" golfer, told my dad he would give him ten strokes and do all his putting with a driver. The bet was one hundred dollars and, of course, Dad accepted.

The following morning we met at Turtlefoot Golf Course in Portage Lakes, a beautiful course surrounded by water. On the 1st hole, Jimmy Ray hit a sweet drive, high and long, and straight down the fairway. Dad's drive sliced OB. I cringed and thought, *Here we go again.*

After Dad's misfortune on the 1st hole, he settled down and played pretty well. Jimmy Ray didn't putt as well as he'd thought with his driver.

Dad had lost all of the shots Jimmy Ray gave him by the 15th hole. They tied on holes 16 and 17. The last hole was a par-4 straight away with an elevated green and trees lining both sides of the fairway. At this point in time, the match was tied. Jimmy Ray hit his drive left center and had a flip wedge to the pin. Dad hit an awful slice deep into the woods where it rested on a huge clump of dirt that was the remains of a tree that was removed. By this time a few of Jimmy Ray's friends had wandered onto the course to watch the match.

I stood at the edge of the woods where I saw my dad climb onto this mound of dirt and debris and address the ball. In my heart, I figured Dad was about to lose another one hundred bucks. I felt rotten, and even worse for my dad. Just then I heard a *crack* echo through the woods that sounded like a cherry bomb going off under a pop can. The leaves parted, and to my amazement, the ball came out of the woods like a bullet, hit the bank in front of the green, bounced twenty feet in the air and came to rest two feet from the pin. This might have shook Jimmy Ray up a bit, for he chili-dipped his next shot. Jimmy Ray then chipped up within five feet and made the putt for par.

Dad needed his two-footer to win the match. As I walked up to the green, beaming with pride, I handed Dad his Bull's Eye putter so he could finish off Jimmy Ray. Dad walked past me and gave me a wink. He went to his bag, pulled out his driver and proceeded to knock in the two-footer!

The drive home was one I'll always remember. We drove straight to Montgomery Ward where he bought me my first set of golf clubs and a cool green, yellow and black plaid golf bag.

I'm still playing golf and running a small driving range in Mount Vernon, Ohio. Dad passed away in '93, but sometimes when I visit family in Akron, I play Turtlefoot. Whenever I come to the last hole, regardless of my score, I always feel good; for on this hole, I witnessed the greatest shot of my life.

Del Madzay

Sweetness

Every generation has those incredible humans that seem to excel at every sport they play. Focus, intensity, humor and an iron will are all part of the basic tool kit. I consider myself fortunate to have experienced such greatness firsthand.

Our paths crossed when I had been working on a project with some former professional athletes; that's how I met the NFL's all-time rushing leader and arguably the best football player in history, Walter Payton. His legendary eye for business was evident at our first meeting. His energy impressed me.

Growing up in Chicago, I watched Walter destroy defenses for years with the Bears. His upper body strength, agility and love for contact were a thrill to watch. Now here I was—actually working with Walter Payton and his staff on projects that would benefit his foundation for children. As passionate as Walter was about football, he was even more so on behalf of children, all children.

Whenever I took my young son Andy into his offices, business became secondary. In no time I would find Andy in Walter's office, both of them on the floor playing some made-up bowling game with golf tees and golf balls. I remember having a hard time figuring out who was having more fun. Walter smiled that galactic grin and all was right in the world of a child.

In 1993, I was playing in Walter's celebrity tournament (though I was far from being a celebrity at the time, Walter made sure I was treated like royalty). My foursome included Tony Galbreath from the New York Giants, the late Winford Brown, an incredible singer/songwriter and an executive from the World Wrestling Federation. Walter's guest list had Hollywood superstars mixed in with top executives and a healthy dose of athletes, of course. Walter drove the course in a golf cart that was a replica of an old railside Ford pickup. As our foursome approached a par-3 hole, heading directly toward us behind a tree line was Walter Payton in his little truck, followed by an army of television crews, reporters and fans.

I have never professed to have mastered the game of golf. I have the power to send the ball 300 yards; however, sometimes the ball charts its own course mid-drive. If this has never happened to you, I assure you, it's very upsetting. But this was a simple par 3, about 160 yards at the most. I teed up the ball, took a couple of practice swings and zeroed in what was sure to be a hole-in-one.

Well, I launched a rocket when all that was needed was a small firecracker. The ball went right between the tree line to my right, setting its sights on the head of one Walter Payton, just as he was stepping out of his cart. Only his catlike reflexes saved his noodle from a certain pounding. Missing his head by only inches (and scattering the crowd of media and onlookers), the ball whizzed into the next fairway. Of course I had yelled "fore" and broke for the trees, walking toward the Hall-of-Famer in apology.

A huge smile split Walter's face and he said, "John, John, no problem. Let me show you how it's done." We proceeded back to my tee, followed of course by a couple of dozen reporters, media and guests, and now a gathering group of other celebrity golfers.

By this time, Tony and Winford were sitting in the cart waiting on me to tee off, and I could just imagine what was going through their minds seeing my new entourage. They burst out laughing, which didn't help matters. I had really been working to improve my game, focus on good shots, read every *Golf Digest* I could find and what did it get me? The near extinction of the greatest football player that ever played the game!

So Walter stepped up, I tossed him a ball, and in one swift motion he takes a tee out of his pocket and plants the combination in the ground at the perfect height. By now there are over a hundred spectators craning their necks to see this shot. Silence falls on the crowd.

Walter studied the shot for a second, pulled the club head back slowly, deliberately, and delivered! And the ball rolled about a foot! The crowd went crazy! I turned around to see Eddie Payton, Walter's brother, nearly on the ground in tears. Mr. Universe, Tom Platz, was head down, huge shoulders shaking in cackling laughter. The Million Dollar Man, Ted DiBiase, wore this huge grin. Walter, however, was unfazed.

"Must be the ball," he murmured, taking a new one out of his pocket and parking it on the still standing tee. "You gotta have the right balls for this game, John."

Of course by this time the crowd had grown still larger. News cameras trained on Walter and me; Dan Marino parked his cart nearby to check it all out. Richard Roundtree, Pat Morita and even Linda Blair were egging Walter on. How could a simple afternoon of golf have gone so wrong?

He teed up for the second time and again silence fell like

a fog over the gathering. Walter eyed it up, took his swing, and *bam!* The ball went all of five feet!

Mayhem broke out. Pro athletes were leaning on Hollywood celebrities for strength, unable to stop the belly laughs and hooting. I could barely raise my head to look at the throng. All around me was the equivalent of a pack of golf hyenas, yukking it up real good. *Oh boy,* I thought. I will be forever scarred from this terrible lambasting on the links.

But then came the gift. I looked up just enough to see Walter wink at me. While the gallery was in the midst of the diabolical break-up, Sweetness teed up and launched a perfect shot that landed less than six inches from the cup! A collective "wow" rose from the spectators, and we all knew we were in the presence of greatness. He could have done that at any time. He walked over, gave me a big hug and whispered in my ear. "It's all about what is on the inside—outside circumstances play no part in golf or life. Never forget that." Walter sauntered away, followed by his legions of fans, and I stood there stunned. I had been folded, spindled and tucked away and it became one of the greatest moments of my life. A small piece of paper tacked on Walter's office wall came to mind. "All change, no matter how small, requires courage."

John St. Augustine

[EDITORS' NOTE: *Walter Payton passed away November 1, 1999, from cancer at age forty-five.*]

Winnie's Barn

No one becomes a champion without help.

Johnny Miller

I was raking my yard on a warm autumn afternoon when Arnold Palmer phoned to say Winnie had passed away that morning (November 20, 1999). He said he wanted me to know before I heard the news on television or from someone else. I thanked him and asked if he was okay. He sighed, and his voice cracked. "I don't know," he said. "I feel like I just took 12 on the opening hole."

Golf, to say nothing of life, would never be the same for anyone who knew Winnie Palmer, least of all her husband, Arnold.

Being invited to help Arnold Palmer craft his memoirs was a dream come true for me, because like millions of you, decades before I actually met the man, Palmer was my sports hero, my personal god in golf shoes. As the mortals of Greek mythology learned the hard way, though, mingling with gods and heroes comes with certain perils. The private great man is seldom as engaging as the public one and, at least in my professional experience, rarely as nice. The good news in Arnold's case was that he turned out to be everything he appears to be and then some—as warm, thoughtful, open and honest as I dared to hope he might be, an autobiographer's ace. The best thing I can say about my golf hero is that I liked him even better after I got to know him.

The unexpected bonus of the three-year project, however, was Winnie Palmer.

Almost from the moment we met, we became good friends and devoted allies in the task of putting Arnold's oversized life on paper. It was really Winnie's book, as I came to think of it, something she understood the golf world needed but Arnold would never seriously undertake on his own, and I quickly learned that the best way to convince Arnold Palmer to do anything was to get Winnie Palmer behind the idea.

A marriage, someone said, is like a medieval morality play. There are things you see on one level, currents you feel on another. After spending nearly eight hundred days slipping in and out of Arnold's and Winnie's lives, being granted poignant proximity to the ordinary ups and downs of the extraordinary Palmer family life, I began to understand what a unique and powerful partnership Arnold and Winnie really were. Their marriage had been tested in almost unfathomable ways, and perhaps because they'd been through so much together—the trials of fame and the dangers of fortune—they often appeared to cling together like shipwreck survivors on a beach.

You could see it in the way they instinctively clasped hands while moving through large crowds or relaxing with intimate groups of friends, you could feel its currency when Arnold affectionately called her "Lover" and teased her about running his life and bossing him about. Whatever else was true, when Winnie spoke about a subject that mattered, Arnold truly listened. The truth is, he relied on her opinions on just about everything for the simple reason that he would have been crazy not to. She was a crack judge of character, a no-nonsense advisor with an Ivy League brain, an unfaltering follower of the heart.

Besides Arnold's memoir, the other great project Winnie had in mind, well over a year and a half before being diagnosed with cancer of the intestinal lining, was the restoration of an old barn adjacent to the golf course in Latrobe. She jokingly referred to it as her "mink coat" while Arnold simply called it "Winnie's barn."

One gorgeously flaring summer afternoon she drove me to the high hill above the barn, overlooking the golf course, and explained that someday she hoped to convince Arnie—that's what she called him—to build a cozy "retirement" cottage up there for just the two of them, if and when he ever agreed to retire. The night before at dinner, out of the blue, Arnold had revealed his latest brainstorm: He was thinking of planting a vineyard and starting a winery on the hill adjacent to the barn. This was news to Winnie. She had looked at me and rolled her eyes with deep amusement as if to say, "Arnold the Dreamer at work again."

Now, Arnold, who happened to be playing the par-5 14th with a group of visiting corporate bigwigs, spotted us and sped up the hill in a golf cart, grinning suspiciously. He asked what the devil we were doing up there, and she replied cheekily, "Why, just checking out the view from the living room of our retirement house."

"Winifred, I'm going to build that house for you," he bellowed good-naturedly at her. "Just you wait and see!"

"Right, Lover," she teased gently. "Will that be before or after the winery?"

With that, she laughed that great laugh of hers, sounding every bit like the smoky, polished, dark-haired, underage beauty who kept her father Shube Walzer's accounting books. She was studying to become an interior designer and dreamed of traveling the world when a handsome, smooth-talking, largely unsuccessful paint salesman from Cleveland, who happened to be the new National Amateur golf champion, reached beneath the dinner table at Shawnee-on-Delaware. He impulsively took her hand and audaciously suggested that she marry him, three days after their introduction.

Strong-willed as a spring colt, she said yes in a matter of hours, beginning golf's most durable love story, and spent the next four decades shaping the views and interior life of the modern game's most commanding figure.

By her own design, Winnie Palmer was one of golf's most private people. Even at the height of Arnold's fame, she walked outside the ropes and a few steps behind, never asking nor tolerating any special privilege, as comfortable among the caddies as the VIPs, often invisible but always watching. "Arnie's the people person," she would say. "I'm a person person."

That was true. One-on-one, Winnie had a way of making everyone feel unique and deeply valued in her sphere. Her home was simple and unpretentious but as gorgeously made and richly hued as an Amish quilt, always dressed immaculately for the season.

There were private times with Winnie I will cherish most. Sometimes, after Arnold and I finished up one of our productive early-morning research sessions, he would jet away to fulfill an obligation, to film a commercial or appear at a function or charity tournament, at which point Winnie would take me under her wing for the balance of the day.

Several times after lunch we slipped out and took long drives with Prince, their retriever, through the countryside. One afternoon she drove me to see Unity Chapel, a two-hundred-year-old Presbyterian chapel sitting on a hill outside Latrobe. She told me its history and explained how the chapel had once fallen in disrepair but thanks to a number of people who loved the place, Unity Chapel had been restored to its simple grandeur.

I realized later that Winnie was one of those special people, but she wouldn't have told me that in a million years. The fact is, she loved going to church—almost any church—and sometimes she took me with her. She enjoyed old hymns and a sermon that made you think. She worried about the world her grandchildren and yours and mine will inherit. She took her quiet faith very seriously but never herself overly so.

I took professional insight and personal wisdom from these moments of easy companionship when we roamed around, went to church, talked about everything—God, books, children, art, dogs, music, history, the passing scene or the passing landscape. Occasionally, we even talked about golf and Arnold. I learned she loved the paintings of Andrew Wyeth and David Armstrong, the piano of Doug Montgomery, Andy Rooney commentaries and a well-made Fitzgerald old-fashioned. The rest of the short list included her daughters and seven grandchildren, icebox cake, good manners, peonies, her brother Marty, London's West End, Augusta galleries, cozy hotels, museums of any kind, early suppers, British golf writers and phone conversations with her partner-in-crime, Barbara Nicklaus.

Speaking of crime, the woman seemed to have read every other book published in the English language, especially mysteries. She was keen for a foggy night, a door left ajar, a crime unsolved. Somehow, she also found time to read half a dozen or so magazines and regularly corresponded with friends by way of handwritten notes packed with clipped articles she thought they should read. I used to kid her that if golf failed to pan out for

Arnie, she could support them both by starting a journalism clipping service.

I loved her Moravian sense of economy and value. After my children and I lost our retrievers to old age, Winnie set out to help me find the right replacement. She introduced me to a woman she'd heard about who bred champion goldens. A month or so later the woman rang me up to say she had the "perfect" dog for us: a three-year-old spayed female, beautiful disposition, papers, the whole nine yards, and a real bargain at just eighteen hundred dollars. When I reported this news to Winnie, she thundered, "Don't you dare buy that dog or I'll reach into this phone and break your arm!"

Her funeral service at Unity Chapel, on a stunning Indian summer day, was a simple and beautiful affair. The music was Bach and Beethoven. A few prayers of thanksgiving were read, the navy hymn sung. Her granddaughter Emily read a few passages from Proverbs. There was no eulogy under Winnie's strict orders—but none was necessary because each of us sat there writing our own eulogies in our heads for the new patron saint of golf wives.

After a little while—Winnie hated services that went on too long—we all filed out and drove to Latrobe Country Club for lunch. In the din of conversation, I was pleased to see Arnold laughing again, gently needling Jack when he pulled out a cellular phone to see how Gary was doing at the PGA Tour Q School. A few minutes later, I saw him lead George and Barbara Bush out the grillroom door, and I knew exactly where he was taking them—to see Winnie's barn, now fully restored, sitting in the autumnal sunlight like a David Armstrong original.

The truth is, some of us stood there worrying about how Arnold Palmer will fare without his Pennsylvania original, Winnie. I was lost in these thoughts, I confess, selfishly thinking how I was going to miss Arnold and

Latrobe and most of all, my weekly phone conversations with Winnie, when a large, strong pair of hands suddenly settled on my shoulders. I turned around and it was Arnold, looking at me with what Winnie once called his "Deacon look."

We hadn't really spoken up to this point. Perhaps I'd even consciously evaded him a bit—and maybe him, me. He knew what I thought of his wife, how we were all a bit in awe and in love with pretty Winnie Walzer. He thanked me for coming, and I asked him for the second time in two days if he was okay. Arnold's look softened. His eyes began to glisten.

"I'm okay for now," golf's most public man said softly of his most private loss. We both knew it would be the early mornings and evenings to come that would be toughest for him to get through, when Winnie's presence filled their house with such warm abundance.

He cleared his throat and managed a smile. "The good news is, she left me good instructions on how to live the rest of my life," he said, still squeezing my arm with those huge blacksmith hands of his, perhaps picturing Winnie that gorgeous summer day on the hill above the barn. Remembering her as I always will.

"Very firm instructions," he said.

James Dodson

4

GOLFMANSHIP

Never do anything to compromise your
integrity. Anything worth achieving is worth
an honorable and honest effort. There are
no short cuts to becoming a champion.
You will never take any trophies or medals
with you when you leave this life, but your
character will be with you always. Be true
to yourself, and keep in perspective the fact
that even if you can't be the world's best
athlete in your chosen sport every day . . .
you can be your best person every day.

Mike Reid

Snakes Alive!

Golf is temporary insanity practiced in a pasture.

Dave Kindred

Dave Harris, my roommate and golfing partner in college, was almost a scratch golfer. He would have been
invited to play on the university team except for one
frailty; he was an incorrigible practical joker. Sometimes
it was the duck call he blew during somebody's backswing, but mostly it came from the collection of rubber
snakes in his golf bag. One afternoon, a burly freshman
from Spokane lined up a putt on the 6th hole, but backed
off when, out of the corner of his eye, he spied a nasty-
looking articulated python lying on the green. "Harris,"
he said, "you pull this stuff again and I'll part that blond
crew cut with a 5-iron and reduce your fat frame to
blubber!" So Dave laid off for a while, but one afternoon
while playing as a twosome at Green Hill Country Club,
he caused a big black snake with yellow stripes to appear
suddenly at my feet just as I was about to tee off.

Then in the spring of 1947, Dave and I parted company.
I took a job with the Montana State Highway Department,

but he stuck around at the University of Washington to go for his masters; I ended up on a sizable construction job working out of Shelby in northern Montana. Shelby's major claim to fame was having been the scene of the infamous Dempsey/Gibbons prize fight in 1923; a gigantic billboard on the road into town told the passing world about it. Its other notable feature was that it was one of the few prairie towns up along the High-Line to sport a real municipal golf course.

The course was singularly spartan in its configuration. The locals had simply mowed down a few acres of buffalograss for fairways, set the mower as low as it would go to make greens, dragged in an old granary for a starter's shack, and voila!—instant golf course. But they had to dig the cups about two feet deep so the wind wouldn't blow the flagsticks over, and most short putts were conceded because nobody relished the idea of reaching up to the elbow into those dark recesses for a ball. Also, a lot of the mowing and some of the fertilizing was accomplished by allowing a local rancher to graze a few scrawny old cows on the place. I had tried playing the course twice but gave up in disgust both times, once after nicking the dickens out of a brand-new 8-iron on a rock and the other because the tumbleweeds, running before a Wild West wind, sailed across my line of sight every time I set up to swing. But there was no waiting, since the course was always completely deserted until the weekends, when one of the cattle owner's kids kicked the cows out to another pasture and then opened up the starter's shack and accepted two-dollar green fees from a few hardy souls.

Dave and I had kept in touch, and one evening he called saying he was working at Glacier Park for the summer and invited me up for a round of golf whenever I was free. "Davey," I said, "I'd love to, but we're working seven-day weeks right now. But, heck, we've got a perfectly good course right here in Shelby; I can take off a little early one day and we can play some twilight golf. After all, it doesn't get dark up here until about ten during July, and you're only a two-hour drive away."

"Great! How about this Wednesday? Thursday's my day off."

"Fine. See you then, ol' buddy."

First I reserved a room for Dave at the hotel, then made a small purchase in the novelty section of the drugstore and dropped in for a short chat with Tom, proprietor of Tommy's Bar and Grill. Then I located Jimmy, the kid who insisted on riding shotgun whenever I went out of town because he loved to watch heavy equipment move earth.

"Jimmy," I said, "do you think you could find a couple of snakes somewhere by Wednesday afternoon? Any kind, as long as they are good-sized and not rattlers."

"Sure. How about gopher snakes? There's a bunch of 'em living under our chicken house."

"Beautiful," I said, and handed him a piece of paper with instructions along with a dollar bill. "And there's another buck in it if you do a good job."

Dave showed up at the hotel right on time, and on the way to the golf course he said, "Bob, I know I used to give you strokes back in Seattle, but here you have all the local knowledge, so how about playing this round even-steven and just for a couple of beers?"

I said okay, and while Dave surveyed the course from the 1st tee with a certain air of misgiving, I said, "Davey, you're a city guy and this is a country course, so I think I owe you some pointers. First of all, I notice the cattle are grazing out here this evening, so I'd suggest you either take off or cover up that red shirt. Also, if your ball comes to rest on or within six inches of a cow it can be lifted without penalty. And I should point out that this is rattlesnake country, and they start coming out this time of day, so please watch your step; the nearest antivenom clinic is ninety miles away."

So, although it was still about eighty degrees in the shade, Dave pulled a blue sweater out of his bag. Then, despite glancing over his shoulder at the cows every five seconds and scanning the grass for snakes, he managed to hit to within a couple feet off the green in three on the par-4 1st hole. He sank a twenty-foot chip. "Bobby," he said as he pulled out the pin, "I think I've already begun to figure out your little course." But when he reached for the ball and his fingers encountered the cool coils of a big snake moving around looking for daylight, he flung his 6-iron away, tried to run but stumbled, fell on his behind and lay there gasping for breath. "Bob," he whispered, "I think there's some kind of snake in there!"

I looked in the hole, reached down, grabbed the animal by the neck, turned him loose to the prairie and, as he slithered away, said, "Heck, Davey, he's just an ol' gopher snake. Wouldn't hurt a soul. In fact, folks like to have 'em around because they eat mice and rats."

On the next hole, another par 4, Dave regained composure, hit a lucky shot out of a clump of cactus and actually scored a birdie. Then on the 3rd, a 175-yard par-3, his tee shot landed in the only "sand trap" on the course, a natural alkali seep which had probably been there for a few thousand years, and Dave ended with a terrible lie. But he laid open a sand wedge, blasted out to within three feet of the pin, and was about to putt out when the handsome head of another gopher snake poked itself over the edge of the hole, stuck its tongue out at Dave, and then fell back. "Hey, Bob," he yelled, "there's another one of your pet snakes trapped in here!"

I trotted up to the hole, peered in and said, "Davey, this one happens to be a rattlesnake with six rattles on his tail, and I don't understand why he didn't buzz at you. But if you had come any closer, we might have been on our way to the clinic in Great Falls. So for the rest of the round, why don't we just concede any putts under four feet? And I hope that wasn't a new ball." Then while Dave shakily marked down the scores, I reminded myself to slip little Jimmy an extra buck. He had performed well.

After that, all the wheels came off Dave's game, and at the end of nine holes he flung away his sweater, gazed at his new white shoes covered with cow dung and said, "Well, Bobby, I've had it with your damned country golf course, and the beer is on me."

Later, sitting at the bar in Tommy's Bar and Grill, Dave lifted his first mug of cold suds, hesitated, looked again into the glass and then reeled back in disgust. There in the bottom rested a little rubber snake, coiled and ready to strike.

After a couple of deep breaths, he looked around the room at all the quiet, expectant faces, reached into the mug with two fingers and extracted the snake. Then he drained the beer and said loudly, "Tommy, would you put a head on this? But you don't need to be so fancy with the next one. I'll just have it plain without a snake." The regulars, primed ahead for this event, gave him an ovation. One anonymous patron must have been really impressed, because somebody picked up the dinner tab that night.

I said good-bye to Dave early while he was in deep conversation with Lucy, the waitress, because I had to get up at five in the morning. The next afternoon back at the hotel, Bill, the desk clerk/manager/owner, hailed me in the lobby and handed me a note from Dave:

"Dear ol' buddy—I got to know little Lucy pretty well last night, and she ratted on you. It was all nicely orchestrated, but did you really need to get half the town involved? Anyhow, you made your point. Looking forward to another round on a course as far away as possible from yours. —Dave."

I tucked the note in my shirt pocket and started for

the room and a shower, but Bill stopped me and said, "By the way, your friend must be into novelties or toys or something."

"Nope," I said. "He's a dumb engineer like myself."

"Well, it's strange. He didn't check out until just before noon, and when Hilda finally got in to make up his room, she came down all excited because he left a dozen rubber snakes in the wastebasket."

Bob Drust

"Better grab your snake wedge."

More Trash Talk Than the NBA

When you are ahead, don't take it easy, kill them. After the finish, then be a sportsman.

Earl Woods—to his son Tiger Woods

Being a typical sportsman, I pride myself in being able to play a good game. But, almost as important, I am a typical man, and I pride myself in being able to talk a good game.

I learned from a master.

I don't mean to brag about father, but if there were a Hall of Fame for trash talkers, my dad would be right up there with Charles Barkley, Xavier McDaniel, John Starks, Reggie Miller and every professional boxer who ever lived. He might even be up for a lifetime achievement award. I mean a bronze statue and everything.

In other words, Dad knows how to "talk the talk" and "walk the walk" of a champion. He could be on the basketball court with Michael Jordan and find something wrong with his jump shot.

It's not so much a matter of simple bragging—it's the subtle little things he says and does. The latest "psych job" took place during a semifriendly family golf outing over a holiday weekend.

First, he forced the enemy (me) to watch the seemingly endless early-round coverage of a pro golf tournament on television, analyzing what each golfer did right and wrong along the way. Dad even offered an explanation for the putting difficulty Jack Nicklaus experienced at one point. Something about a follow-through technique he read about in *Golf Digest.* I dunno. Jack himself probably wrote the article, but Dad would have you believe he coauthored it.

Then came the actual family outing itself. The site of this mock PGA event: a rundown par-3 where most people play winter rules year-round. The "championship flight": my dad, king of the jungle; my mom, who lets her game do her talking; me, the personification of the term "weekend hacker"; and my sister, 60 handicap.

Dad wasn't too concerned at first—he kept the discussions of his recent league tournament wins to a bare minimum as we headed to the 1st tee box.

After all, I had never come close to testing my dad on the links—except for that time when I was twelve and my mulligan limit at least double that number.

But this time was going to be different, I convinced myself. Tension grew thick as I reached two of the first three greens and played par golf. Dad, on the other hand, struggled, failing to even make par on any of the first three holes.

I thought about exclaiming, "Can anybody beat a 2!?!" after I birdied the 3rd hole, but that would have been too cocky and bold. It might have awakened the beast within The Master. So, like an awestruck Luke Skywalker in the presence of the Supreme Jedi Yoda, I bit my lip and moved on.

As time wore on, however, I could see the pressure getting to ol' Dad. He even tried coaching Mom on the read of the No. 5 green—a nearly fatal slip of the tongue.

I cringed and looked away as he said, "It looks like it'll break a little left, Dear."

Now, just calling my mom "dear" was enough to throw off the poor woman until at least next week, but telling her how to read a green!?! Better to tell Leonardo da Vinci to use longer strokes! Better to tell Cindy Crawford to lose the mole! Better to tell Jordan to keep his tongue in his mouth! The very idea!

From past experience, even dumb ol' me knew not to even talk to my mother during any sporting contest. I mean, if you so much as breathe during her backswing, you can expect to dine on the club head of her choosing. Yes, this was a definite mistake and a sign that The Master had lost his grip—not only on his golf game, but on reality and sanity itself.

Sweat beads poured down my dad's forehead on the No. 7 tee box—still one stroke down to the kid whom he once said had "absolutely no athletic ability." I again reached the green. It was time for Dad to pull out all the stops.

As I reached down to pick up a stray ball in the fairway, my dad shouted, "No!"

I moved on, without the ball, knowing full well that nobody on the course would claim it.

While my mind worked on the reason that it was a punishable sin for me to pick up this lost ball, you see, I could not concentrate on my upcoming putt. Dad had done it again! I three-putted and walked off in disgust.

"Well, at least you got a 4!" said Dad, in the cheeriest voice imaginable.

I was still chewing on the mental breakdown from No. 7 when Dad mentioned to Mom—just loud enough for me to hear—something about the stiff wind we'd be hitting into on No. 8.

I promptly decided against my 6-iron, pulled out the

5 and launched a shot well over the green and into the driving range area for a one-stroke penalty. Reality set in. Dad was going to get my goat again.

Dad added insult to injury on the No. 8 green, giving me a backhanded compliment about how good my long game was, but at the same time telling me how horrible my short game was. He'd be happy to give me putting lessons.

Dad had everything in the bag as he took a one-stroke lead into the final hole. Taking nothing for granted, he laid up short and avoided trouble on the back of the green. I, however, airmailed the green (into that "stiff wind").

Dad tapped in for a bogey while I sat thirty feet away from the hole, putting for par on the slope of a steep hill.

"Well, it all comes down to this—if I make this putt, I tie you, Dad," I said, getting a good read. "How's that for motivation?"

With Dad in the background of my vision (another psych-out technique, probably picked up from my Uncle John), I stroked the ball and looked on with anticipation. Oh, how smoothly the ball rolled over those thin blades of grass! Oh, how satisfying a tie would be!

"OH! YESSSSSSSS!" I screamed, much louder than I wanted, dropping my putter and pointing at Dad with the index fingers on both my hands. "YES! I TIED YOU!"

I quickly threw my hand over my mouth, realizing that at least three other foursomes were staring in my direction. I realized that, if only for a moment, some hellish energy from deep within my dad's competitive soul had invaded my normally calm demeanor. For a fleeting moment, I had become The Master of Maliciousness.

And then, it was gone. I was back to myself again, apologizing for my absurd behavior and thinking about challenging Dad to a playoff hole, where I could purposely lose and somehow restore order in the universe.

But, glancing at Dad, I realized it wasn't necessary. He

smiled and appeared truly at peace. He was actually glad, in his own way, that I'd tied him and earned a moral victory. And it was then that I understood . . . that maybe the only mind games taking place that day were the ones inside my own mind. And maybe, just maybe, Dad wasn't such a bad sport after all.

Dan Galbraith

Your Cheatin' Heart

If you think it's hard to meet new people, try picking up the wrong golf ball.

Jack Lemmon

The one thing to be said about my Uncle Steve was that he never let a rule stand in his way of winning. I first witnessed this behavior when I challenged him to a game of Snakes and Ladders. I was only a mere child of five, but that didn't keep him from using his warped logic to win. He argued that since he was not afraid of snakes, he should be allowed to climb the beasts as well as the ladders. This comment, of course, begged the question: If my uncle would go to that much effort to win a child's game, how far would he go for something important?

By the time Steve was in his early thirties, he had become an adequate golfer whose handicap was that he still hated to lose. Because of his attitude and temper he was often forced to play alone, which did not keep him from playing as though his life depended on a victory. Rules became suggestions for people with limited imaginations. He would take a one-foot gimme and then whirl around to see if I was going to argue. I, of course, had long since learned that reminding my uncle of the rules meant a small tip.

I turned fifteen the summer Pine Greens Golf Club held its fiftieth annual championship. Pine Greens was the oldest business or club in the area and therefore was viewed with reverence. The Golf Trophy, a truly unimaginative name for the award, was the most prestigious prize in the county, and my uncle was geared up for the victory.

"Al, my boy," he said, "this year the Golf Trophy is mine and you'll be my caddie."

I hesitated to remind him of his promise to never play in the tournament again. This oath had been made after calling the tournament officials fascists for refusing to allow him his multi-mulligan rule.

"Are you sure you want to play?" I asked cautiously. "After all, you did offend quite a few people last year."

"Water under the bridge," he assured me. "I'm a changed man."

This appeared to be true. As the tournament wore on, my uncle demonstrated levels of self-control that would have put a Zen master to shame. He followed, without the slightest complaint, every rule he had ever dismissed as archaic. What made the situation even more unbelievable was that he managed to keep his anger in check.

At the 8th hole, he missed a three-foot putt and smiled. Everybody in the group, myself included, had fallen to the ground in preparation for the ritual tossing of the putter. "What gives?" I asked as I placed the putter back in the bag. "You're acting like a good sport. You should have lost your temper back at the 1st hole."

"I told you I was prepared this year," whispered Steve. "I went and got myself hypnotized last night. According to the Amazing Freddie, every time I would normally get angry, I focus the energy on the next shot. Considering the quality of my last drive, my tee shot should be a beaut."

It was. The hole was a dogleg left, 350 yards. Steve was on the green after his first shot and sunk a long putt for eagle. He smiled politely as the rest of his party bogeyed.

At the end of the day, Steve was tied with Angus Popovitch, a man whose reputation for cheating made Steve look like an amateur. According to club rules, they would face off the following day in an eighteen-hole match.

It was a lovely fall day as the two golfers prepared to tee off. Word had spread as to who won in the final, and a huge crowd had assembled. They had not come to see a great round of golf, but rather to witness what had the potential to be the first brawl in the history of Pine Greens.

The first sign of animosity occurred at the 2nd green. Angus's shot was within three feet of the cup, and he bent down to pick up his ball. Steve asked his opponent what he was doing, and Angus replied that anything under three feet was a gimme.

"Anything under three feet is a pygmy," snarled Steve. "Now putt the ball."

Thus the floodgates were thrust open, and those who had come to watch flagrant breaking of the rules were not disappointed. Angus drew first blood when he swore the wind from his practice swing had knocked the ball off his tee. It was not until Angus and his caddie were prepared to sign a sworn affidavit that Steve dropped his complaint.

At No. 3, Angus's second shot bounced into the rough among some daisies. It was not a difficult shot to recover from as the weeds offered a minimum of difficulty. Angus, however, was not one to take chances. He plucked a handful of daisies and dropped them in front of Steve's face.

"Wind appears to be from the west," he laughed.

There was a murmuring of displeasure from the gallery at what was generally considered poor decorum. Steve surprised everyone by not saying anything.

My uncle's second shot at the 6th hole saw his 5-iron take him into the rough. It was not a totally bad shot except that his ball landed behind a small boulder. Steve surveyed the ball from all angles, as did Angus. The shot was difficult, if not impossible, as the ball was less than an inch away from the rock. Angus showed his usual compassion. "Drop the ball and take a stroke. It's getting late."

Steve was ready to comply when he was struck with an epiphany. He reached down and grabbed the boulder with two hands and slowly lifted the rock off the ground. The boulder must have weighed about two hundred pounds, and Steve only managed to lift it waist-high. Before Angus could utter a protest, Steve tossed the rock away from his ball.

"You're right, Angus. The wind is westerly," Steve said, and he proceeded to hit his ball onto the green.

This time the gallery gave a polite round of applause at what it deemed to be poetic justice. Steve doffed his cap, leaving Angus to complain to his caddie.

At last the combatants arrived at the 18th. Angus had the lead by one stroke, and the par-3 offered little hope for my uncle to mount a comeback. Still, he did his best as his tee shot landed twenty yards from the green. We waited as Angus prepared for his tee shot and were rewarded by a drive that trailed left, toward the woods.

"Keep an eye on him, Al," warned Uncle Steve. "Angus will try to drop a ball in play if he can't find his."

We walked toward the green and watched as Angus and his caddie searched for the ball. I joined in the search, but Steve wouldn't move from where he was standing. It was not easy to look for the ball and watch Angus and his caddie. I was about to suggest that Steve help when I heard a shout of joy as Angus found his ball. It was a feat just short of a miracle, I thought, as I had searched the same piece of ground just moments earlier. I rushed back to Steve.

"We got him," I whispered. "That's not his ball."
The prestige of winning the tournament and the trophy disappeared with Steve's sharp retort. "I know," he answered. "I'm standing on it."

Alan Broderick

Check Your Bag

My brother Maurice and three of his buddies—Sam, Renwick and Earl—have a regular golf game every Friday during the summer. In order to make the game interesting and even, they use handicaps. As a result of this, Maurice and Brian are partners, and Sam and Renwick play together.

Maurice never walks the golf course and is always trying to get one of the other guys to ride with him. This particular Friday in July, it was very warm, and he asked Renwick to ride with him.

It just so happens that Renwick had been on a health kick for a couple of months, so he told Maurice that he would prefer to walk. Renwick had lost about twenty pounds and had just purchased a carry bag from the pro shop, deciding that toting, rather than using a pull cart as he walked the course, would help him stay in shape.

Maurice candidly cautioned Renwick, "Remember, you are fifty-eight years old. Walking the course is one thing; carrying your bag for eighteen holes is something else."

Nevertheless, Renwick insisted on walking, and off they went.

After nine holes, Renwick said to one of the other guys

who was walking, "I think Maurice was right. Carrying this bag is wearing me out."

Naturally, the other guy suggested that Renwick ask Maurice for a ride in the cart, to which Renwick stubbornly replied, "Not a chance. If you think I will admit this to Maurice, you are crazy."

They continued on. Renwick struggled but refused to give Maurice the satisfaction of giving up.

At about the 12th hole, Sam confided in Maurice, "Renwick realizes carrying the golf bag was a bad idea, but will not admit it to you because he knows he will be in for a real good ribbing."

Shortly after hearing this, Maurice called Renwick over and said, "Are you getting tired of carrying that golf bag? Why don't you take a load off and put the bag on the cart?"

Renwick grimaced but replied, "No thanks. It's not bad at all."

With a sly grin, Maurice continued, "Then why don't you unzip that side pocket and lighten your load?"

Knowing he'd been had, Renwick unzipped the side pocket, where he discovered two rocks—slightly smaller than a couple of footballs—that he had been carrying for twelve holes!

Needless to say, Renwick had some choice words for Maurice, while Sam and Brian were rolling on the tee, laughing until they were crying.

And rest assured, Renwick now checks his bag for foreign objects before every golf game . . . particularly on Fridays.

Robert Lalonde

Play It As It Lays

When it comes to the game of life, I figure I've played the whole course.

Lee Trevino

When I turned fifty, I discovered three essential facts of middle age: periodontia, bifocals and golf.

Golf?

Let me explain. I once assumed that golf was a sport for elderly Country Club Republicans. The sort of men who wore green pants with whale belts and protected their clubs with fuzzy duck head covers.

Golf was Dwight David Eisenhower. My family was Adlai Stevenson.

In my twenties, I thought golf was God's way of telling you that you had too much time on your hands.

In my thirties, I decided that a low handicap was admissible evidence of child neglect in any custody dispute.

In my forties, as a fairly decent tennis and squash player, I couldn't imagine hitting a ball while it was standing still. Quite frankly, it seemed unfair.

But somewhere along the way, somewhere between Bill

Clinton and Big Bertha and Tiger Woods, between chiro-
practors and knee surgery and Advil, I had an epiphany
(that's something close to a muscle spasm) that said: Golf
is my next sport. To wit: my last sport. I better learn it now.

This decision was aided and abetted by a quirky nine-
hole golf course in Maine where people still stroll and stop
to look at the view.

It was also aided and abetted by a quirky husband
(more Bobby Kennedy than Adlai Stevenson) who enthu-
siastically gave me all his clubs. This was an act of gen
erosity that I didn't immediately recognize for what it
was—a ploy for him to get new equipment.

Now, as I approach Columbus Day weekend with a full
set of clubs and big plans, I feel fully qualified at last to
offer up my views on why golf begins at fifty.

Yes, I know that one sign of a new and erratic duffer is
the penchant for turning golf into a good walk through
midlife spoiled. For reasons that remain unclear, golf has
spawned more philosophical rambles than fairways.

Nobody compares tennis to life. A love game? Ken
Burns and several million fans talk about baseball as the
collective field of youthful dreams, but there's no senior
tour on the diamonds.

Today there are, I hasten to add, some 25 million golfers
and 16,010 golf courses. There are speed golfers and net-
working golfers and boring golfers. There is even, for reasons that escape me, a golf channel. All golf, all day long.

There is a business writer who actually correlated the
handicaps of CEOs with their stock performance. And
there are the very, very serious golf professionals who sit
around discussing whether they should ban new
improved clubs because they are making the game too
easy. Say what? But from my perspective, golf is the
midlife sport of choice for very different reasons. First of
all, it's easier to reach your goals. In midlife, after all, it's a

snap to have a handicap below your age and a score below your weight. And getting easier all the time.

Golf is like midlife because only now do you realize that the course you have set upon is governed by rules so vast, so arcane and so arbitrary that the average person—you— will never figure it all out.

Golf is like midlife because it is absolutely unfair. As a young person, you carry the illusion that if you do your homework, study and work overtime you'll get it all right. By middle age, you know that every time you've got it all together—work, family, putt, pitch—some piece is about to unravel. Promise.

Golf, like midlife, is played against only one opponent: yourself. By the time you reach fifty, you had better figure out that doing well doesn't depend on others doing badly. You don't have to wish them ill. They're not the reason you are shanking the ball.

Golf is like middle age, because—ah, you knew this was coming—in these years you really do have to play it as it lays. You don't get to start everything all over again. The most you get is a mulligan. If it's an unplayable lie, every- body sympathizes, but you still have to take a penalty.

Ellen Goodman

The Best Golfer Tantrum of All Time

*Golf is a game that creates emotions that some-
times cannot be sustained with a club in the
hand.*

Bobby Jones

Workers at the Riverside Golf and Country Club in
Portland, Oregon, were taking down some of the golf
course's towering poplars when they came upon evidence
of what appeared to be the enraged-golfer tantrum of all
time. Forty feet up in one tree was a 10-iron that looked as
though it had been thrown right through a ten-inch branch.

Closer examination, however, revealed that the club,
which is of the era when they first started making steel
shafts, was probably thrown about forty years ago. It
seems to have lodged in a high crotch in the tree, and
since that terrible moment, the branch has grown around
the club and the poplar itself has grown taller.

The cut section of tree—complete with club—will be
kept on display at the pro shop.

Rod Patterson

"I've been wondering all morning
why he carried that club!"

Reprinted by permission of George Crenshaw, Masters Agency.

Character Building

I take the revolutionary view that all this talk about the virtues of practice, for the average club golfer at any rate, is a snare and a delusion. "Practice makes perfect," they say. Of course, it doesn't. For the vast majority of golfers it merely consolidates imperfection.

Henry Longhurst

I was playing golf at the local course in my hometown when I sent an errant approach shot into the parking lot adjacent the clubhouse. It took one hop and plowed right into the side of a pickup truck parked in the lot. To make matters even worse, the owner was sitting on the tailgate changing his shoes. Of course, my first reaction was to slink the other way and hope that nobody would know where it came from. But, I decided, I had to own up, take responsibility for my actions.

Taking a deep breath, I walked over to the truck and sheepishly apologized for what I had done. To my surprise and delight, the man smiled and told me he learned long ago that sometimes you get the better of the game, and other times the game gets the best of you.

With a heavy sigh of relief, the weight of the world off my shoulders, I reached down to retrieve my ball from its location near the front tire. However, as I bent over, the shift in weight caused my bag of golf clubs to swing around, smashing into the side of his truck. I looked up at the man, and with a smile that was beginning to flatten out he said, "Now I'm starting to get mad."

Enough character building for one day. I grabbed my ball and took off.

Jim King

Perfect Stroke—for the Car?

Actually, the only time I ever took out a 1-iron was to kill a tarantula. And I took a 7 to do that.

Jim Murray

About twenty years ago, when we lived in Tulsa, Oklahoma, my husband Harold bought a new car and gave me his, a 1973 Ford LTD. It ran very well, and I had no trouble with it until one day while out doing errands.

I came out of the grocery store, sat in the car and turned the key. Nothing happened. I tried again. Silence. The car had apparently died a quiet death while I was in the store.

I went back in the store to a telephone and, fortunately, Harold was home.

"I need you," I said after telling him my plight.

"Where are you?"

I told him.

"I'll be right there."

He came, sat in the car and turned the key as if he had to prove to himself that I was right, and I wouldn't have been surprised if it had started for him. I'd had this experience before, you see. But the car remained inactive.

Next he popped the hood and puttered around a bit, then opened the trunk. After rummaging around, he pulled a club out of my golf bag and tapped on one of the battery cables.

"See if it'll start," he said, looking confident.

Sure enough the engine purred like a satisfied kitten.

"Well," I said, "in case this happens again, I guess I need to know what to do."

"If it does, use a 5-iron." He grinned and winked.

I've had golf lessons before, but never one on this particular use of a 5-iron.

All went well with the car until a week or so later when it stalled right in the middle of a busy intersection. I remained undaunted, knowing exactly what to do this time.

I popped the hood, opened the trunk, took out my 5-iron and tapped that battery cable just like a pro. I sat in the car, turned the key and the engine purred again. Several well-intentioned men had come to my aid and watched the procedure with obvious wonder. When the car started, one of the men came up to my window, grinned and asked, "Hey lady, I have to know—what club did you use?"

Marci Martin

Old Jake's Shrewdest Trick

The older you get, the easier it is to shoot your age.

Jerry Barber

The news that Old Jake had the incurable unmentionable got around the club pretty fast. Members spoke in whispers when they said his days were numbered, or so they understood.

I asked a friend if he'd heard about Old Jake, and he said, yeah, it was a terrible thing—he understood his days were numbered. I asked how long, and the friend said he'd heard six months, maybe nine.

I said, "Well, there goes the Member-Guest and the Club Seniors again."

The friend nodded. He knew what I meant. Old Jake had time to win two more trophies before he checked out.

Old Jake was a 12 who carried a 23.

He'd collected so many tournament trophies over the past ten or fifteen years—I won't say "won"—he'd been forced to build another room on his house.

I often wondered how Old Jake described the trophies

when he took visitors on a tour of the room.

"Here's the Steuben bowl I screwed everybody out of in the '88 Member-Guest. . . . Here's the silver plate I stole in the '91 Club Seniors."

That kind of thing.

I first met him when we were paired together in the first round of the thirty-six-hole Club Seniors in '89. Me with my 10, him with his 23.

When we both turned the front nine in 5-over-par 41, I knew it was all over. He eventually won by fourteen.

There was another year we were paired together in the last round of the Club Seniors, and for once he appeared to be as out of contention as I was, like eight or nine strokes off the lead as we stood on the 12th tee.

"Dang, I better get started," he said.

Whereupon, his swing suddenly got smooth and he shot one under over the last seven holes to win by two.

"Luckiest darn golf day I've ever had," he explained.

Old Jake had style to go along with his handicap. Always acting hung over, limping along, tired, weary, coughing, wheezing, saying how lucky it was he'd hit that 245-yard 4-wood onto the green from out of the rough. He didn't see how he was playing so well today, much as he drank last night.

One afternoon, I complained about Old Jake's absurd handicap to another guy at the club, and the guy said, "Hey, don't knock Jake. I've won six Member-Members with him."

In the Member-Guest or the Member-Member, you could count on Old Jake for two things. If his partner was on the green, he'd be in the water or out-of-bounds. But if his partner was in the water or out-of-bounds, Old Jake would be on the green.

He seemed to be an expert at never shooting better than a 95 when he played a recreational round with other members, even if he constantly had to find new ways to make a 15 or 16 on one of the last few holes.

Guy came in the grill laughing one day, saying, "You can't believe what Jake just did on 17. He got the shanks with his 9-iron. Couldn't get out of 'em. He put one, two . . . he must have put five, six balls in the water. Boy, he was hot. Darnedest thing you ever saw."

"What did he make on 18?" I asked.

"On 18? Oh, he birdied 18."

Two years ago the club tried a new event: the Open Match-Play Championship for the first 128 players to sign up. Full handicaps were allowed, if a guy was a 4 and you were a 10, he had to give you six shots. A guy was a 16 and you were a 10, you had to give him six shots.

If they'd had a way to bet on it, I'd have laid it all on Old Jake and his 23, and borrowed a wheelbarrow to get it home.

With his handicap, Old Jake got one stroke on thirteen holes and two strokes on five holes. He didn't have a close match till the final, when he ran into Big Stu, the club champion, a long-hitting scratch player.

That's where Old Jake was pretty hard-pressed to nail him, 6 and 5.

Not long ago, just when I was having a change of heart, and thinking our club was going to lose quite a bit of color when Old Jake checked out, it began to get around that Old Jake's unmentionable was curable, after all.

Then it was confirmed that he'd never had the incurable unmentionable in the first place.

But his handicap was now up to 27.

Dan Jenkins

The Accidental Purist:
Diary of a Beginning Golf Junkie

I am a public school girl from Pittsburgh. I played varsity basketball and tennis, and I had always maintained
that golf was an elitist sport. A borderline sport at that.
People can play it wearing a belt, for crying out loud.

I was a reverse snob. And then I got a job as a senior
editor at a golf magazine. I never seriously considered that
I would take up the game. I dropped the elitist riff, though,
and just told people that I was a working mom with two
young children and they immediately seemed to get why
I didn't actually play.

This began to nag at me, though. Because, one, I AM an
editor for a golf magazine, and it's a little embarrassing
explaining how I can do what I do and not play golf. Since
the day I took the job, I had read every golf publication I
could get my hands on. I've become familiar with Herbert
Warren Wind and Arnold Haultain and, of course, Dan
Jenkins. I can't seem to get through *Golf in the Kingdom*, but
I think you get the picture. I know golf manufacturers and
golf professionals. I know women who knit golf head covers for a living. I have Sign Boy's home phone number, for

Pete's sake. I have ridden around Clint Eastwood's golf course in Carmel with the man himself. I have witnessed John Daly playing guitar with Lisa Loeb and Dweezil Zappa. I have interviewed David Duval and Tom Lehman. I've talked to the likes of Ray Leonard, Terry Bradshaw, Joe Mantegna, Branford Marsalis and Mario Lemieux about golf. I notice how much guys LOVE talking about golf. It is not lost on me that most men cannot remember where the butter is in the refrigerator, but they can tell you precisely what clubs they used and give you play-by-play action of a shot they hit ten years ago on some course in East Podunk, Ohio.

I am doing everything with golf that a person can possibly do. But I am beginning to tire of explaining—with a smile, for the thousandth time—how I can do what I do without actually playing the game. The idea taunts me like low-hanging fruit until I just can't take it anymore: It's a sunny day in Colorado, and I call this golf school near my house. I have a noon appointment. I am Eve and I am about to be damned. Bring on the golf lessons.

Lesson one:

Mike Schlager, my instructor, walks me to the range, hands me a 9-iron and watches me swing. He knows I'm a skier and explains that like skiing, balance is important in golf. He tells me that the set-up in golf, what goes on before the motion, is more important than the actual swing. He teaches me about where my hands should be— in the center of my body, on a straight path from my sternum—and where they should hang. He gives me two drills to practice with my eyes closed. One's about finding the center of my body that involves holding a golf club over my head and doing a kind of deep knee bend. Then he tells me to swing the club back and forth as fast as I can and only come off of my feet at the end. It feels like a samurai golf swing. We chip a bit and he gives me a chipping drill. We also putt. He says to practice making short one- to two-foot putts. The more it goes in, the more confidence I'll have. I take this all home with me.

Cost (gulp), one hundred dollars. This is a lot of green for a mother of two looking at college tuition for 2013. This is a lot of green for someone whose favorite store is Target. But somehow, I don't think twice.

I have one club at home, some kind of wedge, and I start doing my drills. I've taken to putting with the wedge even while I'm on the phone. Every time I lean my neck in to hold the phone so I can make a stroke, I end up hanging up on someone. I hung up on my boss three times in one conversation. I hung up on Phil Mickelson's agent (don't tell my boss). I take my mystery wedge with me on a ski vacation to Steamboat and do my exercises religiously. I putt at the coffee table.

Lesson two:

I arrive early, and Mike sends me out to the practice area. I putt and putt and putt. I am a two-foot wonder, which I know is good because Mike told me in my first lesson that someday I'm going to play in a scramble and everybody loves a woman who can make a putt.

Mike says, "Let's go up to the range." I tell him that's what I'm scared of—going up to the range. But I press on. I find my balance and swing. It feels pretty good. Mike says it is pretty good. I hit several decent shots, and at one point he laughs and says, "You don't know how good these are." I decide I like Mike a lot. He helps me adjust my grip. He notices my small hands and suggests more of a baseball hold. I practice with the new grip, and the ball starts going a fair amount farther. "Over the pin," he says with a degree of satisfaction like Master Po used to use with the Grasshopper on the old *Kung Fu* TV show.

We go to pitch around the green with a sand wedge. At first, I am smooth, I get the motion, but then I lose it completely. Some piece gets mixed up in my head. Mike makes me stay until I hit a decent closer, and I'm down another C-note.

Lesson three:

We head out to a driving area on a part of the course where I've never been. I get out of the cart and face the wrong way, which cracks me up. I am a blind person on a golf course. Correction: I am a blind person who has never played golf.

We work on my set-up. Mike makes me talk about my mistakes. He wants me to be able to figure them out. There is one other person on the range, a young woman who Mike says is the hardest worker on the University of Colorado golf team. He asks me to look at her swing and explain what's wrong. To my surprise, I know. She hesitates so much in her backswing that she's losing all her momentum. Like life, in golf, it's much easier to look at somebody else and know what's wrong.

I, however, am having problems of my own. Mike gives me a practice drill. He holds two clubs, one to my left side and one to my right, waist-high. Both are parallel to the ground. Then he tells me to swing. I am thinking that Mike is a pretty brave guy because I have no qualms about taking the club back hard, though I can't for the life of me figure out how I'm going to actually swing. I somehow make contact and hit the ball right into Mike's foot.

Eventually, I start whacking the hell out of the ball. Mike then introduces me to a 5-wood. I make minimal contact, and the ball skids a bit forward. So I step back and just take some swings. After I get the feel for a solid swing, I set up and whack the ball. It's practically out of the ballpark. "Jesus," is what I say because I am so stunned by the flight of that little monster. And then I apologize for my language. "How's that feel?" Mike asks. But he already knows the answer.

I am one happy girl. I am so excited that I'm just aching for my clubs. I've ordered a set from my friend Stephanie at Cleveland Golf. When I get home there's a message from her asking if I have received them. When I call to tell her that no clubs have arrived, she calls UPS to discover that someone named Hubert at West Dillon Road signed for them. I live at 902 Sycamore Lane. I tell my husband I'm going to put the kids in the car and go find Hubert. He puts the kibosh on the idea and says I should let UPS do its job. Of course, I'm thinking that I *did* let them do their job, and they gave my clubs to Hubert.

The next day the UPS guy is heading down my street and I flag him down. "Hey," I say. "Whaddya do with my golf clubs?" "Cleveland?" he asks. "Yeah, that's right," I say. He says he dropped them at the La Quinta on Dillon Road. So I call the La Quinta and tell them I'm on my way—no more waiting for UPS. And there they are, behind the counter. MY CLUBS. My first clubs. I grab that beautiful brown Cleveland box, and it's Christmas morning.

I'm itching to desert my family for the range, but my father-in-law is visiting from New York, so I can't exactly just jump in the car and zoom off. But at four o'clock when he's on the sofa with the girls watching the *Wild Thornberrys* on Nickelodeon, I head into the yard with my 9-iron and my 5-wood. I am swinging away with my very own clubs in the Colorado sunshine, and it feels, well, divine. My husband opens the glass sliding door and says, "I can't believe this." And the funny thing is, I can't believe it either. In the course of three lessons, I have become a golf addict. Somewhere my friends are going to start wondering, *What happened to the old Kate?* Somewhere, my late father is going to be rooting me on and telling me not to lose my patience. Somewhere the golf gods are smiling. They've converted another heathen.

Kate Meyers

5

GOLF LINKS
A FAMILY
TOGETHER

Golf is like fishing and hunting.
What counts is the companionship
and fellowship of friends, not what
you catch or shoot.

George Archer

Remembering My Father

Romance fails us and so do friendships, but the relationship of parent and child, less noisy than all others, remains indelible and indestructible, the strongest relationship on earth.

Theodor Reik

I never met anyone more competitive or more intense than my father. My eighth-grade basketball team was playing on the road in the regional finals. As usual he was sitting in the crowd, letting the official know exactly what he thought of every single call. I guess since he himself had refereed basketball games after graduating from college, he felt he had the authority. No doubt he had the voice. It was so loud you could hear him from any part of the arena, and he knew it.

Finally, one of the officials, tired of being abused by some obnoxious stranger in the stands—and who could blame him?—called a technical foul. My coach went berserk. "Who is that technical on?" he shouted. "That man up there in the orange sweater," the referee responded. *Thanks a lot, Dad,* I felt like shouting at him. I couldn't hide far enough away on that bench. How could he do that to me? I vowed right there and then that I would never do that to my children.

So much for the innocent vows of youth. I recently did exactly the same thing. I screamed at the umpire during my son's baseball game. As exasperated as the official twenty-five years ago, the umpire turned around and said, "Any more out of you and you're out of here." I laughed, flashing back immediately to eighth grade. Yes, I had become my father. You know what, I'm glad. Because that man, wiser than I ever realized, taught me how to compete and how to care passionately about whatever you're doing, which, in my profession, is absolutely essential.

I certainly brought a lot of passion to the golf course, probably because my father made me so mad. When I missed a short putt one time, he chuckled and said, "You got your right hand in there." The next hole, when I missed another short one, he started laughing even louder. Nobody got to me like that. Years later, I figured out that he was showing me that the game and life itself would always be filled with distractions. You either succumb to them or you survive them. He taught me how to survive them.

On the golf course Dad was more my friend than my instructor. A few years into my marriage, however, he handed my wife a sheet of paper filled with scribbled instructions, such as: "Watch Payne's head. Make sure his left foot is back and his right foot is up. Watch his address. Make sure he finishes high. Watch his speed on putting," and so forth. Soon afterward we found out he had cancer. Did he already know that at the time? Were the notes his parting gift to me? I don't know. I'll never know. I still have the sheet. My wife framed it for me one Christmas.

My dad hated golf carts, so we had plenty of time to talk on the course. One conversation I clearly remember is when I was preparing for my freshman year at SMU. He figured the moment had finally arrived to give me the famous father-son, birds-and-the-bees talk. So what if he was five years late? Maybe he needed the extra time to compose his thoughts.

I'm so much like him. I am also a traveling salesman of sorts, hopping from one town to another to do my job. I know how painful it is to be away from one's family for a long period of time. That's why I marvel at the way he was able to endure it. He left Monday mornings and returned Thursday evenings, sometimes Friday evenings, but he always devoted plenty of attention to us when he was home. What I experienced as a child has helped me be more sensitive to how my kids feel when I'm away for weeks at a time.

Money never meant that much to my dad. That's probably because he didn't have a tremendous amount of it. My father provided us with everything we needed, but the dollar never became an almighty object of adoration, as it is for so many people these days. He once looked at the new house I had built and said, "Why do you need something like that?" He couldn't understand excess. That was his generation. My generation is different. We swim in excess. But even though I've accumulated many toys—I think I've always understood, thanks to him, that money is not the answer in life.

Did my dad enjoy his work? I don't know. It's not the kind of question one thinks about as a kid. I hope he did. I know, like many others who grew up in the Depression, it was very important to him that his children go to college, and no child of Bill Stewart's was going to drop out of college to go to work. He never allowed me to downgrade education. I grew up knowing that if someday I couldn't hit 4-irons anymore, at least I would have a college degree to fall back on.

He prepared me for everything. Everything, that is, except his death. That, he neglected. The one memory that immediately pops out from his fight with cancer is the last day my father and I saw each other. My wife and I had just learned that she was pregnant with our first child. I was so excited, I couldn't wait to tell him. I also felt that the timing could not have been any better. I was sure it would cheer him up.

He was sleeping in his favorite chair when I walked up to him and whispered; "Dad, I got a secret to tell you. I'm going to be a daddy." His eyes opened up and he smiled. He was going to be a grandfather. I expected him to congratulate me, to express his joy, to say something poignant, perhaps even to break down. But, I swear to God, the first thing he said was, "Don't buy expensive baby furniture." That was such a typical Dad thing to say.

I probably should have been a little annoyed, but I wasn't. That was his way of expressing love. I gave him a big hug and kiss for the last time. Funny thing is, I never cried at the funeral, which no one could figure out. I'm a very emotional person. I suppose that as the new man of the family, I had to show strength. Six months later I took my baby daughter back home to Springfield. We went to the cemetery and sat down. I finally had my big cry.

Payne Stewart
as told to Michael Arkush

Fear of the Father-Son Tournament

It is in the blood of genius to love play for its own sake, and whether one uses one's skill on thrones or women, swords or pens, gold or fame, the game's the thing.

Gelett Burgess

No words strike greater fear in the occasional playing offspring of the inveterate golfer than these: father-son tournaments. For years, my father's mistaken assumption that I needed a valid handicap kept me off the hook. But when he learned otherwise, there was no escape. A date was set, a starting time inked.

Occasional playing is probably an overstatement, though years ago (fourth and fifth grades) I did live on the 15th hole of an Oklahoma City course. Consequently, I learned a lot: how to duck, and that some of the worst shankers in the world reside just east of the Texas panhandle. I had my first taste of the game then. Dad would take me out after dusk, and we'd play the closing holes. If I shot my age on a hole, I was thrilled.

My game peaked a few years later when I tagged along

on my neighbor's trips to South Carolina every summer. We played almost every day. There's no pressure to perform in front of someone else's dad. What do they care if you stink? It's not a reflection on their gene pool.

Outside of one glorious 94 in high school, my game has been in decline ever since. I play once or twice a year, three times if I'm lucky.

Dad, on the other hand, plays once or twice a week. He's a legit 12 or 13 handicap who's known for his long drives, despite a backswing that cannot be captured by time-lapse photography.

He assured me that we would get out on the course a few times before the tourney. And sure enough, two days before the big day, I set foot on the tee box for the first time.

It wasn't pretty. My scorecard sported more snowmen than a Minneapolis suburb in January. The putting display was the worst you'll see this side of a drunk on a miniature course at two in the morning. And, yes, despite using a driver half the size of my head, I whiffed, which, in terms of athletic ineptness, is surpassed only by striking out in kickball.

Still, there was hope. I didn't bean any deer. I found more balls than I lost. And off the tee, I wasn't looking too bad.

Have you ever tried to cram for the dentist? You brush, floss and gargle your brains out for two days trying to make up for six months of neglect. Well, this was me hours before the tournament. Poring over golf magazines, I'm putting in the basement and perusing the tube for tips— or at least a rerun of *Dead Solid Perfect, Tin Cup* or even *Caddyshack.*

Given my antics, you'd think my father was exerting a lot of pressure on me. Not at all. Sure, doing well would enhance the experience, but he just wants to have fun. Step onto that tee, though, and it's Little League all over again. You want to do well in front of Dad. Back when I was in high school we played tennis against two guys who together were about a century and a half old. They cleaned our clock as I sprayed balls everywhere but on the court. And tennis is my better sport.

D-day rolls around and the weather is beautiful. I discover that Dad has put me in for a 26 handicap, even though the last time I saw the 90s was, well, the '80s. Add his legit 13 handicap, multiply by 40 percent, and we get sixteen shots. It won't be enough.

While at the pro shop, he tries to buy me a new pair of golf shoes. My game doesn't deserve it, but one of the man's great joys in life is buying athletic footwear for family, so I relent. Without the old fifteen pounds of foot gear, the only thing left to keep my head down is a self-imposed burden of expectation.

We arrive at the 1st tee, and my fear of being paired with Johnny Miller and son disappears. It's a mother and son, and they're getting twenty shots. Maybe this will be okay after all.

The format: Both partners hit tee shots and then you alternate shots from the better of the two. After a spectator makes the requisite mulligan crack, I step up and pop up to short right. I half expect someone to invoke the infield fly rule, but no one does and the ball lands safely on the edge of the fairway. The mighty Casey has not whiffed!

We play my drive. Dad sticks it on the green; I almost drop the putt. Par! I crush the tee ball at the 2nd, and we make another par. We bogey the 3rd and then make a third par. Images of a net 54 and a club championship dance through my head. I am Tiger Woods!

Then reality rears its ugly head, and the train wreck begins: double bogey, bogey, triple, double, double. We briefly recover on the back nine and then fade. As the rain begins to fall, we struggle home with a 90, net 74. The mother-son combo takes us by two.

I have not led us to greatness. Nor have I let us down. I've simply been the mediocre golfer that I am, sharing a cart, a score and an all-too-rare afternoon with my old man. And that is plenty.

Besides, there's always next year. I might take lessons, hit the driving range and trade my running magazine subscription for golf. Maybe hit the course every Sunday and get that handicap. Then again, perhaps I'll just dust off my clubs (and those new shoes) in time for next year's tournament.

Mike Pennella

Corky's Wedge

Parents lend children their experience and a vicarious memory; children endow their parents with a vicarious immortality.

George Santayana

It was one of those moments that makes a golfer rejoice in the fact that the game is a part of his life, a moment only a golfer would be silly enough to get sentimental about. The prelude to the moment occurred when I was with my children at my parents' home, the house I grew up in, which borders a public golf course. The course, in suburban Philadelphia, was built by two members of the famed Whiz Kids, the 1950 Philadelphia Phillies. As a kid, the owners were nice enough to let me go out onto the range at twilight and hit all the balls I wanted, as long as I hit them at the flag in the center of the range. That little spot of land is where I learned how to strike a golf ball with approximately the same lack of skill I do now.

I was in the house with my parents when I happened by the kitchen window and saw the three children with golf clubs in their hands. My parents are not golfers in the sense that they play a lot. Typically, they play a few times a year, mostly when they go to Florida to visit my mother's sister and my uncle. Nevertheless, the garage of the house on Fairway Road still has a lot of clubs scattered about, remnants of the days when the five brothers who lived there claimed any club, ball or bag offered to us by someone at the club where we caddied. The kids had found a few rusted old weapons, grabbed a few muddy balls from an old bucket in the garage and were now giving those balls what-for in the backyard.

As you might imagine, the ground was getting it worse than the balls. With little two-handed chops at the ball, only the oldest, my ten-year-old daughter, was making occasional contact. The other two, a girl and a boy ages seven and five, were doing a proper job of tilling the soil. It was the first time I had ever seen them with clubs in their hands, though I suspected their actions were born more of boredom than genuine interest.

It was an admittedly odd moment for me. Because the game means so much to me, and because nearly every minute of my working life has involved the game in some manner—be it as caddie, editor or writer—I had long ago made the decision that I'd let my children decide for themselves if they wanted to play golf. I knew I couldn't be objective and feared I'd become one of those tennis or Little League fathers who becomes obsessed with his child's golf game. It's uncommon, but that type of person does exist in golf. I occasionally encountered them as a junior, and once saw a man bring tears to the eyes of his very talented son during a match in which the boy was whipping me handily. It just wasn't good enough for the father. You never forget things like that. Once in awhile, somebody will bring up that boy's name (although I suppose he's a man now) and mention that he is a very competitive amateur in the area around Philadelphia. I automatically think of his father. I realize now that he was probably a good man who just lost sight of the true purpose of the game. Back then he simply seemed like a mean guy.

"Why don't you go out there with them?" asked my mother, and so I did. I sat on the back porch and said things such as "Way to go" and "That's a great try, buddy." And that was it.

The moment happened the following way. We were at our home in rural Bucks County, Pennsylvania, and we were packing up our possessions to move to a bigger house just a mile or so away. My oldest daughter found an old wedge in a closet she was cleaning out, a wedge that had served me faithfully for years. Fact is, it wasn't actually a wedge. Years ago I discovered I was a lousy bunker player and decided it was because the flanges on sand wedges were too big for my liking. About that time, I stumbled upon an old 9-iron in my parents' garage. It was a Spalding Bobby Jones model, with a rather large, offset clubhead, and I noticed when I hit it full bore it only flew about 110 yards. It had a wonderfully thin sole, so I wandered out onto the course and hit a few bunker shots with it. Perfect—for me at least. So I went back to the garage, cut about an inch off the top of the shaft, put a new grip on it and had the wedge I'd been looking for.

As time passed the already dilapidated club became even more battered looking, but that just added to its appeal. The club was the one constant in my bag. I changed drivers, irons and putters every few years, but the wedge was with me wherever I traveled. It launched me out of the fearsome bunkers of Pine Valley, it (not I) executed the best recovery shot of my life from a steep hillside at Royal Dornoch, it bailed me out from desert lies in Phoenix and Palm Springs and the thick rough of Baltusrol and Westchester Country Club. Once in Florida, from the driveway in front of a clubhouse, it hit a beauty that landed two feet from the hole and stopped like a dart. I could even remember a shot from the fairway it played, to the 1st green at the Old Course. Even I couldn't miss that fairway. And then it ended up in the farthest reaches of a remote closet for a few years, an ignoble end to its career, no doubt initiated by one of my kids.

I was immersed in those moments as my daughter stood before me with the wedge. "Daddy, could you make this shorter so I could use it?" she said. *Could I make it shorter? Voluntarily destroy a link to my past, a landmark tool in my personal golf history? Are you insane, kid? Bad enough you lost it in the first place. Now, you want me to ruin it?* "Sure thing, kiddo," I said. "We'll do it tonight, right after dinner."

And so we did. In the last breaths of a late summer evening, when the only sound to be heard was the Delaware River on its slow but relentless march to the sea, Michelene Corcoran, with a little help from her old man, made her first golf club. Take care of it, I told her, and she assured me she would.

The next afternoon I saw the grip end of the club sticking out of the edge of our fish pond. I pulled it out and found a rope tied around the clubhead. It appeared someone had been trying to hook a big one with the club. *Oh well,* I thought, *as long as they were having fun.*

Mike Corcoran

DENNIS THE MENACE

"After we look at your toys,
can we look at some of mine?"

A Matter of Course

Morning sun clearly defined the mountains, promising a pristine day, and luring him to answer the call of the links. He had left the house early, but not too early. Not before helping Mary through their daily routine.

Lionel wiped the dimpled ball, nestled it on the green of the 9th hole, and picked up his marker.

Not before gently lifting her in and out of the bathtub. Not before shepherding her back to the bedroom. Not before erasing the ravages of another sleepless night by combing her hair into place.

Lionel gazed at the lush grass as he bent his knees and gripped the putter.

Mary would love walking the course, listening to the hushed stillness. He could point out the geese gliding on the pond and the fragrant crabapple trees laced with blossoms. A love of the outdoors and God's creations. That was something they shared.

And they shared a lot. Six daughters. Twenty-two grandchildren. Allegiance to church. Devotion to each other. That hadn't changed, but other things had.

Lionel lowered his head and hunched his broad shoulders over the extra-long club.

Once, Mary's slender athletic body complemented his rugged six-foot-five-inch frame. Now, crutches supported her stooped shoulders.

Once, she agilely whirled with him on the dance floor. Now, the only spinning she did was a turn through the shopping mall in her wheelchair.

Once, her nimble fingers flew at the sewing machine, tucked a blanket around a slumbering child and tidied the house. Now, crooked and gnarled, they sat—idle—in her lap.

Lionel stiffened his wrists.

Rheumatoid arthritis invaded their union only nine years into their marriage. He watched it ravage his wife's body. The changes it made were both immediate and gradual, until—quite clearly—the disease determined their course in life.

Lionel closed his stance and shifted his weight forward.

Some people thought he carried quite a load. But as Mary was able to do less, he simply did more. He merely broadened his definition of husband, the job title he considered most sacred. After all, it was a pledge he had made to Mary before God. So he took upon himself new roles: cook, housekeeper, beautician and chauffeur. Even nurse.

He and Mary were good together. They should be. They had perfected their teamwork through twenty-four surgeries. He knew better than any health-care worker how to lift her, turn her, tend to her personal needs. That last hip replacement came at a high price for them both: a permanent infection that added a new element to their routine. Now his large hands tenderly applied fresh dressings twice daily to the draining wound.

Lionel drew the putter into a slow backward stroke.

He rarely glanced back at their old dreams. Instead, together they forged new ones. Like purchasing a self-contained motor home so he could assist her in the bathroom, something just not acceptable in public restrooms.

Lionel completed his putt with a firm follow-through.

And they could travel. They could visit their kids. They could attend the important family events most precious to them: baptisms, graduations, weddings, funerals.

Lionel watched the ball roll forward in a gentle arc and rim the cup. He listened to its satisfying drop and thonk. *He made par.*

Mary always said other husbands would have left long ago. She even called him "her good-hearted man." But he liked to remind her that those wedding vows some forty-five years past were sincere—and binding.

As his stubby shadow nudged the rich turf, Lionel glanced at the late morning sun. He leaned down and, with his thick fingers, plucked up the ball, brushed it on his pants and tucked it into his pocket.

There would be other days to play golf. But, for now, home beckoned. Home—and his Mary.

Carol McAdoo Rehme

Wake-Up Call

I was sitting in a bathtub full of moldy sheetrock when my thirteen-year-old son asked the question. "Can you take me golfing sometime?" he said.

I had a bathroom to remodel. It was fall, and the forecast for the next week was for 100 percent chance of Oregon's liquid sunshine. I wanted to say no. "Sure," I said. "What did you have in mind?"

"Well, maybe you could, like, pick up Jared and me after school on Friday and take us out to Oakway."

"Sounds good."

Friday came. The showers continued. Looking out the window, moldy sheetrock seemed the saner choice. But at the appointed hour, I changed from home-improvement garb to rain-protection garb and loaded the boys' clubs and mine in the back of the car. In front of the school, Ryan and Jared piled in. Ryan looked at me with a perplexed expression.

"What's with the golf hat, Dad?" he said.

It was, I thought, a silly question, like asking a scuba diver what's with the swim fins.

"Well, I thought we were going to play some golf."

A peculiar pause ensued, like a phone line temporarily gone dead.

"Uh, you're going, *too*?" he asked.

Suddenly, it struck me like a 3-iron to my gut: I hadn't been invited.

Thirteen years of parenting flashed before my eyes. The birth. The diapers. The late-night feedings. Helping with homework. Building forts. Fixing bikes. Going to games. Going camping. Going everywhere together—my son and I.

Now I hadn't been invited. This was it. This was the end of our relationship as I had always known it. This was *"Adios,* Old Man, thanks for the memories, but I'm old enough to swing my own clubs now, so go back to your rocking chair and crossword puzzles and—oh, yeah—here's a half-off coupon for your next bottle of Geritol."

All these memories sped by in about two seconds, leaving me about three seconds to respond before Ryan would get suspicious and think I had actually expected to be playing golf with him and his friend.

I had to say something. I wanted to say this: *How could you do this to me? Throw me overboard like unused crab bait?* We had always been a team. But this was abandonment. Adult abuse.

This was Lewis turning to Clark in 1805 and saying: "Later, Bill. I can make it the rest of the way to Oregon without you." John Glenn radioing Mission Control to say thanks, but he could take it from here. Simon bailing out on Garfunkel during "Bridge over Troubled Water."

Why did it all have to change?

Enough of this mind-wandering. I needed to level with him. I needed to express how hurt I was. Share my gut-level feelings. Muster all the courage I could find, bite the bullet and spill my soul.

So I said, "Me? Play? Naw. You know I'm up to my ears in the remodel project."

We drove on in silence for a few moments. "So, how are you planning to pay for this?" I asked, my wounded ego reaching for the dagger.

"Uh, could you loan me seven dollars?"

Oh, I get it. He doesn't want me, but he'll gladly take my money.

"No problem," I said.

I dropped him and Jared off, wished them luck and headed for home. My son was on his own now. Nobody there to tell him how to fade a 5-iron, how to play that tricky downhiller, how to hit the sand shot. And what if there's lightning? What about hypothermia? A runaway golf cart? A band of militant gophers? He's so small. Who would take care of him?

There I was, alone, driving away from him. Not just for now. Forever. This was it. The bond was broken. Life would never be the same.

I walked in the door. "What are you doing home?" my wife asked.

I knew it would sound like some thirteen-year-old who was the only one in the gang not invited to the slumber party, but maintaining my immature demur, I said it anyway.

"I wasn't invited," I replied, with a trace of snottiness.

Another one of those peculiar pauses ensued. Then my wife laughed. Out loud. At first I was hurt. Then I, too, laughed, the situation suddenly becoming much clearer.

I went back to the bathroom remodel and began realizing that this situation is what life is all about: change. Fathers and sons must ultimately change. I've been preparing him for this since he first looked at me and screamed in terror: not to play golf without me, but to take on the world without me. With his own set of clubs. His own game plan. His own faith.

God was remodeling my son. Adding some space here. Putting in a new feature there. In short, allowing him to become more than he could ever be if I continued to hover over him. Just like when I was a kid and, at Ryan's age, I would sling my plaid golf bag over my shoulder and ride my bike five miles across town to play golf at a small public course called Marysville that I imagined as Augusta National.

I remember how grown-up I felt, walking into that dark clubhouse, the smoke rising from the poker game off to the left, and proudly plunking down my two dollars for nine holes. Would I have wanted my father there with me that day? Naw. A boy's gotta do what a boy's gotta do: grow up.

I went back to the bathroom remodel project. A few hours later, I heard Ryan walk in the front door. I heard him complain to his mother that his putts wouldn't drop, that his drives were slicing and that the course was like a lake. He sounded like someone I knew. His tennis shoes squeaked with water as I heard him walk back to where I was working on the bathroom.

"Dad," he said, dripping on the floor, "my game stinks. Can you take me golfing sometime? I need some help."

I wanted to hug him. Rev my radial-arm saw in celebration. Shout: "I'm still needed!" I wanted to tell God, "Thanks for letting me be part of this kid's remodel job."

Instead, I plastered one of those serious-dad looks on my face and stoically said, "Sure, Ry, anytime."

Bob Welch
Previously appeared in Chicken Soup for the Father's Soul

The Miracle Ball

True miracles are created by men when they use the courage and intelligence that God gave them.

Jean Anouilh

There is no shortage of testimony to the power and magic of the Titleist golf ball, which is far and away the number-one choice on the PGA Tour. As guys like Phil Mickelson, Davis Love and Ernie Els relate in a current television commercial, the Titleist was present for all their special tournament moments.

None of their Titleist success stories, however, is as heartwarming as that of young Samuel Rachal. Sam would qualify as Titleist's youngest spokesman, except for the fact that at less than six months old he's still pretty much into baby babble.

So we'll tell the story for him.

Born five weeks premature on March 15, 2001, to a couple of Port Arthur, Texas, natives—Tom and Denise Rachal, who now live in Dallas, Texas—Sam started life with what in golf terminology would be an unplayable lie.

His heart arteries were crossed, meaning he would need something called an arterial switch to survive.

The surgery proved successful, but Sam's handicap was a heart so weak that he had to be put on a heart-lung machine. Then a kidney problem developed. Much agonizing followed for Tom, the son of Pat and Mary Helen Rachal, and Denise, the daughter of Sam and Billie Jo Henry.

Baby Sam, though, was not about to WD from this high-stakes game to which he'd just been introduced. Helped along by faith, prayer, hope and a Titleist 1 that remained in his bed throughout the entire ordeal, he overcame the life-threatening obstacles in his path and is expected to live a normal life.

Now about that Titleist 1.

Tom, an avid golfer, had spotted the ball in his car on the way to the hospital for Sam's delivery and thought he would stick it in his pocket for a good luck charm. Later, on a whim, he put the ball in Sam's bed at the hospital.

For the next eight weeks, while Sam was transferred from Presbyterian Hospital to the Children's Medical Center of Dallas, the Titleist 1 was his constant companion. Day after day, week after week, as he battled through a series of hazards tougher than Pete Dye could conceive, the Titleist 1 was always there.

"It's hard to explain but that golf ball kind of became a focal point for everybody," says Tom. "The doctors and nurses would always look for that ball when they came into his room. The ball was just sort of a symbol of hope."

Now that Sam is home, healthy and happy, the Titleist 1 sits on Tom's desk as a constant reminder to him and Denise of what they went through. One of these days, if Sam desires to give golf a try, Tom has already decided it will be the first ball he hits.

But it certainly won't be the last Titleist at his disposal.

Thanks to George Sine Jr., Titleist's vice president of golf ball marketing and strategic planning, Sam is well stocked. After receiving a letter from Tom relating how the Titleist 1 proved to be a positive symbol during his son's crisis, Sine responded with a heartfelt letter, 144 Titleist 1 balls personalized with Sam's name and birth date, and a pair of baby Footjoys.

"It was really a nice touch on his part," Tom says of Sine's letter. "We were so surprised when that care package arrived."

Sine, a father of four young children, was obviously touched by the story about Sam. He wrote, in part, ". . . While I am confident that it was your faith, prayer and hope that resulted in Sam's wellness, not to mention a dedicated medical team, the fact that a single Titleist 1 was along for the journey is indeed a proud moment for the brand.

"The round which you have described is unparalleled by any major championship, coveted trophy or record score, as it was not a game of honor but rather a game of life at stake. . . . So that you may permanently enshrine the now famous Titleist 1 which accompanied Sam on his journey, I am enclosing a supply of new No. 1s. . . .

"The enclosed are personally imprinted for that first occasion when you and Sam approach your first tee box, place the tee in the ground and cherish what is certain to be your first of many father-and-son moments sharing not merely a game but rather a milestone together that will not be forgotten."

Sounds like Titleist needs to get baby Sam and his dad under contract for what could be a powerful TV spot.

Bob West

Links Between Fathers and Sons

Dear Dad:

This year I won't be sending you expensive golf gear for Father's Day. I suspect you may be surprised. I suspect you may also be relieved.

Fact is, for purely selfish reasons I've spent a small fortune in recent years trying to prop up your ailing golf game. First I sent you a set of "super senior" graphite-shafted irons guaranteed to put the life back in your swing.

But they must have arrived DOA because when we played next you were still using the same beat-up irons. You said you were just too sentimental to let them go. I donated the space-age wonders to the church summer auction.

Next, after watching your drives grow shorter and shorter, I doled out for the latest high-tech metal woods that were supposed to forgive your fading strength. You sent them back with a polite thank-you note and scarcely a grass stain on them. Now they're in my bag, forgiving *my* erring ways.

The real kicker, though, came when I paid for private lessons with a crack young woman pro whose specialty is helping aging golf stags steal a few more years in the sun. It didn't hurt that she looks better than Helen Alfredsson—but geez, Dad, you never showed up for lesson one. What gives?

Actually, we both know what gives. You don't have to whack me over the head with Chairman Penick's Little Red Book.

After more than half a century, your once-splendid golf game is fading fast, heading for keeps into the clubhouse turn, finally going gently into that golf good night.

Though you clearly love the game, I get the distinct impression that the thing you desire most is to be left alone to play out the round at your own pace, without advice or meddling from me or anyone else, for however long the USGA official-in-the-sky grants you before darkness closes and the warning horn sounds a final time.

You're what, seventy-five . . . seventy-six? It's kind of embarrassing how you refuse to act your age. I know you still clock a fifty-hour workweek, go harder on the job than your twenty employees and think "retiree" is a four-letter word.

You're the only geezer I know who still cleans out his own gutters, mows his own lawn and would happily tee off at 6 A.M.—if the pro could just manage to haul his young backside out of bed.

Ironically, it's only in your golf game where your mortality is beginning to shine through like the seat of a worn-out suit. I suspect it's the thing that hurts you the most. If that's so, you should see what it's doing to me.

So, out of deference to your "advanced" age, I'll spare you the pro-shop sermon and declare a moratorium on further merchandise. After all, P. G. Wodehouse said, "No man can know the peace that passeth understanding until he giveth up golf."

So, how about if I give you a little peace and quiet and

the right to play golf—or give it up—according to your own internal clock?

This gift is conditional. I need to get a few things off my chest. We've been playing golf together for thirty years and I can't get it out of my head that when you decide it's finally time to toss in the towel for good, I won't just have lost my best friend and fiercest competitor.

I'll have lost my best golf. We hear a lot these days about golf being a family affair. Did you happen to catch the AT&T Pebble Beach National Pro-Am on the tube this year? You might have thought you were looking at a family reunion with a little golf thrown in for fun, what with all those Nicklauses, Floyds and Stocktons loitering about.

Mark O'Meara is on record as saying the happiest moment of his playing career occurred when he won at Pebble Beach with his dad as his amateur partner.

Payne Stewart has six Tour wins and two majors under his belt, but the tournament that means most to him was his first win at Quad Cities in 1982—because his father, Bill, who died of cancer a short time later, was there to witness it.

Every time Tom Watson reminds himself to hold his head still, he hears his father's voice.

Golf is a game about links—the kind made of grass and the kind made of blood. It's not just a game that binds fathers to sons, but also sons to mothers, and dads to daughters.

Was it simple coincidence or something fateful in the stars that Paul Azinger's mother carried him in her womb when she won a women's club title in western Massachusetts? Or that JoAnne Carner's father did odd jobs at a country club just so his daughter could have a good place to play to prepare for a national amateur title?

About the only thing Rush Limbaugh and Jesse Jackson

agree on is that a lot of what ails modern America could probably have been prevented if a caring father had been around somewhere when it counted.

Those of us who grew up with full-time dads should probably count our lucky stars they were around to scold us when necessary, to cheer us up when it was needed most.

People tell me I laugh just like you, Dad. Wish I had your short game and velvet touch around the greens. I know you developed that touch because the only club you owned as a teenager was a hickory-shafted 5-iron you paid a buck for.

You were caddying on the sly because your old man thought golf was a game for rich playboys. I think it was pretty ironic that your job in the Eighth Air Force during the war permitted you to play most of the great courses in Britain and that after winning a few tournaments here and there you came to believe that golf was anything but a game for rich playboys.

I grew up listening to you mouth all these corny platitudes about following the Rules, policing yourself and playing it as it lies. You were a field general about the basic courtesies of conduct, politeness, proper ball marking and so forth.

For years, I thought you were such a square. But I was a temperamental twit who had the benefit of starting out with a supportive father and a full set of clubs.

The first time I threw a club in anger, you simply walked off the course and told me to notify you when I was through being a jackass. When you caught me shaving my score, you explained that I better get used to playing alone because nobody liked a cheater.

The words stung. But they stuck. To this day, even playing mulligans makes me queasy.

I'll spare you a detailed regurgitation of all the good

it could well be our last turn around the track. So I had better make it count—with sticks and words.

I once heard you say to a playing partner that when your allotted time was up you hoped you would just keel over cold as an alewife somewhere on a golf green— preferably after making a ninety-foot sidehill putt to close a tight match.

No lingering nurses and dehumanizing life-support systems for you. Just a neat, clean exit—stage left—with a birdie in hand. Real life, sudden death. Wouldn't even slow up play, probably.

I must admit, I was deeply shocked when you said that, but I was a kid of thirty who expected to live forever. Now, I'm forty and have my own kids who someday may realize that a golf club is something other than a useful tool for clocking an unsuspecting golden retriever over the head.

You'll probably be long gone by then, but if it's any comfort to know, your granddaughter shows flashes of being a genuine putting prodigy. No doubt in my mind where she gets it from. So, rest easy. The family tradition you started fifty years ago will far outlive us both.

Which gives me an idea, Dad. Let's make one final father-son pact. Whoever gets to heaven first has to book the tee time. Make it 6 A.M. on the Champion's Course.

You've earned it.

James Dodson

times we had playing together as grown men—hacking balls and batting the breeze about everything from Nixon's tapes to Madonna's bloomers.

We were lucky, Dad, even charmed. We must have quit seriously competing sometime around Reagan's second term, but I somehow forgot to notice.

A few years ago came the news that your regular foursome of fifteen years was breaking up for good. Your partner, still smarting from a putter-thrashing you gave him in our last father-son match against him and his son, decided to start playing with "younger" men. Another moved to France with his new wife. The third suffered a coronary and wouldn't play on cool mornings.

That left you, your fading game and a lot of empty Saturday mornings. No wonder your enthusiasm plummeted.

I thought I was doing you a favor when I invited you to join me and two friends for a round at Pinehurst No. 2. It was a cold, blustery day. You topped your first drive and it got worse from there—a blur of double and triple bogeys.

Your once-invincible short game was gone. A wind gust almost blew you over in a sand trap. At one point I noticed both your hands trembling. On the drive home you apologized and I told you that was complete rubbish— that we all have lousy days.

We finally had a laugh about it, but I was scared. I'd seen the future of golf mortality, and I didn't like it. That's when I hauled out the checkbook and literally tried to buy us some more time.

That scheme, as we know, utterly flopped. So I have nothing left to give you this Father's Day except peace and quiet—and my heartfelt thanks.

I don't know if a son's gratitude counts for much these days, but I'm haunted by the fact that every time we play

I Was in My Wife's Gallery

Women can be vivacious. We are allowed more varieties of facial expression and gestures. Men must be rocklike.

Gloria Steinem

My wife was playing in a golf match the other day, and I was in the gallery.

Fortunately, I'm never nervous on such occasions.

They teed off, and my wife's opponent dropped a magnificent putt for a birdie and won the 1st hole. A man in a yellow jacket kept following along beside me and he turned to me:

"What are you doing?"

"I'm writing down the score," I told him.

"Hadn't you better turn the pencil around? The lead is on the other end."

"Thank you," I said with dignity.

My wife lost the 2nd hole and was 2-down. A woman in a long-peaked cap came up to me.

"Things aren't looking too bright, are they?" she said sympathetically.

"Oh," I said airily, "it's nothing to be upset about. After all, it's only a molf gatch."

She stared at me a moment. "Yes," she said. "Yes, of course."

Neither my wife nor her opponent won either of the next two holes. Then they came to a short, par-3 hole. My wife was about to hit her drive. The man in the yellow jacket was beside me again.

"She's about to drive," he said. "Aren't you going to watch?"

"I have to tie my shoelace," I told him.

"You've been tying that shoelace during every shot for the last three holes."

"It's an old lace," I told him. "Very slippery."

Finally the match stood all even after six holes. Then my wife hit a shot into a bad piece of rough.

"Don't be jittery now," said the man in the yellow jacket. "She can still get out of it all right."

"I'm not the slightest bit jittery, and I wish you wouldn't keep talking about it," I told him, edging away.

"Hey," he said. "Watch where you're—"

Two gallery marshals helped me up out of the sand trap and brushed the sand off the back of my shirt.

"I ought to penalize your wife two strokes," one of them said darkly. "It's against the rules for a competitor to use any implement to test the consistency of a sand trap."

Around the middle of the match my wife took a one-hole lead. The tension grew. It was blazing hot on the course. I reached down for my handkerchief and mopped the perspiration off my brow.

"Do you always," asked the man in the yellow jacket, "use your tie to wipe off your face?"

"There are so many other matches to watch," I told him. "Why don't you go find one of them?"

My wife won another hole and was 2-up with only a few holes left.

I was standing at one side of the fairway, in the shade of some trees. The woman in the peaked cap came up behind me.

"Well," she said, slapping me on the shoulder. "How do you feel now?"

"Fine," I told her from ten feet up in the tree. "Just fine."

"That's good," she said. "Don't try to get down. I'll go find a ladder."

The sun grew hotter and the tension tighter. But as it turned out my wife won the match on the 16th hole. Someone went up to congratulate her and asked her how she felt. "I'm hungry," she said.

And I'm proud to say that I maintained my own icy calm right up to the final moment of the match.

In fact, I never felt more relaxed than I did as they carried me into the clubhouse.

John L. Hulteng

The Y2K Crisis

In order to get as much fame as one's father, one has to be much more able than he.

Denis Diderot

Some of you may be unaware of the crisis on our horizon. Let this be the moment you learn.

As the new millennium approaches, a threat looms—a threat so ominous and far-reaching, its reversal will require every ounce of ingenuity, every fiber of resolve and every corpuscle of human courage. Otherwise, panic—and ultimately devastation—surely will ensue.

I'm referring, of course, to the situation in my household—more specifically, to the nasty business with the younger of my two sons, Scott.

I remember back when Scott was eight years old, an age when every nonsclaffed shot was cause for joy, when to ride in an E-Z-GO was to live large and when the world's number-one golfer was Dad.

Oh, how things have changed. I forget whether it was Mark Twain or Will Rogers who said, "When I was fourteen, my father was a complete idiot. By the time I reached twenty-one, I was astounded at how much the old man had learned." Well, Scott is now fourteen.

And so is his handicap. In two years he's shaved twenty strokes. Although he can't hit the ball as far as I can—at least he couldn't last year—his swing is far smoother and produces better contact. His short game is sharper than that of any other 14-handicapper I know, and his putting nerves are, well, those of a fourteen-year-old. And he knows it.

So these days, when I hit a drive long and straight, I hear no "Wow!" from the sidelines, just an occasional snort. And when my three-footer rims the cup, he doesn't commiserate, he snickers.

Scott and I are no longer teammates, we're enemies. Indeed, for almost a year now, the little snit has been laboring under the gross misconception that, over a given eighteen holes, he can actually beat me. Beat me! Even up!

You can't imagine how annoying it is when, every time you tee it up with a person, he announces, "Today, you're going *down*." Well, let me tell you, that is just not going to happen. At least not any time soon. After all, despite creeping decrepitude, I can still scrape it around my home course in under 80 as often as not, while Scott's best is well, okay, 81—but let's face it, that day the fairways were hard as rocks, and he also drained everything he looked at.

Anyway, near the end of last summer I became so fed up with his insolence that I issued a solemn oath. "Scott," I said, "you will not beat me this year. You will not beat me next year. Indeed, you will not beat me this century or, for that matter, this millennium. I will hold you off until at least the first day of 2000."

Smart aleck that he is, he immediately smirked, "The year 2000 is part of the twentieth century, Dad."

"Fine, you will not beat me in any year that starts with 1."

And so the battle has been joined. Filial piety is dead, intergenerational strife reigns, as father and son gird themselves for a season of grimly serious combat. An Oedipal thing is going on, too, as my dear wife has positioned herself firmly behind her son.

I don't care. There's no way that half-pint is going to dethrone me. He might get lucky for nine holes again, the way he did last fall, but hey, neither of us had ever seen that course, and he needed an ignorance-is-bliss 38 to do it. And I can assure you I will never again allow him to take a three-stroke lead with two holes to go. I was incredibly distracted by office stuff that day. Besides, he flat-ass choked on 17 and 18.

Believe me, it ain't gonna happen. Scott won't start playing regularly until school's out, while I plan to get in at least a dozen rounds before then, maybe even a quick lesson. I think I may need a little less loft on my driver, too. But I'll get that all fixed, rest assured.

Yep, as long as he doesn't hit his growth spurt before June, as long as he keeps sand-wedging shots that should be bumped-and-run, and as long as no one tells him his irons need regripping, I like my chances.

In fact, nothing gives me more pleasure than the notion of battling that little bugger for the remainder of this century—and a long way into the next.

Come and get me, Son.

George Peper

[EDITORS' NOTE: *George Peper held out until late November of 1999 when he choked on the 18th hole with a double-bogey to lose to his son for the first time. But that was during a vacation trip to Japan, so he decided it didn't count! Then in the last week of December, his son threw a 74 at him to beat him soundly. At this writing their handicaps are both five, but George's is on the way up and his son's is coming down.*]

"Wow! How can you swing so fast and hit it so short?"

A Little Slice of Heaven

Imagine, as a parent, your worst nightmare. You lose a child. For William Nobbe of Waterloo, Illinois, that nightmare came true the evening of Super Bowl Sunday, 1990. "About 12:30 that night, the minister and the coroner were at the back door," remembers Nobbe. "You kind of know something ain't right when you see those two people."

What Nobbe learned was that his eldest child and only daughter, Ann, had been killed in a car accident.

While a parent might harbor a wide range of emotions after such an event, Nobbe came to one important decision in the days and months following his daughter's death. He would continue to build, and then operate, a golf course—a facility envisioned by his daughter, crafted in her memory and named in her honor: Annbriar.

The real story of Annbriar actually began two years before Ann's death. Nobbe had been a third-generation car dealer, selling Chevrolets and Buicks. When General Motors told him in 1988 that he had to spend a bunch of money to upgrade his dealership, he said no and sold the business. He decided to retire to his 345-acre farm in a rural area southeast of St. Louis.

Understand that William Nobbe, fifty-nine, is a big man—

mostly heart. At six-foot-three and 250 pounds, he has hands the size of baseball gloves. He loves working outdoors. Having been a car dealer, he is also mechanical. After selling his dealership, he was engrossed in his farm and helping out his neighbors.

That lasted until Ann came home one night from her job in real estate and told her dad, "I've been thinking about it. How about building a golf course?" Ann, after all, was a good athlete who had recently taken up the game. She was hooked. She also recognized a need for public facilities in the St. Louis area.

Nobbe was floored. "I didn't play golf then," he said. "I thought golf was for people who had nothing to do."

Ann wouldn't let the idea die. "I didn't know anything about golf," her father lamented, "but I got to thinking about it, and the more I thought, it made sense."

Nobbe did his homework. He talked to architects and possible partners. Not until Nobbe met Bob Kelsey, owner of Crystal Highlands Golf Club in Festus, Missouri, did he decide to move forward. "He was wonderful," said Nobbe of Kelsey. "He showed me his books and everything."

By late 1989, everything was in place. Nobbe had hired course architect Michael Hurdzan, and although there were some concerns about routing, Ann's dream was seemingly going to come true. Nobbe had found the money he needed to fund the course, some through friends and some by offering equity in the course in exchange for labor. Ann was ready to quit her job and help her dad run the course.

Then Ann Nobbe died. After the tragedy, Nancy, Nobbe's wife, didn't believe the course should move forward. "Ann and her mom were real close," says Nobbe of his wife. "But there was no doubt in my mind. I had to. It was her [Ann's] idea." Work on the course started that May.

Enter Dana Fry, Hurdzan's design partner and the

on-site person selected to oversee construction of the course. "The guy [William Nobbe] is just literally as good of a man as I have ever met in my entire life," says Fry. "I'll never forget the first time I went there and met William and Nancy. William tells me the story of what happened to his daughter, and by the time he's done, everybody's crying. He told me how important this golf course was and how they need to build it in her memory. It just became way more than a job. It became part of your heart."

Fry was on-site for a year and a half. He and his crew moved almost 1 million cubic yards of earth to fashion the course. "Everybody who worked on that job is personally attached to it because of William," says Fry. "He was just like one of the guys, [he] did everything."

Annbriar Golf Course opened for play on May 28, 1993. Since then, it has garnered rave reviews both locally and nationally. Annbriar is public, and no homes will ever be built around the course. Nobbe wouldn't have it any other way.

Since the opening, Nobbe has been a fixture at the course, sometimes spending twelve to sixteen hours a day to ensure everything is right. He's been known to cook breakfast or make lunch for customers, even change flat tires in the parking lot. He absolutely loves what he does. "People come in here for fun," Nobbe says. "They're coming in the right frame of mind." He feels his job is to have them leave the same way.

The experience has turned Nobbe into an avid golfer. He and his wife travel constantly, comparing their course to others more well-known. "I wouldn't trade even-up for Torrey Pines," says Nobbe. "I'd trade for their scenery."

William Nobbe is honest, caring and outspoken. He maintains fierce pride in his facility and a huge soft spot in his heart for why it happened. "If you think it's good and you know it, that's all I need," says Nobbe about the course. "I really think this has been the best ten years of my life."

The only way they could have been better is if Ann were alive. But Annbriar, William Nobbe's personal legacy, thrives in her absence.

Gordon Wells

6

OUT OF THE ROUGH

You are a fortunate person, indeed, if you can begin each day accepting the fact that during that day there will be ups and downs, good breaks and bad ones, disappointments, surprises, unexpected turns of events.
At the same time, wise golfers have learned to accept those adverse conditions of the golf course as representative of real-life challenges.

Roy Benjamin

Reprinted by permission of Aaron Bacall.

Charging Back

For a guy who comes wrapped up in such a nice, warm package, he has a fire that could light up a whole city.

Peter Jacobsen—on Paul Azinger

It takes a lot to get my mind off golf. Like most members of the Professional Golfers' Association, I eat, sleep and drink the game. That's the life of a pro. Or at least that's what I used to think.

Dr. Lobe called me unexpectedly on Friday evening after the second round of the 1993 PGA Championship at Inverness Club outside Toledo, Ohio.

At the time, I had the dubious distinction of being known as the best player in the world never to win a major. Sure, I had come a long way from salad days struggling to make the qualifying cut at the PGA tour school. Back at the 1987 British Open, I had held the lead all week on the misty, windswept fairways of Muirfield in Scotland, only to suffer a devastating loss to Nick Faldo on the last hole. Though I won a lot of other tournaments, a major title still eluded me.

At age thirty-three, I was at the top of my game and feeling pretty invincible. I was in good shape going into the third round at Inverness, just a couple of shots off the pace behind Greg "the Shark" Norman, an Australian. My family was in Ohio with me, which made golfing even more of a pleasure. It was a heady feeling competing for a $300,000 purse in front of a global television audience. The pressure was definitely on. That's why it was strange that Dr. Lobe would call me at my hotel. My wife, Toni, handed me the receiver with a quizzical look and hushed the kids.

I had been having trouble again with nagging pain in my right shoulder. Dr. Lobe, one of the premier sports physicians in the world, had operated on my shoulder in 1991, and I had recently seen him in Los Angeles about the recurring soreness. Now he came right to the point: the x rays he had taken concerned him. "Paul, I want you back in Los Angeles for a biopsy as soon as possible." *Biopsy?* I thought. *Is he crazy? I'm in contention here. I have the rest of the tour to finish and the Ryder Cup. I can't take time off now!*

Dr. Lobe finally relented and agreed that the biopsy could wait until later in the fall, when I would be in California for a tournament. Until then I would survive on anti-inflammatories, aspirin and prayer. *Tendinitis,* I told myself, and banished it from my mind.

I went out the next day, a boiling hot Saturday, and shot a solid 68 to climb one stroke behind Norman. At the end of Sunday's final eighteen holes, I was in a tie with the Shark for the Wanamaker Trophy. Then, on the second hole of sudden-death play, Greg missed a tricky putt for par and I made mine to become the PGA champ. I had my title! Not one to take things mildly, I leapt into the air. Next I gave thanks to the Lord, which is what I had always promised to do when I won a major. With Toni and our daughters, Sarah Jean, seven, and Josie, four, at my side, I went to raise the regal trophy high for all to see. Suddenly a sharp pain sliced through my right shoulder. It was all I could do to lift the silver cup.

I was determined not to let the pain lessen the thrill of victory or undermine my plans. I went to England and played with the U.S. team against the Europeans for the 1993 Ryder Cup, which we retained that year. But the pain never went away. By late November, when I finally saw Dr. Lobe in Los Angeles, I was barely able to operate the stick shift in my car. In fact, sometimes I drove and depressed the clutch while Toni shifted gears. As I sat on the table in Dr. Lobe's examining room that Monday morning at Centinela Hospital, showing him the spot on my shoulder that was now red-hot to the touch, he was irritated that he let me talk him out of doing a biopsy earlier. He took a pen and gently drew a line across the hot spot. "I'm going to make the incision right here," he said thoughtfully. "Don't shower that line off tomorrow morning."

As I dressed, for the first time I felt a stab of fear. *Come on, Zinger,* I reproached myself. *It's probably nothing.* That's what I told Toni that night back at the hotel while we talked quietly in our room and the kids went to dinner with Mildred, their sitter. What was the worst it could be? A stress fracture or some infection? I would be back on the course in no time. The next morning Dr. Lobe scraped out about a capful of tissue and bone for testing. We waited a few days for the results.

That week—a week of worry and prayer for Toni and me—I thought a lot about our life together and how intertwined with golf it was. We married in our home state of Florida in January of 1982 as soon as I got my tour card, and Toni was a golf wife from the start. In those hard, early years Toni and I traveled the country in an old camper, chasing the tournaments. In the off-season back in Florida, she worked as a bookkeeper while I practiced, practiced,

practiced. It might be my name up there on the leader board when I'm playing well, but really, Toni's should be there, too. She's been as much a part of my success as I have.

When Toni and I went back to see Dr. Lobe, I dispensed with the usual pleasantries. "How am I?" I blurted out.

He looked me right in the eye. "Paul, you have cancer." One simple word. Cancer. Impossible. It was a good thing I was sitting. Toni gripped my hand, and I rocked back and forth in my chair, shaking my head. I had been worried about my career, not about dying. Suddenly everything changed. "Paul, if the cancer is still localized, then it is treatable."

Something like a silent explosion overwhelmed me. "I need the restroom," I gasped, rushing out the door and down the hall. Bent over in that tiny bathroom, I put my head in my hands. I thought about Toni and the girls, about our life. I thought about golf. *Dear Lord, help me. I'm scared to death!* Then I cried until I heard Toni knocking on the door, asking gently, "Paul, are you okay?"

After I pulled myself together, Dr. Lobe brought me in to see an oncologist, Dr. Lorne Feldman, who put me through a battery of tests to determine if the cancer had spread beyond my shoulder. Late in the day, Toni and I went back to our hotel to struggle through a weekend of waiting for the test results. As I played with the kids I thought about the PGA title, and what a cruel twist it would be if it turned out that I should have been in the hospital instead of competing with Greg Norman in the heat and humidity at Inverness.

We took Sarah Jean and Josie to a mall on Saturday to take our minds off our situation, but all the Christmas decorations going up just made me more anxious. Early Sunday morning a false fire alarm roused us from bed. Toni noticed a sign in the lobby announcing church services in one of the ballrooms. "Want to go?" she asked me.

Toni and I had become Christians back in the days when we were bouncing around the country in our old camper—happy, carefree, uncomplicated days, they seemed now. Sometimes when you have the least you are most aware of how much the Lord provides. We always managed to put enough food in our mouths and gas in the camper. We took turns driving and reading aloud from the Bible.

Now Toni, Mildred, the kids and I slipped quietly into the back of the ballroom where services were being held by a local church whose regular facilities were under construction. The big room was full and smelled of cut flowers. That false alarm had not been so false after all. There was a fire in the air, a spiritual charge I felt throughout my body. I sensed I was face-to-face with God, and an excitement I hadn't felt in years came over me. I knew that Christ wanted not just my cancer, or my golf, or my fears about my family, but all of it—my whole life, if only I would give it to him and recommit myself to faith. *I need you now more than ever, Lord,* I whispered silently.

That afternoon my parents flew in from Florida, and the next day we heard the news from Dr. Feldman that as far as they could determine the cancer had not spread beyond the right scapula. I was immediately scheduled for six chemotherapy treatments, one every four weeks, administered right there in his office, starting that day. Between treatments I could return home to Florida.

That first chemo session was a doozy. I suffered intractable nausea and got so dehydrated that I had to be rushed back to the hospital for emergency treatment. But after a few days, Toni and I flew home. Coming home is always a relief to a professional athlete, the real reward at the end of the game. This time it was even more so.

Anyone who has seen me golf knows I am not a player who disguises his emotions. You don't need the television commentator to tell you if I am happy or upset with a shot. I'll let you know. That's me, not exactly Mr. Mellow. Yet the first few days home, I found myself spending hours in our backyard just looking at the flowers and the trees, or watching birds through binoculars. I was turning so mellow it was beginning to scare me! "Maybe the chemo went to my brain," I told Toni, joking.

The phone rang regularly with well-wishers, including President Bush and even my PGA competitor Greg Norman. I found out that the Shark has a soft side.

Then one morning while I was getting ready for the day, something happened. I stood in my bedroom praying, wondering in the back of my mind what would happen if I didn't get better. The sun was forcing its way through the blinds when suddenly a powerful feeling swelled over me like a huge, gently rolling wave lifting my feet off the sandy bottom of the sea. I stopped everything I was doing and experienced an incredible, peace-giving sensation. I knew that God was with me, and I felt absolutely assured that I would be okay. It wasn't that God told me what would happen next or that the cancer would go away. I simply felt positive I was in his complete and loving care no matter what.

I am blessed to say that today, six years after my diagnosis, the cancer is gone. I'm back on the tour trying to shake the rust off my golf game. Dr. Lobe said it was probably a good thing I didn't rush out to California right after the PGA title because at that time, the number of cancer cells in my body might not have been sufficient to show up on a biopsy. I guess, in a way, my competitive drive saved me after all, but what keeps me going most these days is the chance to be an example for others who are struck by disease, to help them see that God is there for them no matter what. That's all you need to know to get through anything in life. That is the real "major."

Which is not to say, of course, that the next time I find myself in a playoff with the Shark you won't be able to tell how I feel about a shot. I am the way God made me, and I don't think the Lord is interested in tinkering with my golf game.

Paul Azinger with Ken Abraham

The Luckiest Golfer Alive

Whenever I play with Gerald Ford, I try to make it a foursome—the president, myself, a paramedic and a faith healer.

Bob Hope

No golfer worthy of his titanium driver would dare complete a round without complaining. The greens are always too hard, the pin positions too difficult, the rough too high and the sand traps too deep. The unwritten code of behavior dictates that every golfer must voice such complaints.

Either that, or admit the real reason for lack of success on the golf course: your own ineptitude.

But even while joining the griping session, I know deep down I am the luckiest golfer alive. I haven't holed a chip shot to win the Masters on extra holes. I haven't canned a sand shot to win the PGA. But I am lucky.

Just how lucky I am was brought home by an item in the Golf Plus edition of *Sports Illustrated*, which read:

"A golf course is the fifth most likely place to suffer a heart attack, but one of the least likely places to survive one—about 5 percent of stricken golfers survive."

But here I am. I twice beat the statistics. And on the same course. I had what was described as a cardiac arrest on the 3rd hole in February and on the 5th hole in November. Improved, huh?

I survived, I am convinced, because of having good friends. In the foursome immediately behind me when I keeled over in February was Dr. Bob Bullington, a retired cardiologist. Behind that group were Cotton Fitzsimmons, former coach of the Phoenix Suns, and two of the Suns' current players, Joe Kleine and Dan Majerle. They called 9-1-1.

Bullington used chest compressions to revive me. I remember coming to, laying on the apron in front of the 3rd green and hearing another doctor tell Bullington he couldn't get a pulse.

"Isn't that nice?" I said.

I then suggested we let Cotton's group play through. I was too late. They already had skipped around me. I was lucky they didn't give me a two-stroke penalty for slow play.

In November, I holed a fifty-foot putt on the 5th hole. I was short of breath, possibly from the excitement of the putt, but made my way to the golf cart and passed out. My cartmate, Paul McCoy, immediately recognized my problem and raced to the group ahead of us, which, get this, included the same Dr. Bullington.

This episode was more serious. Bullington thought he had cracked a couple of ribs pounding on my chest. I didn't regain consciousness until reaching the intensive care ward. My problem apparently has been remedied by a new drug and a pacemaker.

One problem: Bullington won't play golf with me now. Says he wants to finish eighteen.

Bob Hurt

The Power of Charity Golf

When our little hero Ryan Dant speaks, he sounds like a chirping bird—only happier. "Yes, sir, we had a game today," he says.

He's thirteen years old, a baseball player, four feet, seven inches tall, eighty-five pounds of excitement.

"I hit a ball out into center field, and I got on base."

He plays second base and left field for . . .

"The Bombers."

Maybe because he lives near Dallas, Ryan's favorite team is the Texas Rangers. His favorite player is . . .

"Alex Rodriguez. He's a good shortstop and hits the ball really hard."

Behind Ryan's house there's an open field that runs toward a small creek in front of tennis courts. Back there he plays catch with his father, Mark, a police lieutenant in Carrollton, Texas.

"I hit golf balls out there, too."

The first time Ryan had a golf club in his hands, he went behind his house and thought it would be neat to hit a golf ball so far it flew over the field and over the creek and into the tennis courts maybe 120 yards away.

"Golf, it's easy," he says.

The ball just sits there.

"Easier than baseball."

Try as he might, though, his longest golf shots stayed on this side of the creek.

In October 1992, the Adams Golf Company was three people and one telephone with nobody calling except wrong numbers and insurance salesmen.

For staying-in-business money, Barney Adams, the boss, left the shop every afternoon to do club-fittings and repairs. On his door Adams hung a sign: NO SOLICITATIONS.

Mark Dant walked past the sign. The year before, at a routine physical checkup, a pediatrician thought Ryan Dant's head and liver were abnormally large. So he sent the boy, then three, to a geneticist whose tests showed Ryan had a genetic disease, mucopolysaccharidosis, known as MPS 1.

Because his body lacks an enzyme that breaks down sugar, his cells were overwhelmed by deposits of sugar molecules. MPS 1's damage is progressive and complete. Joints lock up. Organs fail, including the brain. By age six, Ryan suffered headaches so severe he would throw up until he fell asleep, exhausted. He was small; he ran with a stiff-legged gait; he couldn't raise his arms to take off a T-shirt; he couldn't hold a baseball bat, because his fingers were fixed in a curl toward his palms. All the while, Ryan's parents knew it would only get worse. "We were told Ryan would not live past ten," Mark Dant says.

The day they heard those words, Dant and his wife Jeanne went home and began a period of sorrow and grieving that lasted months. "We didn't do anything," he says, "but close the door and cry."

By October 1992, grief had been supplanted by the Dants' determination to give their son a chance to survive a disease that seldom allowed any child to live past his or her teens.

The Dants had done enough homework to know that such a chance would come only if science found a cure for MPS 1. They also knew that scientists rarely find a cure unless someone else first finds money for research.

That's why, despite the NO SOLICITATIONS sign on the door, Mark Dant walked into the storefront shop of Adams Golf. Not that he expected much. He'd been playing golf for only a year; he knew nothing about some company working out of a shopping complex. Dant had turned to the Yellow Pages and looked up "golf" because he'd heard that golf tournaments were a good source of charity money. Certainly, the Dants needed to do better than the $342 raised at their first event, a bake sale.

Barney Adams remembers: "I was walking a box of clubs to the front of the building when this young guy came in. Mark had been going door-to-door trying to raise money. He told me Ryan's story, but at that time I probably had less money than he did; our annual sales may have been $150,000. So I said, 'Why don't you auction off some clubs and make some money?' We gave him three or four clubs."

The Dants' first weekend golf event raised $25,000. That's small change in the high-dollar world of scientific research. But to the Ryan Foundation for MPS Children—established by the Dants after a visit to a conference of MPS children and their families—the $25,000 was huge.

It meant hope.

Golf tournaments became the Ryan Foundation's primary source of money, the proceeds rising from $25,000 to $75,000 to $150,000. Early on, the money went to the National MPS Society. "Every year Mark would come by," Adams says, "and we'd give him more clubs."

It was always a struggle. In 1994, because he had used

all his vacation time going door-to-door, Dant wrote letters to ninety golf companies.

"All 'no's,'" he says. "I was about to give up."

Worn out, dispirited, Dant came home from work one evening and on his porch he saw some boxes. "They were Tommy Armour irons and 288 sleeves of Wilson Staff balls," he says.

"It was a sign. It was stunning. It said, 'Do not give up.'"

Soon he heard about work done by a California scientist, Emil Kakkis, a Ph.D. in biological chemistry with postdoctoral training in genetics. "Dr. Kakkis had found a way to make the enzyme that's missing in MPS children," Dant says. "But he was running out of money. He was two months from closing his lab."

Life's moments are rich with coincidence so wonderful as to seem ordered up. How else do we explain the intersecting lives of Emil Kakkis, Mark Dant and Barney Adams? Consider . . .

Just when he needed big money quickly, Dant again turned to the boss of Adams Golf—only by then Barney Adams was no small-timer. He'd become a golf industry sensation by creating and marketing Tight Lies fairway woods. And he was eager to help Ryan.

"I asked Mark how much it would take to accelerate the research process," Adams says. With the figure $200,000 in hand, Adams called a friend, Tom Fazio, the golf course architect. "I told him Ryan's story and said, 'I need X dollars from you to help me underwrite this.'"

That day, right then, Fazio wrote a check. "I had a big lump in my throat," Fazio says. "I have six kids myself, and I thought, 'What would I do if a doctor told me what that doctor told Mark Dant?'"

Without the Adams/Fazio contribution, Dr. Kakkis's research likely would have ended. Instead, as Kakkis's work gained greater notice, the biotechnology company

BioMarin Pharmaceutical gave him $5 million, in hopes of bringing a treatment to market.

"Not to be melodramatic about it," Mark Dant says, "but if not for Mr. Adams, Mr. Fazio and the entire golf industry, my son would be deceased. Golf's a game, I know that. But golf has given my family life."

On February 13, 1998, Ryan Dant was the third of ten MPS children to receive Dr. Kakkis's enzyme-replacement treatment. A week later, standing in front of a mirror, his shirt pulled up, Ryan shouted, "Wow! Mom, Dad! Look how much smaller it is." His stomach was no longer grossly swollen.

Three years of four-hour weekly infusions haven't cured Ryan; what they have done is give him his body back. With the treatment, he has grown five and a half inches, gained thirty-five pounds and is again an athlete. He spent a week in June participating in a baseball camp.

"We're halfway now, and it's been a miracle," Mark Dant says. "But what the doctors tell us now is that what's happened to the body also has happened to the brain. There's the possibility of mental regression. The next step has to be gene-replacement therapy."

Barney Adams is aboard. "They say the gene-replacement research will cost $2 million. I told Mark, 'Okay, let's do it again.' I've never talked about my company's involvement, nor has Tom Fazio talked about his, but now we have this ulterior motive. We want to raise $2 million for Ryan Dant."

On February 13, 2001, the third anniversary of his first enzyme treatment, Ryan Dant went into his backyard with a new Tight Lies 5-wood that bore his name on its sole plate.

He teed up a ball, took a look at the creek way out there,

took a look at the tennis courts way farther out there and he whaled away.

The ball bounced off the tennis court fence.

"Wow, it really went," Ryan says.

Did he hit another?

"No, sir. I took my club to my room. I want to save that power."

Dave Kindred

A Profile in Courage

Pete Farricker never played in a U.S. Open or won a state amateur, although he was a scratch handicapper who could get up and down from a bird feeder when he had to. Before arteriolateral sclerosis (Lou Gehrig's disease) began wrecking his body years ago, he was a terrific golfer and twice as good a person, a master of humor and compassion who changed the lives of everyone who knew him. And hopefully, the lives of a few who never will.

His death at the age of forty-five was, of course, a tragedy—this wonderful man cut down in his prime by an illness as mysterious as it is vicious. That Pete left behind a wife and three-year-old son is sad enough. That two of his life's greatest accomplishments—starting a family, becoming the equipment editor at *Golf Digest*—occurred after he turned forty is snarled fate. Pete's time atop the mountain was far shorter than the climb.

It would be nice to say something remarkably profound about Pete, except the eulogies delivered at his funeral were beautiful and simple, reflective of a guy who didn't ask for nearly as much from this world as he gave it. Long after being diagnosed with ALS, Pete played every horrible lie without a complaint, made us laugh and made us cry, made us live and wonder why. Sitting in an office next door to his for six months was one of the best things that ever happened to me.

Employed as a carrier pigeon in the affluent suburb of reality known as the PGA Tour, I'm reminded that courage isn't the guy who makes a five-footer on the seventy-first hole or knocks it stiff to a back-left pin on Sunday afternoon. Courage is coming to work four days a week after your arms have taken the rest of your life off. Courage is letting somebody stick a spoonful of tuna salad in your mouth, then looking your little boy in the eye and telling him it's good to be alive.

Courage is asking somebody to follow you into the men's room so they can pull up your underpants after you've used the toilet. Just the other day, I was watching NBC's telecast of the U.S. Senior Open, where the word "patience" was used to describe men who make long strings of pars or hit their ball into the center of a three-tiered green. Excuse me for getting a bit oversemantical, but I've seen patience. It looks nothing like that.

Patience is needing fifteen minutes to go from your bed to your wheelchair, another ten minutes to get from your wheelchair to the van, then wondering if you can't talk because your throat is dry or because your vocal cords have permanently shut down. Patience is needing forty-five minutes to leave work at the end of the day, twenty of which you spend hoping your ankle will stop quivering. Patience is waiting for someone to turn the corner so they can help you off the floor.

One of the worst things about ALS is that your body turns into a puddle of applesauce while your mind stays totally functional. Driving Pete home one evening, I asked him what he felt like inside. "Like a 110-year-old man," he gasped, not sounding a day over 90. Near the end, his speech had become so slurred that when he said something, you'd have to ask him three or four times to repeat himself. Believe me, it was always worth it.

The last time I saw Pete he was so weak that his toes were curled up and frozen in different directions. He couldn't lift his head, couldn't eat, sleep or drink. Someone had to feed him ice chips to keep him hydrated. You knew the end was near, and so did he, but inside that ravaged body, there was a hearty, healthy, bulletproof soul.

"How's life on the tour?" he asked me five or six times before I understood him.

Not half as good as life with you, Pete. Not half as good as life with you.

John Hawkins

Making Contact

Driving back to New Orleans with his cousin Bill Kyle after attending a wedding in Baton Rouge, Louisiana, Pat Browne's thoughts drifted to a round of golf he planned to play the next day. It was late afternoon on Saturday, February 26, 1966, and Kyle was driving, so the thirty-two-year-old Browne, who had played on the golf and basketball teams at Tulane University in his hometown of New Orleans, did not have to concentrate on the road.

Suddenly, though, he saw a car driving at a high rate of speed from the opposite direction. As it got closer, it swerved out of control, crossing a small median divider.

"Look out, Bill!" Pat Browne screamed. As he did, the other car slammed into the auto Bill Kyle was driving. The force of the impact drove the hood of Kyle's car through the windshield, sending shards of glass into Browne's eyes and severing his optic nerve.

The teenage driver of the speeding car, which had been stolen, was killed instantly. But both Browne and Kyle survived with serious injuries. "Seeing that car jump the divider was the last thing I ever saw," Browne recalled thirty-five years after the accident which left him blind along with a fractured collarbone, jaw and knee cap and cost him several front teeth.

How in the world am I ever going to play golf again? Browne thought to himself when doctors told him that he would never see again. *And how can I bear not seeing my three daughters again?*

At the time of the accident, Pat Browne was married with three young daughters, aged eleven, nine and seven, who were the joy of his life. He also was a lawyer with a large law firm in New Orleans and a well-known athlete. When he was able to find time, Browne also excelled on the golf course, shooting in the 70s and holding a 3 handicap, which was 2 less than the one he possessed while playing on the varsity golf team at Louisiana State University. Occasionally, the six-foot, four-inch 210-pound Browne also played some pickup basketball. As a player at Tulane, he had gone up against such Half-of-Fame players as Bob Pettit of Louisiana State and Sam and K. C. Jones while they were winning back-to-back national championships at the University of San Francisco in the mid 1950s.

Indeed, Pat Browne had a lot going for him until, suddenly, the lights went out forever on that winter afternoon in 1966.

"Depressed? I guess I was for a while," said Browne, whose weight dropped from 210 pounds to 165 during his convalescence. "But I knew I had to get on with my life and was convinced that, even though I had lost my sight, I would still be able to do most of the things I did before the accident, including maybe even play golf."

Following months of hospitalization and a long convalescence, along with learning how to get along in a world that had suddenly gone dark, Browne returned to work with the law firm of Jones and Walker on a part time basis in June of 1966, four months after the accident. "In September, when I was back working fulltime, I tried my first case," he said, "and realized that I could still practice law effectively."

The following spring two friends, Bobby Monsted and Doc Schneider, convinced Browne to try to hit a few golf balls at the New Orleans Country Club to which the three men belonged.

"Come on, Pat, let's give it a try," Monsted said.

"Bobby, how in the world am I going to hit the ball when I can't see it?," Browne said.

"Don't worry, you'll do fine," Schneider said. "You're still going to be a good golfer."

At the club, after Browne had taken a few practice swings, Monsted placed a ball on a tee, set Browne in position, handed him a driver and set the club back on the ground directly back of the ball. "You're all set, Pat," he said. "Now all you've got to do is swing and hit it."

Browne, apprehensive and unsure of himself, swung easily and lofted a drive about 150 yards down the middle, about 100 yards shorter that he would normally hit his two shots before his accident. "That impact felt good," he told Monsted and Schneider. "Where did it go?"

"Right down the middle," Schneider responded. "Not bad for the first time out."

"Let's hit some more," an enthused Browne said.

For the next fifteen minutes or so, with Monsted and Schneider lining him up for every shot, Pat Browne struggled. Most of his wood shots went straight, some as far as 200 yards. But most of his iron shots sailed wide to the right—shanks, as they're known in golf.

As they left the driving range, Monsted said, "Pat, that was great for the first time. I think you ought to keep at it. After all, you were practically a scratch golfer before the accident, and you still have a great swing, good coordination and excellent reflexes."

"Maybe you're right, Bobby, and thanks a lot to you and Doe for your help today," Browne said to his friends as they walked towards the clubhouse. "Maybe if I really work at my game, I can still play reasonably well."

As it developed, Browne played more than reasonably well. Henry Sarpy, a member of the same law firm, volunteered to be Browne's coach, as the people who line up blind golfers for their shots and lead them around the golf course are known. Together, along with other friends, they played scores of rounds of golf together over the next two years. Then one day, Sarpy said, "Pat, I think you ought to consider playing in the national blind golfers tournament.

"A golf tournament for blind golfers?" Browne asked incredulously,

"Yes, they have it every year," Sarpy said. "Charlie Boswell is the head of the Blind Golfers Association, and the way you're playing, I'm sure you would do well."

Browne knew about Boswell. He had been an outstanding football and baseball player at the University of Alabama before losing his sight in World War II. After taking up golf following his blindness, Boswell had written a book entitled, *Now I See.*

With Sarpy as his coach, Browne played in his first blind tournament in Chattanooga, Tennessee, in 1969. At the time, the blind golfers' field was dominated by Boswell and Joe Lazaro, who, like Boswell, had been blinded during World War II, Browne finished fourth, shooting between 100 and 108, which is excellent in blind golf competition. "I know I can do better," he told Sarpy after the tournament ended. And he did, winning his first national tournament in 1975, and then, from 1978 through 1997, winning it a phenomenal twenty years in a row with Gerry Baraousse, a former All-America golfer at Washington & Lee, as his coach.

During that period, and into his sixties, Browne established himself as the best blind golfer in the world. Playing under U.S. Golf Association rules, he performed better than most sighted golfers, even very good ones. He carded an 80 at the very difficult Pinehurst course in North Carolina, a 76 at his home course, the New Orleans Country Club, and then, incredibly, put together four consecutive rounds in the 70s, including two in which he shot 74, in 1982 at the very challenging Mission Hills Country Club in California. By the 1990s, as the blind golf circuit expanded internationally, Browne was winning scores of other tournaments, both in the U.S. and abroad. At times during the mid-1990s, his "coach" often was his teenage son, Patrick, who had developed into one of the best junior golfers in Louisiana.

Numerous honors have been bestowed on Browne who served as president of the U.S. Blind Golfers Association from 1976 to 1992, when he was succeeded by Bob Andrews, who lost his sight in Vietnam. Browne has received the Ben Hogan Award from the Golf Writers Association of America and been inducted into the Tulane Hall of Fame and the Louisiana Sports Hall of Fame.

"I think I've been blessed," said Browne, who for the last twenty-five years has been president and chief executive officer of a savings and loan association in New Orleans. "I've played at some of the world's greatest golf courses in England, Ireland, Scotland, Australia and New Zealand, which I may never have played if I hadn't lost my sight. And I've met some wonderful people along the way, particularly the other blinded golfers. I've also been to the Masters six or seven times since the accident and played the Augusta National Course. Now that's golfing heaven. And to think I've played it twice. I imagine that some people wonder why blind golfers play. But they don't understand that the thrill of hitting the golf ball is what counts. And you don't have to be able to see it to enjoy doing it."

Jack Cavanaugh

A Thoughtful Gift

My husband, Richard, is an avid golfer and likes to practice his golf swing on our lawn. Often, during the summer, he breaks a window or two. "Oh, well," we always say, "at least it was our own window." And we have the glass replaced.

One year when he had trouble with his slice, he broke a grand total of four windows. The following spring, a parcel arrived, addressed to him. It was a box of a dozen golf balls, and the enclosed note read, "Have a good season. From Mike, your Window Guy."

Kay B. Tucker

A Childhood Passion Strikes a Chord

I waited until my mother had driven away. Then, after opening the front door, peeking down the road and seeing her white Ford Falcon disappear, I lined up my 8-iron shot. Standing smack in the middle of the living room, with a plastic golf ball sitting on the carpet, I took dead aim through the small opening that skirted the chandelier and led through the back door to my target, a square of screen at the back of the porch.

At thirteen, I had been hitting balls inside for well over a year. Eight-iron shots were my favorite—even plastic practice balls zipped off the club face at an ideal trajectory. I loved the unique contour of that particular club, its braveness as it stood distinguished from the rest of the set. It had none of the angular assertiveness of the 7-iron (which reminded me of a proud slice of pie), or even the bulbous, bloated roundness of the wedges. No, the 8-iron, viewed at address, appeared to be exactly what it was: a jewel-like machine of measurement.

Over the past year, a small worn spot had begun to appear on the carpet, and while the blemish didn't please my mom, perhaps some thought that one day I would make millions on tour and buy her a dream house had made her overlook it.

My next swing, however, would prove a swipe no one could ignore. The backswing seemed ordinary enough, a decent little turn. And the transition was good, too. Other kids had dogs; my swing was my faithful servant. The club dropped into the slot just as it was supposed to, and with a well-timed release, I squared the blade forged out of steel.

Next to my living-room practice tee sat the family piano. Now, a plastic practice golf ball yields a soft, light sensation when struck reminiscent of patting a balloon. On that fateful swing, I felt that little whiff, alright, which was followed by a most unexpected *thud.* I had caught the side of the piano solidly with my 8-iron, which had gone on to bury itself deep within the instrument's chamber, leaving only the silver shaft exposed. With my grip horrifically frozen in place, the image must have resembled a tableau in a French farce.

I didn't like to think of myself as a delinquent child. I was a good student, a good athlete. I ate my vegetables, didn't smoke and felt compassion for kids less fortunate than myself. But knowing that I had done something wrong, the criminal instinct took over.

Off I went on my bicycle to the candy store, then the art supply shop across the street. I saw my mom's car parked in the supermarket lot, and recalled her saying she was going to stop by her friend Phylis's house after shopping. So I figured I had an hour and a half to carry out my plan.

Back home there wasn't time to lose. I chewed a wad of gum and stuck it in the vertical "divot" slashed in the piano. Then, with the ecstatic freedom of Van Gogh, I painted the pink gum brown, hoping to match the hue of the instrument.

The end of this unfortunate escapade came swiftly.

Mom walked in, groceries in hand, spotted the oozing gum dripping cheap watercolor paint on the side of the family treasure and threw a fit. My dad, who on the golf course crooned over every great golf shot I hit like a tenor warbling "Sonny Boy" with a pint of Guinness in his hand, suddenly rejected the idea that golf encompassed spiritual values. My backside made the abrasion on the piano seem like the surface of a mountain lake at dawn. The scar in the piano never healed, but mine did, and I grew up to be a golfer. I even played scratch for many years while teaching school in Memphis.

My passion for golf, though, goes beyond the mere enjoyment of the game. It penetrates to the root of the word *passion* itself, with its base in the idea of suffering. From the recognition of the pain of others, we develop compassion. Every time I play golf, I see my own frustration mirrored in the exasperation of my partners, and I remember what I learned when I was a kid swinging in the living room—that the world is not a stage but a golf course.

Andy Brumer

Laboring to Fulfill a Dream

*Ted Rhodes was the best golfer I ever saw, and
that includes Arnold Palmer and Jack Nicklaus.
If they ever let him play on the PGA Tour, he
would have won everything.*

Charlie Sifford

One morning in 1926, the small boy William Powell
walked seven miles down a railroad track. He found his
future. Not that he knew it. He knew only that he loved
what he saw that morning. He saw a golf course. My, my.
What a thing. He'd never seen so much green.

"Beautiful," he says now, seventy-five years later. Only
he says it better than that. He says it sweet, soft, slow.
"Beeyoootifulll," he says.

One morning in 2001, the great-grandson of Alabama
slaves sits in a cart near the 1st tee of his very own course.
He built it with his hands, with money from his factory
job, with eighteen-hour days, with his wife and children
working alongside.

People drove by on Ohio's U.S. Route 30 and saw
William Powell on his wild land yanking out tree stumps

as if they were bad teeth. They saw him hacking, tugging, burning, bulldozing, pulling up fence posts and picking up stones, planting, watering, mowing. He sweated rivers.

"We had seventy-eight acres, a dilapidated barn, a milk parlor in shambles, chickens in the weeds, no plumbing, no heat and a big ol' white tomcat chasing rats as big as it was," Powell says. "Whatever the 'pioneering spirit' is, we must've had it."

His body aches. Asked if he still plays golf, he laughs. "I take it." He's five inches shorter than the five-foot-nine Wilberforce University fullback of his youth. "At 190, I looked 175."

He pats his windbreaker. "Got a stomach now for the first time."

He can talk. My, my. He sits three hours, talking. He drives a visitor on a tour of Clearview Golf Course, talking great good sense: "I'd rather fail trying than be successful doing nothing."

The way he tells his story, it's a lesson in American history. He worked on his golf course not for months or years. He worked for decades.

When he started, late in 1946, the pro golf tour enforced a Caucasians-only clause. Jackie Robinson hadn't joined the Dodgers. As Powell worked, Rosa Parks was arrested, Emmett Till beaten to death, Martin Luther King Jr. shot. Watts burned. Four young girls died in a Birmingham, Alabama, church. Bull Connor loosed the dogs of racial war.

William Powell kept working. His daughter, Renee, a former LPGA Tour player and now Clearview's club pro, asks, "How do you stick to something for fifty years when you have obstacles thrown in your path because your skin is the wrong color? My father's story is, 'Never give up.' I got death threats on tour, and I'd call home crying, and y'know what? My parents never said, 'Come on home.'"

Bankers wouldn't lend him money, not even a GI loan.

An insurance man told him to keep quiet about his plans or white folks would build a course next door. Vandals plundered his meager place. He kept working. "Even black people thought I was a kook," Powell says. "Who wants to fight a racist, apartheid society all the time? But I had golf in me. And I had to bring it out."

Golf got into him that morning in 1926. Willie Powell and his friend George set out from their little town of Minerva, Ohio. They followed the railroad tracks to see a golf course, though they had no idea what a golf course was.

They hurried through a quarter-mile tunnel before a train could squeeze them against the side walls, those walls crumbling with stone jiggled loose by locomotives rumbling through.

The boys saw railroad construction done with giant steam shovels. They heard dynamite blasts. "So exciting," Powell says. "Like they were digging the Panama Canal."

Then they saw the golf course—beautiful—Edgewater Golf Course. All day they hung around. Powell inspected a Model-T Ford made into a tractor/mower with twelve-inch-wide steel rear wheels and a chain drive with three-fourths-inch flat metal studs. He saw golfers hit balls into the sky and he was amazed how far those balls went and he wanted to try it himself—if his mother ever would let him out of the house again.

Night fell before the boy retraced those seven railroad miles. He tried to sneak into bed, only to hear his mother say, "Willie! Go get me a switch!"

She wanted a whippy switch off a willow tree in the front yard. She used it to great effect. The boy, now a man eighty-four-years old, William Powell yet squirms on the seat of his golf cart and says, "That's a switchin' I'll never forget."

But golf had him. He caddied, thirty-five cents a loop. He became a player who in a different time might have been a professional: "I had the game. But like John Shippen and

Teddy Rhodes and many others, not the opportunity. We had to pay the colored tax."

During World War II, U.S. Army Tech Sergeant Powell organized truck convoys in preparation for the D-Day invasion. He used downtime to play golf throughout Great Britain. But at war's end, back home, no golf.

"I had put my life on the line for this country," he says. "I'd just left a country where I was treated like a human being. Now I was supposed to be satisfied to be treated like dirt? I couldn't play any local events. I knew I ought to be allowed to. But there was nothing I could do about it."

Nothing? Powell had been captain of his college golf and football teams. He led men in the army. He often quoted grade-school principal R. R. Vaughn: "Billy, you know you are a little colored boy, and you have to realize you can't do things just as good as a white boy—you have to do them better!"

He would do something. "I couldn't stand being controlled by a certain part of society—you know who I mean—when they didn't come up to my standards."

What he'd do is build his own golf course. "It was necessary," he says. "I had to do it for my own pride. Necessary. I had the right to exist."

All these years later, William Powell knows why he wanted to build Clearview. But he doesn't know why he thought he could. He had no money, no land and no idea how he'd get either. "Then, miracles," he says.

He and his wife, Marcella, had admired land they saw while driving from East Canton to Minerva. They soon saw that land for sale. He made two doctors his partners; his stake came in a loan from his brother.

Clearview is now eighteen holes on 130 acres of rolling, verdant hills decorated with dogwoods and sassafras, oaks and maple. A cool breeze crosses the land transformed from wilderness into parkland. At the 1st tee, a sign calls it

"America's Course." On February 16, 2001, Clearview was placed on the National Register of Historic Places.

Jeff Brown, an Ohio historian who finished the writing of Clearview's register nomination, says, "It's an amazing story, the only course in the history of America designed, built and owned by an African American."

"The lesson of Mr. Powell's life," says Dr. Obie Bender, assistant to the president of Baldwin-Wallace College and a Clearview player for thirty-five years, "is 'Never let other people define you.'"

Powell's wife, Marcella, died in 1996. His son, Larry, is course superintendent. Daughter Renee runs the shop, teaches and, like the rest of the family, is involved in the Clearview Legacy Foundation, preserving the course's history.

The Powells need a museum just for awards: An honorary doctorate from Baldwin-Wallace. The National Golf Foundation's Jack Nicklaus Golf Family of the Year Award in 1992. A Tiger Woods Foundation scholarship in the name of William and Marcella Powell. A lifetime PGA of America membership.

All nice, if late. "Those honors are beautiful," Powell says, there by the 1st tee fifty-five years after he drove off U.S. Route 30 and down a dirt lane to his life's work, "but they're empty, because Marcella's not here. She'd never say, 'This is not going to work.'"

He takes a visitor around the property, the afternoon light golden, and he talks about this tree stump, that creek, those flowers.

He drives to a new tee on the 5th hole, where the PGA of America is lending a hand in renovation, and he points out three maple trees now in the fairway rather than beside it.

"We'll take those down," he says.

"Might be interesting," the visitor says, "if you left one to get in the way."

Suddenly, William Powell raises his chin. His eyes brighten. "Maybe we could," he says, his old man's voice alive with a boy's excitement.

Dave Kindred

Start of a Love-Hate Relationship

I'd like to see the fairways more narrow. Then everybody would have to play from the rough, not just me.

Seve Ballesteros

Apologies to the property owner on South Mountain, the one who must've wondered if a comet had crashed through the drywall. Honestly, I didn't know a little white ball made so much noise when hitting a house.

Apologies to the man who came into view just after I made contact, the one who suddenly appeared in my fairway and came within inches of not finishing his life, much less his round. I really must learn to say "Fore" a little earlier.

And sincere empathy goes out to a certain female, the one currently wondering about the return policy on husbands.

Yes, I did a very bad thing on vacation. I learned how to play golf.

I'm not sure what precipitated such madness, but one day, I was scanning the Internet, printing out pages on how to swing a golf club. The next few days were spent in a ridiculous cocoon: Trips to the cash machine, trips to the driving range, midnight swing sessions in the driveway. And then, the binge.

Eleven rounds, nine different courses and, oh, the things I've seen.

I have tasted the euphoria, the intensely satisfying moment when the swing is true and the ball sails forever. I have been slightly alarmed by my shortcomings, especially when the result lies somewhere past a warning sign regarding rattlesnakes in the immediate vicinity.

I have seen a woman stand aghast in her backyard, resentful of the ball that just plunked her tile roof, as if a golf course had suddenly sprouted around her home.

I have barged onto a hidden green, unaware that a foursome hadn't completed the hole. After apologizing profusely, I proceeded to hit one of their balls.

I have played a round in two hours and five minutes. Alone. An exhilarating day when it seemed like the course was empty and I was the only person alive. Naturally, on this day the planets were aligned, the clubs were wands and I was the maestro—a day I craved for witnesses.

Another time, I made the turn after nine holes in three and a half hours, stuck behind a legion of slow-playing foursomes. A tortoise parade that would qualify as golf purgatory.

I have seen men examine long-distance putts for five minutes, only to hit the ball six inches.

I have seen a friend hit the ball sideways, nearly decapitating another friend sitting in the cart. I have willingly raked sand.

And just when you think you're the biggest and only doofus on the planet . . .

One afternoon, while I walked to my ball, which teetered on the last blade of grass separating land from lake, a diver emerged from the black. In full scuba gear. Carrying about six thousand errant shots.

Yes, misery loves company.

And yes, golf is a lot like life. Humbling beyond reason. Laced with a rich bouquet of hope. And in the end, it gives you just enough to keep going.

To be honest, the intent of this experiment was born from curiosity and a desire to become socially equipped. Living in Arizona and not learning to play golf is like living in Paris and not speaking French. I still maintain that any endeavor requiring a collared shirt is not a sport, but for a recreational skill, golf is addictive. Much better than Ping-Pong, and much more than a good cart ride spoiled.

Fascinating game, really. Intoxicating in its solitude, decadent in its consumption of time, a wonderful reminder of how nice it is to walk on grass.

Granted, I still don't get the extensive volumes of etiquette, and I'll never forget the look on my friend's face when I arrived for our initial golf date in a T-shirt. But I quickly learned to love the game, and now I'm ready for the next step.

Because I'm starting to hate the game.

On Friday, I hit three excellent shots in succession, leading to a six-inch putt and the first birdie of my life.

On Saturday, I stepped up to the tee, swung at a ball and missed.

And now I get the joke.

Why do they call it golf? Because @!#@ was already taken.

Dan Bickley

$\overline{7}$

THE NINETEENTH HOLE

A round of golf should permit eighteen inspirations.

A. W. Tillinghast

The Thrill of the Hunt

Finding golf balls is like an adult Easter egg hunt. I relish that juvenile "Hey, cool!" moment of excitement even as I race toward eligibility as a senior golfer. Besides, no one can have too many golf balls. Honestly, the richest I've ever felt was the time I bought a gross of balls. It was heaven. Just grab a couple sleeves of those glaringly white jewels and head for the links. Once, I poured them all on the carpet and batted them around like a cat with a toy mouse. I would grab them by the handful just to feel the heavy, sensuous pleasure of them tumbling through my fingers like overgrown drops of water. Sadly, they vanished all too quickly.

Hey, look, it was my own fault. If I had spent more time practicing with the range rocks, the pretty ones would have lasted longer. Sure, the feeling of a new sleeve is nice, but nothing approached the joy of having a whole gross. *A dozen dozen!* It was wealth of truly biblical proportion: "Thou shalt have pristine alabaster orbs of the finest balata and their number shall be without end" (Book of Arnold, Chapter 4, Verse 72). It's always a treat to find balls. You're out on the course and not having the best day. You carve another high one that clears the right-hand tree line and drops precariously close to OB. You trudge into the woods hoping it's not lost and that by some miracle you'll have a shot. *Hmm, let's see, if I can just punch-slap a little knee-high fade around that pine.* Well, you know what I mean. Suddenly, you stumble across a stray ball and feel a little better. It's sort of like the golf gods have taken pity and are offering up some compensation. Yeah, like they really care. These are the same golf gods that have left your match-clinching putts hanging on the lip against your loudmouth brother-in law. "Nice lag, Tarzan." Or remember the time they let him snap-hook a 4-iron over water, off a rock and on the green for a tap-in deuce while you pure a 6-iron long into the back bunker? Sympathy is not their strong suit. Besides, if you didn't like abuse, you wouldn't play this game. I'm surprised it is not mentioned more often in the personals column of those freebie classifieds. "Wanted: Submissive male in need of discipline and swing advice. Please call Mistress Flog."

So like any good supplicant you shamelessly pick the ball up and stuff it in your bag. Trying to save face you say, "Here's one for the shag bag." Shag bag, right. Like anyone is going to believe that you: a) practice, or b) pick them up yourself. Still no one calls you on it because they've told the same lie. You're like conspiratorial winos in an alley patiently listening to one another swear they're going to quit drinking and straighten up. The truth is, this little nugget will come in handy. Sometime soon, you'll drown one too many of those precious surlyn pellets fresh out of the box and start reaching for the oldies. You're just going to lose them anyway. Why waste the good ones?

Finding golf balls recently took on a whole new meaning. I was visiting a friend in Myrtle Beach, South Carolina. He lives near a course. (Okay, everybody in Myrtle Beach lives near a course.) We were out for an evening stroll with Rover and, lo and behold, there it was: A sparkling white, slightly used, top-of-the-line ball in the right rough, about

220 yards from the first tee. What a find! Have you priced these things lately? Fifty-four bucks a dozen if you can get them! A little quick math says that's $4.50 a ball minus depreciation, which in this case was probably one swing.

"You want this?" I said.

"Naw, you take it," my friend said. "I've got a garage full of them."

I doubted he knew exactly which ball I'd found, but took it anyway. Walking on, we found more. Not all the same type, but mostly high-end balls with few battle scars. I was excited. I was hooked. Wouldn't you be if you just found $5 bills lying around? It was like a golfer's Elysian Fields. I wanted more. "This is great!" I said, "I wish I could do this at home."

He said, "You probably can. Not as much competition back in Charlotte. We've got to get out early down here before the retirees get 'em all."

He was right. How many other people living in an upscale golf community would spend (or waste) time looking for balls? "Pardon me, Barfield, that's not a *used ball* you're playing, is it?" I needed a cover. I needed a disguise. I needed a plan. So I stunned my wife by announcing, "Honey, I need more exercise. I think I'll start taking a walk in the evenings."

I waited until Monday. The course was closed so I wouldn't be running into any late-afternoon golfers. Besides, with a full weekend's play just finished, the woods should be teeming with dimpled fruit ready for picking.

I put on a hat and sprayed myself with bug repellent to ward off ticks and mosquitoes. I wore long shorts and high socks to minimize poison ivy exposure. I grabbed a 6-iron—ostensibly to ward off angry dogs, but perfect for swatting snakes—stuffed a plastic bag in my shorts and headed out.

Moving briskly, I planned as I went. I would have rules. No traipsing around in the neighbors' backyards. They paid big bucks for a course lot and deserved any stray balls on their property—yuppie mineral rights. Lakes were off limits; even I can't bring myself to buy a ball retriever, and it would blow my cover.

I would have to be selective. Unsold lots were fair game, but the prime hunting ground was the right side of hilly holes. You've got to go where slicers lose balls and fear to tread, and be willing to put up with a few hazards like Lyme disease, venomous serpents and twisted ankles.

The plan worked like a charm. My friend was right; I had no competition. I came home with ten balls. The next morning, I lovingly washed and sorted them: Shags, Kids, Everyday and Tournament. It was like Christmas. The next day was better still; my hunting skills had improved.

I have continued "walking" and have never come up empty. Several times, I've found two dozen balls. Not always perfect, but eminently playable. Many are only one bad swing and a little mud removed from the pro shop. For a guy who gave up golf gloves as an economy measure, this was a windfall. That feeling of extravagant but imitation wealth is back. I gladly suffer the opulent burden of choice. "Which of the $50-a-dozen balls shall I play today?"

I even make better grillroom conversation. "That brand is soft, but I prefer the lower spin of this one off the driver," I might muse. "Still, nothing beats this third one for holding its line on putts." I've become a golf ball connoisseur.

My buddies envy the luxury of playing different balls. They wonder if their own games are refined enough to discern such subtle differences. They marvel at my fearless calm as I execute lengthy carries from precarious lies without the temptation to reach for a water ball. My waistline is thinner, my wallet is thicker, and both my cholesterol and scores are lower. Life is good.

Now if I could just figure out where everyone is tossing those new drivers.

Henry Lawrence

Reprinted by permission of George Crenshaw, Masters Agency.

BUSINESS REPLY MAIL

FIRST-CLASS MAIL PERMIT #28 HARLAN, IOWA

POSTAGE WILL BE PAID BY ADDRESSEE

GolfDigest

P. O. BOX 2024
HARLAN IA 51593-2057

Fore!

I know I'm getting better at golf because I'm hitting fewer spectators.

Gerald Ford

I imagine you sports fans are dying to learn the results of my golf tournament.

That is correct: I have a golf tournament. It used to be that you had to be a major star such as a Bob Hope or a Moammar Gadhafi to have one, but now anybody can. It has reached the point where, if you apply for a credit card, the first two blanks on the application are "Your Name" and "Name of Your Golf Tournament."

Mine is "The Dave Barry Classic," and it attempts to raise money for the American Red Cross. I'm a fan of the Red Cross, because after Hurricane Andrew devastated South Florida, the Red Cross provided us with the one thing we most desperately needed: showers. This was a godsend, because after a few days without plumbing, we all smelled like Eau de Athletic Supporter.

And so when the local Red Cross chapter asked me if I'd host a golf tournament, my answer, without one instant of hesitation, was: "I don't play golf." This is true. I don't have anything against golf; it's just that, if I'm going to play a sport, I want one that provides more aerobic benefits, such as "Rock, Paper, Scissors."

But I told the Red Cross people I'd host the tournament anyway, because I sincerely believe in "giving something back" to the community. Plus they said there would be beer.

The Dave Barry Classic was held at Doral Park, which is a residential golfing community catering to people who enjoy combining the pleasure of living in attractive homes with the pleasure of never knowing exactly when a small, hard, white sphere will penetrate your recreation room traveling upward of 140 miles per hour. This happens routinely because golfers, despite the fact that they are using expensive, modern golf clubs made from space-age materials and engineered to tolerances of thousandths of an inch, have absolutely no idea what the golf ball is going to do once they hit it.

I say this after spending a day observing the golfers in my tournament. These were mostly middle-aged business guys who had come out because they truly believe in the ideals of the Red Cross, especially the ideal of holding a golf tournament on a Friday afternoon.

"I would love to stay in the office wearing a tie and talking on the phone with boring people I dislike," they probably told their business associates, "but I have an obligation to the Red Cross."

In addition to the business guys, we had some big celebrities on hand. I do not mean "big" in the sense of "famous"; I mean "big" as in "larger than your junior high school." For example, one celebrity was Charles "Gator" Bennett, a former defensive lineperson with the Miami Dolphins. At one point "Gator" playfully put his arm, which is the size of Keanu Reeves, around my neck, thereby playfully shutting down my trachea for what at the time seemed like an eternity, but which in fact, as I look back on it, was probably only about forty-five minutes. This is exactly why I hated gym class. I was afraid that "Gator" would decide to snap me with a towel, and I would never walk again.

Not that I felt much safer on the golf course. For one thing, there were the killer ducks. The Doral Park course has a large colony of ducks that, after years of eating food dropped by golfers, have become large and aggressive. If you stop your golf cart, they surround you, dozens of them, pretty much demanding that you give them something to eat.

"We can peck you to death," is their unmistakable message, "and the authorities will do nothing to us, because we are ducks."

More than once I found myself stomping on the accelerator and rocketing away at top golf-cart speed ("mosey"), with a herd of irate ducks waddling after me, like a terrifying scene from a Stephen Spielberg movie called *Jurassic Duck.*

But the scariest phenomenon on the golf course, as I noted earlier, is the golfers. Basically, every time they hit the ball, they go through two distinct phases:

Phase One—They are a foursome of serious, middle-aged accountants, bankers, lawyers, doctors, etc., gathering around a golf ball, studying it intensely, as though it were an unexploded terrorist bomb. Then one of them takes a club, stands over the ball, waggles his butt around, hauls off and hits the ball, which leads to . . .

Phase Two—All four golfers instantly transform into lunatics, gyrating their bodies and screaming contradictory instructions at the ball ("STAY UP!" "GET DOWN!" "STAY DOWN!" "GET UP!"). They sound like the deranged homeless people you sometimes see shouting on city streets, the difference being that, at least some of the time, somebody might be listening to the deranged homeless people, whereas the ball never listens to the golfers. It goes wherever it wants, laughing the laugh of the truly carefree.

So what with the golfers and "Gator" and the gangsta ducks, it was a scary day out there on the "links." But I'm pleased to report that we got through The Dave Barry Classic without any unnecessary deaths, although as of this morning there still were several tee shots that had not yet returned to Earth, so if you live within 250 miles of Miami, you are advised to cower under your bed until further notice.

And if, God forbid, something bad should happen, you may rest assured that the Red Cross will be there for you.

Dave Barry

Thank God I Have a Day Job

Standing on the 2nd tee at St. Andrews Old Course, my playing partner and touring professional, Paul McGinley, turned to me with a wink and said, "Congratulations, you just managed to miss the two biggest fairways in golf." I laughed. Strange as it sounds, I had! OB to the right on number 18 and a shanked 3-iron off the 1st tee at the Old Course. Ouch!

We started the day playing off of number 10, and now as a team, were 10 under par after twenty-eight holes. (Yesterday we played Kingsbarns and Paul had gone around in 6 under.) Today, he was on his way to a course record–tying 64. So shank or missed fairway, whatever, nothing could break my humor. I was in heaven.

It was Friday, second round of the four-day Dunhill Links Championship Pro-Am in Scotland. Paul and I, along with Sven Struver and his amateur partner, legendary downhiller Franz Klammer, were playing the Old Course at St. Andrews. Tomorrow we would be heading to Carnoustie, with a fourth and final round to be played back at the Old Course on Sunday—if our team made the cut.

I was here because I had played in Michael Douglas's charity golf event in Los Angeles earlier in the year. There

I met Iain Banner, part of the Dunhill team who sponsored the event in Scotland. He had promised an invitation to all celebrity players involved in Michael's tournament and true to his word, a few months later, I received the invite in the mail for a week of golf on three of the sport's most hallowed tracks. *Are you kidding,* I thought, *I'm in!* I sent the signed application back that same day.

I arrived Monday afternoon from New York, determined to squeeze in as much golf as possible during the practice rounds before the tournament officially got under way on Thursday. The drawing for playing partners was Tuesday night. There were a lot of pros playing, but most were from the European tour. Very few pros had come from America in the wake of September 11. The list of actors from America was comparably short: Michael Douglas, Samuel Jackson, Hugh Grant (from Los Angeles) and myself.

Johann Rupert, chairman of the tournament and a boisterous and generous host, read the names of the pairings. Kyle MacLachlan with Paul McGinley . . . people near me nodded their approval. Great golfer, Ryder Cup, competitive but with an easygoing manner. I just hoped I wouldn't get in his way because we're talking about an $800,000 purse for the winner.

My concern, naturally, was about my golf swing. I was a skillful enough player, having grown up playing golf from an early age. Tutored by my dad and his various golfing buddies, I had developed a pretty good-looking swing in the Tom Weiskopf mode. Upright, with a strong motion down and under the ball. I played on my high school golf team, usually sixth or seventh on the squad, occasionally putting together a decent round of 4 or 5 over. The problem now was playing time. I usually managed about a dozen rounds a year. Enough to remember what I used to be able to do, but not enough to have much of a chance of carrying it off. Visions of a televised disaster on the week-end began dancing through my head. So Friday afternoon, after struggling through my first round at Kingsbarns and a disastrous second round at the Old Course, I threw myself at the mercy of golf wizard Robert Baker and his teaching partner Grant Hepburn.

The tournament sponsors, in their infinite wisdom, had set up a teaching facility next to the practice range for those unfortunate amateurs, like myself, who had lost (or maybe never really had) a swing. Well, after watching my swing and putting it on video, they dismantled me and then proceeded to put me back together in the image of Ernie Els. (He was the swing image on the computer that I attempted to emulate and one of the many pros Robert works with on a consistent basis.) When I say dismantled, I'm not kidding. New grip, new address at the ball, new body position at the top of my backswing—a complete overhaul—and it worked. I began to hit the ball. I mean, I began to crunch the ball. And it was straight! Years of hearing "from the inside out" but never really getting it finally occurred because my new position at address allowed it to happen naturally. Robert and Grant had saved me in one afternoon. I was reinvigorated and deter-mined to put this new swing into practice.

The following morning we drove north to Carnoustie. It was raining sideways. The tournament had been plagued by fog and rain all week. Today we were getting the worst of it, and playing the toughest course of the three. Our team managed to get around in 3 under, Paul playing bril-liantly in brutal conditions, seventeen pars and one birdie. I had a moment of brilliance as well, hitting out of the infamous Spectacles bunker on number 14, and making the putt for a legit birdie. The new swing was still a work in progress (what did I expect?) and I was anything but consistent, but I sure felt more confident.

That afternoon I was back at the practice range for more work. I began to dream about golf shots. The world and its troubles faded away. Outside contact with the real world was limited to a good-night call to my fiancée, who was incredibly supportive of my experience, and my father halfway around the world. I called him each day during my round, and on one occasion, as the cameras rolled, handed Paul the phone to say hello. My father, watching the Golf Channel at 4:00 A.M. in Yakima, Washington, saw himself talking to Paul McGinley on the 12th tee at Carnoustie with his son in the background. That moment alone was worth the trip.

My father had played over in Scotland about ten years ago on a golfing pilgrimage. He spoke to me about "links golf," about the wind, the quixotic weather, about the rugged nature of the Scots and their love of golf. These people really know the game. There is no wasted applause simply because you managed to land the ball on the green, no. You'd better have knocked the ball inside of twelve feet from the rough over some gorse with a 5-iron. Now that's a shot that would get you some well-deserved appreciation.

I had a few of those, but many more of the other variety. Not quite as bad as the shanked 3-iron, mind you, but enough to be grateful I had a day job that wasn't dependent on driving the ball three hundred yards or hitting greens in regulation.

Perhaps the greatest lesson I took away from that week of close observation is this: there is just no way for the amateur golfer at home to appreciate the professional golfer's process during their round. Every shot is executed with the conviction that the ball will do exactly what the pro wants it to do.

And it's not the galleries that create the pressure. It's the elusive dance between the physical and the mental inside the golfer. The continual shedding of tension, moment by moment. The unshakable conviction that you are holding the right club in your hand for the shot, and that the body will perform with the precision that the mind demands. Add your livelihood to that, and the pressure seems unbearable. I watched as Paul McGinley methodically did this over four days of tournament golf, and it has forever changed the way I play, practice and watch the game.

It's the last day and Paul and I have made the team cut, by one stroke. Even more exciting (and nerve-wracking), Paul is tied for the lead with Paul Lawrie at 14 under. This means I will be in the foursome teeing off in the final position from the 1st tee on the Old Course. (My hands are sweating at the computer just thinking about it.)

First tee. 11:27 A.M. I'm standing there with the coleaders of the tournament . . . breathe. No one expects anything from me, right? *Bang!* A good (not great) drive with a little draw down the left side of the fairway, and we're off. Paul McGinley hits an iron to the right and the ball takes an unlucky hop into the burn (creek). He starts with a bogey 5, Lawrie birdies and just like that Paul's dropped two strokes off the lead. I manage a par and would have been content to head back to the clubhouse and bask in that accomplishment. As it turns out, I redeem myself fairly well over the day, hanging in at 2 over after fifteen holes, before the wheels come off. I proceed to knock the ball OB on number 16, take a triple bogey 7 on the Road Hole, and on my old nemesis number 18—you guessed it —OB on the right. A bittersweet finish to a round of golf I would never have thought myself capable of at the beginning of the week.

McGinley struggled during the final round as his putter went cold, watching Lawrie knock in long putt after long putt. I could feel his frustration. It was not to be

McGinley's day, yet he always had a supportive word to say to me as he recognized I was putting up some pretty good numbers. Lawrie played a solid round of golf, holding off a late charge from Ernie Els by sinking a fifty-foot putt from the Valley of Sin on the 18th for a birdie and sole possession of first place. The crowd roared its approval as the putt dropped and Lawrie skipped sideways in triumph. In that moment, it all seemed quite surreal, standing just off to the side of the green, witnessing a great finish by a great player, feeling like I was included in this elite brotherhood.

And just like that, it was over, and a kind of emptiness descended over the course. I didn't want to let go yet; I wasn't ready to return to my world. I said good-bye to my partner and new friend Paul McGinley, wanting to say something encouraging and knowing it would sound ridiculous, so I thanked him for his company and for his words of support that had meant so much to me.

I walked back down number 18. There's something haunting about an empty golf course at the end of the day, with the echoes of the little truths it has revealed to each competitor. I began to think about tomorrow, my trip back home and how my experience in Scotland might resonate in me. New friends, a new appreciation for the game and the men who play it well, and just maybe a new swing that would carry me back to my world and the solitude of the practice range, where believe me, I will be imagining a hundred perfect drives straight down the 18th fairway on the Old Course at St. Andrews.

Kyle MacLachlan

Thursday Is Men's Day

A state judge has put a Massachusetts country club under direct court supervision, saying compelling evidence at trial showed systematic sex discrimination that warranted judicial oversight in the public interest. The judge will personally oversee putting new policies into effect at Haverhill Golf and Country Club.
—News item, January 2000

Owing to a harsh winter and business overload in the spring, it had been close to four months since I'd been out to my country club, so you can imagine my surprise when I drove up and saw all the surreys with the fringe on top. They were lined up where the golf carts used to be.

I parked under an oak and immediately went over to speak to the cart boy, who was now a girl. "Do you work here, miss?" I asked.

"I'm the cart person, yes," she said, eating yogurt out of a cup and leaning on a carousel horse that was attached to a surrey. "I'm Ellen."

"You're new, Ellen."

"Yeah. I was hired after James got karate chopped."

"James got what?"

"He called Francesca 'honey,' or 'babe' or something like

that, so she gave him a karate chop in the neck and fired him."

"Who's Francesca?"

"You don't know Francesca? She's the head pro."

"She is? What happened to Dutch?"

"Dutch who?"

"Dutch Miller. He's been the pro here for fifteen years."

"There's a Dutch who works in the kitchen."

"Dutch is the chef now?"

"I'm not sure you'd call a dishwasher a chef."

As calmly as possible, I said, "Tell me, Ellen. By what set of, shall I say, bizarre circumstances did somebody named Francesca get to be our head pro?"

"I don't know. You'd have to ask Juliette."

"Juliette . . . ?"

"Boy, you haven't been around here in a while, have you? Juliette's the director of golf."

I stormed into the golf shop and went over to a young woman behind the counter. "Are you Francesca?"

"I'm Samantha. Francesca's playing in a tournament this week."

"Where's Juliette?"

"She's playing in the same tournament."

I looked around. The shop was mostly stocked with women's clubs and women's apparel.

Heavy on the sarcasm, I said, "Do you have any fuchsia Titleists?"

"No, but we have egg yolk and lime," she said seriously.

I decided I needed a drink, a double Junior, and went around to the men's grill. Only the large sign above the door said it was now called Emily's Cafe.

"Hi, I'm a member," I said to the woman who greeted me. "I see the room has a new name, but I assume I can still get a cocktail."

"Only on Thursdays, I'm afraid," the woman said.

I countered, "You're telling me I can only come in here on Thursdays?"

"Thursday is men's day on the golf course. Naturally, you can drink and dine in here on Thursdays. You're not familiar with the new club rules? They've been in the monthly club bulletins."

"I guess I should have been reading them."

"Yes, I dare say you should have."

"Are you Emily?"

"No, I'm Dorothy. Emily's playing in a tournament this week."

"What if I hit your palm with a little whip-out, Dorothy? Do you suppose that would help me get a drink?"

"Tipping is not allowed, sir."

"What about begging? Is that permissible?"

"Sir, I will be happy to send a drink around to you in the men's locker room. It's where the women's used to be, of course."

"Of course."

I had my drink in what was now the small and cramped men's locker room, where an attendant told me he could bring me a zucchini and beet sandwich if I was hungry. I declined limply.

When I went outside to leave I found two female security guards standing by my car. One of them said, "You parked in Francesca's spot."

"Sorry," I said. "I didn't know."

"You'll know next time," she said.

I drove home on four punctured tires and desperately started looking in storage closets for my old croquet set.

Dan Jenkins

Reprinted with permission of Jonny Hawkins.

The Old-Guy Game

I went to the golf course alone the other day. There were four carts parked beside the 1st tee, and a young guy in a Greg Norman hat was taking gigantic practice swings in preparation for slicing his drive into the 18th fairway.

The pro offered to run me out to the 2nd tee so I could jump ahead. A group on the 3rd waved me through. I ran into another group on five, so I ducked behind the snack shack and went to No. 7. I had clear sailing for one shot.

That caught me up to a threesome of old-timers, who were moving down the fairway as slowly as if they were worried about land mines. They invited me to play through—many clear holes lay ahead—but I asked if could join them.

I like playing with old guys. My tempo drops out of the red zone, and I stop trying to hit the ball farther than I can—the opposite of what happens when I play with twenty-five-year-olds. I enjoy hearing stories about what the course or the club or the members were like forty years ago, when everything was better than it is now. Every so often, an old guy who can no longer reach the fairway with a driver will turn out to be a former hotshot—as I'll discover later, when I recognize his name on one of the plaques on the grillroom walls.

I like looking into old guys' bags: mismatched irons, woods made of wood, grips resurfaced with electrical tape, chippers, Gintys, Samurais, 23-woods, putters with punch marks on their faces and ball retrievers that extend so far you could use them to rescue your glasses from the Mariana Trench. The guy in the Greg Norman hat would sneer, but to me those golf bags prove that with good luck and the right equipment you can keep playing until the day you drop.

You also need the right swing, of course. Two of my companions the other day had one that I've been studying: a short, turnless lunge—the move you make when you throw dirt with a shovel. It's the old-guy swing, and it's the product of a compromise worked out by old bones, stiff muscles and osteoarthritis. I've been studying it because I suspect that someday it will be my swing. I want to be prepared.

Both players aimed left and hit right. They took their clubs back belt-high, then leaned forward and swatted. Their shots didn't go very far, but we never had to look for a ball except mine. After three 3-woods apiece, they were each close enough to the green to hit pitching wedge, just about the only iron that either of them still used. They drilled their putts, got two strokes and took the hole with net birdies, while I three-putted for a 5.

I still nurse a fantasy that I will wake up one morning and be Ernie Els, or even Morris Hatalsky. But it pays to be realistic, and time is running out. There's a lot to be said for the old-guy game. If my regular foursome wouldn't make fun of me, I would almost be tempted to switch right now.

David Owen

When You Wish upon a Par

Golf is a game in which one endeavors to control a ball with implements ill adapted for the purpose.

Woodrow Wilson

One defibrillator exhibit was okay, but two? I have enough reminders of where my physical health might be heading every morning when I have to suck it up—and in—to button my pants. The thought of emergency resuscitation is not something I particularly like to be reminded of at a merchandise show. Although with what they were feeding us in the media room, knowing at least one of those machines was close by did offer some comfort when stepping back in the chicken Parmesan line a second time.

I've known for some time that what my golf game truly lacks is more gizmos, gadgets, swing aids and nonconforming equipment, so my attendance at golf's version of Disney World—the annual PGA Merchandise Show in Orlando, Florida—was to determine just what it would take to get me closer to the hole and farther away from those defibrillators.

There was a golf glove touted to increase distance ten to twenty yards and prevent a slice. I tried it on, and it immediately slapped me upside the head. Since I've always believed that I could cure my slice and play better if someone would just slap me upside the head once in a while, I have to say the product lived up to its billing. I found another glove called the "Knuckle Glove" that helps you maintain a consistent grip on the club, presumably giving you a nice tasty knuckle sandwich every time you regrip at the top of your backswing.

I next strolled past an exhibit featuring miniature golf consultants. I tried to imagine what one of their sales pitches might sound like. ("Well, the clown's nose and windmill are certainly rich in the traditions of miniature golf, but our research has shown that dinosaurs, action heroes and dragons are trending strong in the market right now.")

Software is big, of course. One program took your golf score, analyzed it and then gave you tips based on what that analysis suggested. In my case, the tip was to buy one of those gloves that slapped me upside the head to cure my slice. I decided not to buy.

Oh, you can now buy antitheft devices for your clubs. I guess with the price of clubs approaching what you used to be able to buy a car for a generation or so ago, I suppose this is a worthwhile investment. Expect one day to see "The Club" in use at bag drops all across the country, but primarily near urban areas.

You can now earn a degree in professional golf management, from an accredited university no less. The B.G. program (bachelor of golf) probably includes concentrations in such critical areas as how to say "$150, walk or ride" with a straight face. "Optimizing the Routing of the Beverage Cart" and "The 400 Percent Pro Shop Markup: Theory and Practice" no doubt round out the curriculum.

A product will tee the ball up for you on the practice tee, thereby avoiding all that pesky bending and reaching when attempting to get a little recreation and exercise. (Note: See "defibrillators" above.) Another product for the practice tee promises to provide up to twenty-six degrees of cooling in the practice area. Oh, and air-conditioned golf carts are available in selected markets as well. It's always been a bit of a struggle to work up a sweat in our chosen sport. Soon, apparently, it will be next to impossible.

Myrtle Beach alert: You will no longer have to set the oven in your efficiency on "broil" in order to dry your shoes after a rain-soaked round. A product available now will not only dry your shoes but remove odor as well. That means Big Al no longer has to keep his shoes out on the balcony or windowsill during your annual hajj to the golf Mecca of the universe. And with wet, smelly shoes a thing of the past, figuring out how to stuff four sets of clubs into that Ford Aspire you rented just became easier with a trunk organizer called the Golf Butler. Figure one day the Golf Butler to be equipped with software that will make tee times for you, as well as change twenties into nice crisp ones for the evening's silicon fantasies at those gentleman's clubs.

And just what I needed: another swing-training gizmo, this one with two laser beams emitting from the bottom and top of the shaft. The theory is to keep the laser beam on a straight line (represented by a piece of tape stuck to the floor) on the takeaway (the bottom beam at the end of the shaft) and at the top of your swing (the top beam emitting from the top of the grip area). A proper swing will show the laser beams from both positions to remain on the tape. In my own experience, that didn't happen, but the salesman did say that with my reverse pivot, outside in, flying-elbow swing plane, I probably inadvertently performed a laser eye surgical procedure on myself.

One outfit extolled the virtues of its strengths in financial planning by claiming its goal was to eliminate income taxes, capital gains taxes and wealth-transfer taxes. Utilizing "offshore strategies" was also one of its boasts. I bit my tongue and chose not to ask if they also knew where Hoffa was buried, lest that also entail me to carry an unidentified package through the Miami airport on their behalf.

Back at the Orlando airport, instead, I was having a brew and trying to digest the product and services overload I had experienced the past four days. I felt completely wrung out, head spinning and thoughts reeling over how much golf stuff is out there driving our economy. What if everyone got as upset as me over rotten play and just quit? Hackers, or former hackers, might just bring down the whole global economy. It was a chilling thought.

I looked up from my ruminations and saw a young mom pushing a stroller with a child awash in Disney stuff. I looked at the mom's face and saw she was the one with the pacifier in her mouth.

I knew exactly how she felt.

Reid Champagne

Humor at Its Best

*I had a wonderful experience on the golf course
today. I had a hole in nothing. Missed the ball
and sank the divot.*

Don Adams

Hartman was a big man. Physically, he was a solid 280
pounds and stood around six-foot-two. He had a presence
about him that demanded attention when he entered a
room, and he had a twinkle in his eye. Oh that twinkle!
Hartman was the kind of man who could talk a half dozen
men into walking outside in the snow in their bare feet,
and still be in position to close the door and lock it, before
he actually had to go out himself.

Hartman was the person who introduced me to golf. He
loved the game. On one occasion, when we were younger,
a group of us rented a farmhouse for the summer. It was a
place where we could go at the end of the week and just
do whatever comes to mind. Hartman suggested one
evening that we go to the local golf course the following
day and play a round. Eight of us agreed immediately and
went off to bed at a reasonable hour, which at the time

was not the norm, so we could get an early start.

The next morning we arrived at the golf course early enough to be the first two groups off. Being a small "farmers field" type of golf course we fit right in. The skill level of all the participants varied from just above beginner to really struggling for a bogey round. Hartman was one of the more accomplished players out that day, but it was obvious that he was struggling along with the rest of us.

Finally, after the increasing frustration seemed to win out, Hartman snapped! He stood up on the tee of the par-3, 157-yard 8th hole and pulled his driver from his bag. With a great deal of drama, for which Hartman was known, he pulled back on that club and pasted that poor ball with every ounce of his 280 pounds. The ball took off as if it knew it was no longer wanted and headed straight for the trees and the river just to the left of the hole. By this time the other group had already joined us on the tee and the seven of us were howling with laughter. No one really tracked the ball except Hartman, who cringed as we all heard the ball hit a tree to the left of the green. What none of us were ready for was the look on his face as he excitedly asked us, "Did you see that?"

"See what?" was the common reply.

"My ball. It came off that tree, bounced off that rock in front of the green and rolled towards the pin. I think I'm close!"

"Yeah, right. That ball was so far gone you'll never find it," I said with a note of finality.

Fully convinced that there was no way in the world Hartman's ball was even on the golf course any more, let alone anywhere near the hole, we watched as Hartman teed up what we considered to be his serious ball. He hit it fat with his 8-iron, and we all started to walk toward the green disregarding everything he had to say about it being a provisional ball.

As we approached the green we were giving Hartman a pretty hard time. It was becoming more and more obvious his ball wasn't on the green. Hartman couldn't believe it.

"I know I saw it head in this direction." he said with absolute conviction.

"Maybe it's in the hole!" suggested Pete in a sarcastic tone.

Pete walked up to the hole, looked down and yelled back to Hartman.

"What are you hitting?"

"Top Flite number 4" was Hartman's reply.

You could have knocked Pete over with a feather as he leaned over and picked the ball out of the hole.

"It's in the hole," was all he was able to stammer.

Hartman was the last one of us to arrive at the hole to authenticate the ball.

"That's it. I don't believe it! A hole-in-one!" he exclaimed excitedly.

The rest of us just stood there with our mouths open and looks of utter disbelief on our faces. It wasn't possible, yet seven of us witnessed it. The most incredible shot in history.

We finished our round in a state of excited numbness, anxiously waiting to tell someone, anyone, what we had witnessed.

Back at the clubhouse we were indulging in a few beers and regaling the story among ourselves and anyone else who would listen. That's when someone suggested we call the local newspaper and maybe get our pictures taken and enjoy our fifteen minutes of fame. While we were planning all the TV appearances and endorsement contracts, Hartman sat at the end of the table with that twinkle in his eye. Oh that twinkle! It was the unmistakable tone of his laugh at that point that removed all doubt. We had been duped!

Being the first group off that morning put us in the unique position of being the first to each hole. Hartman took advantage of that fact when playing the 6th hole, which paralleled the 8th.

Having hit his ball in the narrow stretch of woods between the two holes, no one thought anything of his activities while he was looking for his ball. While wandering around in this no-man's-land he meandered over to the 8th green, casually dropped his ball in the hole and then wandered back to the 6th fairway as if he had just played his ball out of the rough. The rest of that hole and the next one leading up to the 8th was a display of acting on a Shakespearean level, to bring his apparent frustration level to a peak on the 8th tee.

The number of people with the imagination and savvy to pull off a prank of this magnitude and make all his victims feel good about being had are few and far between. This was the case with most of his pranks, the ones who laughed hardest were the ones at the center of the prank. We lost Hartman to cancer at the young age of forty-three, but he left behind a legacy of good-natured humor, a zest for life and a true appreciation of the good friends he had.

I miss the big man.

John Spielbergs

The Ten Inevitabilities of Hacker Golf

It took me seventeen years to get three thousand hits in baseball. I did it in one afternoon on the golf course.

Hank Aaron

It never fails. . . .

1) You're standing in the fairway 220 yards from the green. The group in front of you is still on the green. You know that if you hit the ball you will fly it to the green, send that group scattering, and once again have four angry golfers waiting for you at the bar. So, you wait until they completely clear, then you duff the shot and end up 75 yards short.

2) You're wearing your lucky hat, your lucky socks and your lucky underwear. Things are in your favor. And even though you typically shoot 90, you've had a really good back nine and you are at 76 with only two par-4s to go for your best score all year. Correspondingly, you triple bogey both holes, your only triple bogeys of the day, to end up shooting—you guessed it—90.

3) After careful consideration you decide to hit a high

soft lob shot onto the elevated green just like Tiger might do, but you hit it flat with your wedge and line drive it over the green. On the next hole, faced with a similar shot, you decide to bounce it on with a 9-iron like Sergio might do, but instead hit it straight up into the air and leave it three feet short of the green.

4) After muffing the tee shot, sculling the approach, pitching it into the sand trap and taking three shots to barely get it out and onto the green, you make a forty-five-foot, double-breaking, downhill putt that you couldn't make again if your life depended on it.

5) You place your tee shot right behind a tree so large that it should be named after a president. By some miracle not only do you get your iron shot around the thing, but it hooks right back into the middle of the fairway. On the next tee shot you land fifty yards behind a three-foot-tall sapling no bigger around than your finger. Using a lofted fairway wood, you hit the little tree dead on, the ball pops up into the air and lands five yards behind you.

6) You are playing really well and, therefore, decide to dole out a "bit of advice" on someone else's game. Instantly, your game goes south faster than a Canadian goose in late November.

7) You decide to wear your brand-new, birthday-gift golf shoes to a course you've never played even though they are not broken in yet. Upon arrival, you find out the club has a cart-path-only rule and, subsequently, you end up walking more miles than Lewis and Clark did exploring the Dakotas.

8) You are on the driving range and your buddy lets you try out his five-hundred-dollar driver. You have never, ever hit the ball as far or as straight. So you buy one for yourself. The first time you play with it, your cogolfers nickname you Water Boy, because you shank drives into the lake, the creek and a resort swimming pool next to the

course, before you put the thing away and go back to your fifty-dollar garage-sale driver.

9) After tossing some grass into the air to check the wind, you see that it's blowing left-to-right, so you alter your grip, play the ball back in your stance to keep it low, aim a little left to be safe. Then, after two great practice swings, you hit a wicked slice way up into the wind that lands two fairways to the right.

10) The course is busy, and they are backed up at the 195-yard par-3. The group on the green waves you up. You know the odds of hitting that green with everyone watching are slim-to-nil. So you decide to lay it up. Then you proceed to hit a wicked worm-burner that just keeps going and going, finally rolling up onto the green and stopping just inches from the hole. A dead bug and several blades of grass fall off the ball. The crowd cheers—and, of course, laughs.

What's the good news about these inevitabilities? You get asked to play often, because you are just so darned entertaining!

Ernie Witham

"I'll look for the ball. You look for the club."

The Life and Times of a Golf Ball

I have talked to golf balls all my golfing life. I accept that a golf ball is inanimate; I understand that a golf ball does not have ears or a brain or even a nervous system. But it is, nonetheless, pleasing to see a golf ball pop right out of a bunker at the exact moment you've yelled, "Skip, golf ball, skip!" So, yes, I talk to golf balls; I admit to that. If I had to guess, I'd say we talkers are in the majority.

Michael Bamberger

There is nothing surprising about it—ending up in this trash can behind the golf shop. I suppose it was inevitable from the day they put me in a package back at the factory. Still it's deeply disappointing: Nobody or nothing in the world likes to admit that the end is near. Not even a golf ball.

A golf ball? That's right. So no golf ball has spoken out until now. Well, I'm going to tell my story. It needs telling—too many of us have been sliced, hooked, topped, scuffed and thrown to oblivion without a backward glance from the people we have served so loyally.

My life hasn't been typical, because for one splendid day I had the kind of life few golf balls enjoy—a chance to perform on the professional tour. But, other than that I've been the same as my brothers. Now, battered, bruised and severely cut I have been tossed out—worthless.

My last few weeks were spent on the practice range. A horrid kind of existence. You're poured into a bucket, then dumped onto the ground and clubbed down-range by golfers with talents ranging from lots of it to none at all.

But I was surviving all right until this morning. A lady beginner talked briefly with the pro before picking up the bucket of balls where I was resting. "I never have played golf before, but my husband insists that I give it a try," the lady explained to the pro. I winced.

She was dangerous, the kind who could deliver a fatal blow with one disjointed swing. My only hope was that she would hit the ground behind me so I could dribble along the grass and avoid serious damage. There wasn't a prayer that she would hit me square.

I watched painfully as she chopped away, missing some balls two or three times.

Finally my turn came, and she flailed at me with a 7-iron. It might as well have been an axe. The clubhead hit into my topside, and I would have screamed in agony if the golf ball code of ethics had permitted.

Instead, I needed all my strength and determination to hold my tightly wound innards in place as I skittered along the ground. The pain was almost unbearable, but I turned numb as I rolled to a stop less than thirty yards from the tee.

I took a hurried inventory and learned the worst—I had a mortal wound, a deep and ugly gash that laid bare my wrappings and assured the end of even my driving range days.

Less than an hour later I was picked up by the range boy. He took one look at me and, without hesitation, dumped me in a sack with other discards. A little later he tossed me into this trash can.

But that's only the end of the story, the saddest chapter. I would like to tell the whole thing, including the part about my close relationship with Sandy Douglas, the famous touring pro.

By some kind of a lucky break, I was given to Sandy by the sporting goods salesman. Sandy uses only balls with the number 3 on them, and that's my number. So into his bag I went just two days before the $200,000 Dorado Classic.

Several new balls were in the bag, but not so many that I couldn't be sure to see action. Sandy, like most of the pros, uses a ball for only six holes or so before switching it to his practice bag. I was delighted. I would compete in a major tournament, and then I would serve out my life with Sandy Douglas, traveling in a shag bag from city to city on the Tour.

Well, things started out just as I expected. Actually, they started even better, because Sandy picked me out as one of the first three balls he would use in the Classic. I got in on the preliminary action, too—he used me for his tuneup on the putting green.

Sandy Douglas is all the things everybody says about him. He's colorful, humorous, and he has the kind of charm that draws big galleries: there must have been five thousand people crammed around the 1st tee to watch him. Sandy placed me carefully on a tee and then took his address position. I was tingling all over.

"Okay, little ball, let's just send you out there nice and easy," Sandy said quietly, and then he swung smoothly. The driver came into me perfectly, and suddenly the green color below me was a blur. I reached my peak height and started down. I could feel myself being drawn to the middle of the fairway, and finally, I bumped down and rolled to a stop.

The spectators were applauding, and I could see that we were in perfect position, about 275 yards out and with a clear shot to the green. Sandy and his caddie strolled up, held a brief conference on distance and club selection, and then I was on my way again, this time with a 9-iron. Again the swing was good and I climbed into a high arc before dropping toward the flagstick. Sandy had been a little firm with me, but I managed to dig into the green and curl back to within eight feet of the hole.

A small coin was placed behind me and the caddie gave me a bath before Sandy placed me back on the green and prepared to putt. He wanted a birdie for a fast start, and I wanted to help him get it.

"It looks as if it will break about an inch to the left," Sandy said to the caddie.

"A little more than that, about an inch and a half," the caddie replied.

Sandy didn't say any more. He carefully lined me up and a hush settled all around. Finally, he tapped me, and I rolled gingerly towards the cup. Two feet away I began to break to the left, and I was dead on line. *Plunk!* In I went, and a huge roar arose from the spectators. Sandy picked me out of the cup and held me up to acknowledge the cheers. It was the supreme moment for me.

The 2nd hole was another par-4, and Sandy gave me another good ride off the tee, but with a bit more hook than he wanted. I ended up in the rough, but I managed to crawl into a good lie and there was no problem. A solid 8-iron put me six feet from the hole on a flat portion of the green. It was a straight-in putt and Sandy sank me for another birdie.

Two holes and 2 under par! I could hardly believe it! It was an exquisite experience; I had to be the luckiest ball in the world—or so I thought.

Little did I know that heartbreak was just ahead. What

hurts most is that it really wasn't the fault of either of us.

The 3rd hole is a par-3 of 180 yards with a pond right in front of the green.

"Give me the 6-iron," Sandy said.

"I think a 7-iron is enough," the caddie replied.

Then Sandy and the caddie huddled and I couldn't hear what they said, but when Sandy addressed me I could see he was using the 7-iron. The caddie had convinced him.

The next few seconds turned into sheer horror. Sandy hit me well, but from the moment I left the tee I could see that flying over that pond would be touch and go. If only he had stuck with that 6-iron.

I sailed through the air and started my descent. Everywhere I looked was water! Suddenly I was sick; I wasn't going to make it over the pond. With a knifing dive, I splashed into slimy weeds about three feet from the edge of the pond. I can't describe the agony I felt as I settled into the mud two feet under water.

A few minutes later I saw the head of a wedge poking about near me. Sandy was trying to find me, and I wanted desperately to reach out for that wedge, but of course I couldn't. Moments later, the wedge disappeared. I had been given up for lost.

Such was the end of the exciting part of my life. It was so brief, but so memorable.

What followed was almost predictable. About a week later a young boy was wading in the pond looking for balls. He found me along with a lot of others, sold some of the balls at the golf shop, but kept me. I still looked as good as new.

For the next month I served the boy's father, about a 12-handicapper who beat me up a bit but didn't give me any of those dreaded cuts. Finally he lost me in long grass behind a green. The next time I was found was by a greenskeeper who narrowly missed running over me with his mower. He turned me over to the golf shop, and that started my tour of duty on the driving range.

That's about all there is to tell. I lived dangerously but made it by okay until the other day.

Now I'm buried deep in this trash can, and I can hear the garbage truck coming. I recognize the sound because I've heard it many times in the last few weeks.

It's just a matter of minutes now until they haul me away to the dump. I wonder how Sandy Douglas finished in the Dorado Classic. I wonder how my life might have gone if it hadn't been for that pond. I wonder if that lady beginner ever will learn to hit a ball.

Bob Robinson

Quiet, Please!

She was sitting in the stands at the 15th hole lost in her thoughts. Maybe she was contemplating the previous hole. Or the beautiful Georgia day. Or perhaps she was praying that this would be the year Augusta National relented and allowed her husband to walk away with a green jacket instead of a broken heart.

Then Laura Norman heard those voices. Two men seated near her at the Masters were arguing . . . about her husband's hair. Was Greg Norman a real blond or wasn't he? It couldn't be real, could it? It was too perfect. Too white blond. Too much a part of the larger-than-life image of the Great White Shark.

"One of them said Greg must have stayed up all night bleaching it," Laura recalls, laughing. "They were like two catty women, the way they were going on. It was as if they were jealous of him."

One more crack and Laura had had enough. "It's real," she said.

They weren't buying it. "Yeah, right," said one of them. "How do you know?"

She smiled. "I'm his hairdresser."

Two jaws dropped. "You are? Well . . . uh . . . omigod . . . uh . . . . okay."

Did that stop the thoughtless chatter?

What do you think? Want to bet those guys were at it again a few groups later?

The men and women who follow their spouses on the PGA and LPGA tours know the drill. Walking along outside the ropes with the gallery, they have an opportunity most of us don't have: They get to watch their spouses work. That has its benefits and its drawbacks. On the one hand, the husbands and wives don't have to wait until a spouse comes home and tells them about their day to know if a cranky or ebullient evening lies ahead.

On the other hand, they have to put up with the other people who are watching their spouses at work. People who let everyone know what they think they know. People who voice opinions without a worry about who might be listening. People who offer unsolicited advice to wives, husbands, mothers, fathers, even players—whether they want it or not. No wonder tour spouses generally tuck their "family" badges out of sight and walk alone.

Imagine hearing someone you don't know talk about your personal life, or listening to someone bad-mouth your wife for being last in the field or simply for not being on someone's short list of favorite players. Observing "true fans" is no better, if they are giggling about how cute your husband is or how he—and you—are headed for divorce court. Then there are the "experts" who love to disclose juicy details about the wild party you never threw, or your taste in furniture.

"Today, my daughter told me to hurry up and get over here," Sally Irwin says after walking a round watching her husband, Hale. "They were talking about our house in Arizona. About how big it was, what it looked like. They didn't have anything right."

They seldom do. Just ask Steve Stricker's wife, Nicki. In 1998, she found herself standing behind the 17th green at The Players Championship, five months pregnant and sandwiched between two guys out to impress their wives or girlfriends and each other.

"Steve walked up to the green and one of these fellows started telling the other, 'Yeah, his wife used to caddie for him, but they got in a big fight and now they're divorced,'" Nicki chuckles. "I stood there and thought about whether to say something, but I didn't. They were just trying to sound good for the women.

"When things like that happen, you have to evaluate the situation. Do you want to embarrass them? Or do you just walk away? I just walked away."

Others haven't. Ben Crenshaw's first wife, Polly, routinely joined in the fun. When someone would tell a story about Ben, she would lean in, without a hint of revealing her identity, and say, "Really? Tell me more."

Norman's mother once tired of hearing a fan belittle her son and hit the man with her umbrella. Another time Irene Burns had had enough of one fan's disparaging remarks about her husband, George, so she wound up and hit him with her stick seat. Sue Stadler, whose husband, Craig, has always been a fan favorite and target, was subtler.

"It was at the Kemper Open, and Craig was playing on Sunday," Sue recounts. "These guys had been saying things all day and one of them yelled, 'C'mon Stadler, choke.' He was about four feet behind me when he said it.

"Later, we were all walking along, and I stopped and put my stick seat out. The guy ran right into it. It hit him right in the stomach." Oops. Pardon me.

Another time, Sue was less subtle. Craig was playing with Raymond Floyd when someone called him an SOB. "I held my temper in check and said, 'Excuse me sir, my husband is not an SOB,'" recalls Sue. "The entire gallery laughed at him."

It's even better when the player himself (or herself) responds. During the final round of the 1994 Masters, Jeff Maggert's first wife, Kelli, and his mother, Vicki Benzel, were at the 13th green waiting for him to hit his approach. Jeff was last and playing with a marker, so a few fans started in, calling him "Maggot" and other rude names. Kelli and Benzel were giving the fans a dressing down for insulting their husband and son when a ball hit the green and rolled into the hole for a double-eagle 2.

"I was just praying it wasn't the marker," Kelli says. It wasn't. Maggert had hit a 3-iron 222 yards for the third double eagle in Masters history, the first since 1967 and the first at the 13th. Everyone, including the Maggot men, cheered.

Even the most polite inquiry can be, well, annoying—and a little amusing. Consider the day Dale Eggeling's husband, Mike, was standing beside the 17th green at an event in East Lansing, Michigan. Dale was working on a career-low 63 and had just hit her approach shot eight feet from the flagstick. Just then, a reporter walked up and asked, "Does anyone know which one is Dale Eggeling?"

When Mike pointed her out, the reporter asked if he was sure. Mike said, Yes, he was, that he was Dale's husband.

"Then with all sincerity, the guy—a reporter right?— says, 'Do you know she's leading the tournament?'" Mike recalls. "I was surprised a reporter asked that. I think I just said something like, 'Yeah, she is doing well.'" She won.

Some incidents aren't the least bit amusing. One day when he was in elementary school, Craig Stadler's son Kevin overheard someone in the gallery call his father a jerk. Tears came streaming down Kevin's face as he asked his mother why anyone would say that.

"It broke his heart. It's hardest on the kids," Sue says. "I told Kevin the man didn't know Daddy and that just meant that [the man] was the jerk."

She also taught Kevin and his brother never to root against anyone. Ever.

One scenario is so oft repeated that it's almost like an initiation rite: A husband or wife is walking along early in their spouse's careers when someone comes up and asks who is playing in the group, When the spouse rattles off the names, the fan responds, "Oh, nobody." If they are prepared, the spouse will turn and say oh-so-politely, "Hey, I'm Mrs. Nobody. And I don't appreciate that." If they aren't prepared . . .

"You have to grow thick skin," says Allison Frazar, whose husband, Harrison, turned pro in 1996. "People get excited about this or that, and they mean well. But sometimes I look at what they're criticizing, and see it as a problem I have to go home and help fix."

Which brings up another major hazard of watching someone in your family work: You tend to want to help. Melissa Lehman remembers one particularly tough week when every well-meaning family member turned into a critic or a teacher. They were all staying together, which made it especially hard on Tom.

Finally, Melissa exploded. "I said, 'From now on, Tom is the only person allowed to be elated or upset about any golf shot, understand?'" she said. And the second Tom walked in the door that night, she announced, "C'mon, we're leaving." And they did.

A fair number of stories, though, are just plain silly. Amy Mickelson overheard two elderly men who claimed that her husband, Phil, had broken both his legs in a skiing accident. "They both had to be amputated," the men went on. "And look how well he's walking."

Then there was the man who was seriously explaining why Dallas resident Frazar wore shirts with Byron

Nelson's name on them. "You know, that's Byron Nelson's grandson," he said. "That's why he has Byron Nelson's name over his heart. Byron is his No. 1 fan." Of course, they're no relation. Frazar wears the shirts because he has a deal with E. McGrath Clothing, which makes the line.

Hal Sutton's wife, Ashley, overheard another man telling his companions that Hal had gone to school with his daughter at Arizona State University in the early 1970s. "I laughed at them," she said.

"If he did, he must have been sixteen." Hal went to Centenary College.

Trying to stay inconspicuous is often the best tack to take. Dottie Pepper's husband, Ralph Scarinzi, tries to lay so low that he usually stays about half a hole ahead of Pepper's group and doesn't even look at gallery members who approach him.

Melissa Lehman's favorite story may be one about her. One day, someone came up to her husband's caddie, Andy Martinez, and laid into Tom.

"The man said, 'I thought Tom Lehman was a nice Christian man,'" Melissa says, recounting the tale. 'If he is, then why was he clutching some babe behind the fitness trailer this afternoon? She was dark-haired and on a bike. And she was hot.'

Yes, and she was Tom's wife.

Pardon me.

Melanie Hauser

Nuts to Par

For two people in a marriage to live together day after day is unquestionably the one miracle the Vatican has overlooked.

Bill Cosby

It was a beautiful autumn day, and I decided to play a round of golf. When I called a friend to see if he wanted to join me, his wife answered the phone. "Pat's enjoying himself cleaning the yard," she said. "Right now he's pitching walnuts from under a tree into the vacant lot next door."

"That's enjoyable?" I asked.

"He's using an 8-iron," she replied.

Jerry P. Lightner

CLOSE TO HOME ©1996 John McPherson. Reprinted with permission of UNIVERSAL PRESS SYNDICATE. All rights reserved.

The Finest Gift

It makes a sweet and pure sound. Metallic, and yet at the same time, almost ceramic. And loud, oh yes, it's loud. Like a rifle shot, it'll snap your head around if you haven't heard it before.

Smack! I watched as my friend Carl lasered another golf ball to the back of the driving range. He held his follow-through as the ball soared higher and higher against a fading afternoon sky.

"You know," he said, "buying this club has to be one of the best investments I've made all year." He turned and smiled, looking just a little too cocky.

Knowing Carl's penchant for tech stocks, I wasn't going to argue the point. And besides, I was becoming just faintly aware of jealousy's green tentacles beginning to tighten around my neck. I knew that somehow I had to get my hands on one of those drivers. Carl tried to explain what a scientific marvel it was.

"They call it elastic reticular venting, or ERV. It's the variable face thickness you know; it works sorta like a trampoline."

I nodded, but kept my eyes on the gleaming clubhead as Carl addressed another ball. Was this fair? Why should

Carl have such a nice golf club, and I don't? Sensing my lower lip pushing up into a pout, I checked myself, threw back my shoulders and tried to appear indifferent as we both followed his next shot arching higher and higher until the ball nestled into the upper netting at the very back of the range.

"Yes sir, Jacky. You gotta get one of these little beauties."

"What did it set ya back?" The words sprang from my mouth before I could stop them. I felt my face redden. What did it matter, the cost of so fine an instrument? Would Perlman quibble about the price of a Stradivarius? Would Puck settle for cheap tomatoes? How could one place a price on perfection?

"Bout 290, with tax. I got it down at Reno Bob's. You know, at the mall."

Yes, of course I knew. Reno Bob's was the local discount golf shop where the teenage salesmen casually gossiped about their 220-yard 7-iron shots. I made a mental note to stop by the mall on my way home. But wait, did he say 290!? For one golf club!? My gosh! Hattie would kill me if I even thought about spending that kind of money on one golf club.

"So, you got any plans for the holidays?"

I didn't pick up on Carl's question right away. Two hundred and ninety, for just one club? The number echoed in my head.

"No, we're just planning a quiet Christmas at home this year."

Now, Carl's not a big guy. So maybe it was understandable how watching his next ball sail right over the top of the back fence made me feel just a little depressed.

I went straight home. Hattie was making meatloaf and my little five-year-old, Jennifer, was waiting by the back door, all ready to give her daddy the best hug she could.

Of course that lifted my spirits. She motioned me to bend down, then whispered in my ear.

"You know—it's only four more days."

I could see she was already giddy with excitement.

"Have you been a good girl? You know who's watching, don't you?"

Cupping her hands over her mouth, she looked up at me with those big green eyes and whispered, "Santa Claus."

Hattie saw us and frowned. I knew she was upset with me for stirring up such anticipation in the child. For a week we'd had the same conversation. "Christmas isn't just about Santa Claus, or receiving presents," she kept saying. And she was all business when I gave her a peck on the cheek. She just pointed me at the dining room table. Dinner was great, of course. My Hattie invented meatloaf. She waited until my cheeks were puffed out with food before speaking.

"I need to do some shopping tomorrow. So why don't you and Jennifer go with me to the mall? I understand there's going to be someone special there. While I'm busy, maybe you two can get a picture taken."

I took the hint and hoped that this year's Santa was a little more convincing. Last year, I spent nearly an hour trying to explain how the jolly old elf could have a Jamaican accent.

The next day, when we arrived at the mall, Hattie took off for parts unknown and I was left to stroll the rows of shops, Jennifer tugging anxiously on my hand. The stores were all decorated with twinkling lights, scarlet, silver and golden ribbons of streaming color. We followed the clatter of children, all laughing, running, skipping in the direction of an enormous snow-covered gingerbread house where occasional flashes told me that a photo opportunity lay just ahead. When we arrived, I was disappointed to see that the procession had stalled. A sign read, "Santa is out feeding the reindeer. Back in five minutes."

I suggested that we just walk around until Santa came back. But when we turned the corner, I felt my pulse jump. There it was. Right in the front window of Reno Bob's Discount Golf Shop. There was my ERV driver, glistening, beckoning, calling my name. I felt a sudden weakness in my knees.

"Let's walk over this way, Jenny."

My innocent little one obligingly followed. Could she feel the wave of excitement overwhelming me as we stood there in front of the golf shop? Could she imagine that her daddy might be so excited about some inanimate object? Something so silly as a golf club?

"So there you are!"

Hattie's voice made me jump.

"Have you seen Santa already?"

"No," I stammered. "He's feeding his reindeer." I smiled, feeling a little self-conscious.

"Well, I guessed that you'd eventually wind up here." There was a hint of insinuation in her voice. "It's your favorite store. Right?"

"Oh, yes—right—my favorite. I mean, it's *one* of my favorites. Of course I like the yarn shop, too."

"Oh yeah, the yarn shop. One of your favorites, too."

Clearly whatever I was selling, Hattie wasn't buying.

"Wow, look at that!" She pointed at the shop window. "Look at that golf club."

I nodded. "Yeah, she's a beauty, isn't she?" I was amazed. I never knew Hattie appreciated the finer lines of a good driver. And my ERV was just poised there, looking like a work of art.

"No, no. I mean, look at the price of that thing."

I realized that her finger was pointing at the bright red sales tag dangling from the grip of the club. Her mouth was gaping. She finally composed herself enough to say, "Can you imagine anyone spending that kind of money for a single golf club!? My lord!"

I smiled, but not showing my teeth. It occurred to me that it might be possible to marshal the facts—perhaps compile a list of the essential attributes of a highly advanced ball-striking device like this one. And, of course, I could argue that it's made out of titanium—the stuff of supersonic jet planes. But, I bit my lower lip instead and just stared at the shop window.

"Well," I finally said. "My friend Carl has one, and it's really quite a remarkable golf club, and several of the better players are getting them, and you know, if you really love golf it might almost be worth. . . ."

I stopped. Hattie was giving me her "you must be nuts!" look. I could see that there was no point, so I suggested that we head back to the gingerbread house.

Hattie and I were always quite rational about Christmas. We agreed that neither of us would spend more than $150 on each other's present. She argued, and I agreed, that all the attention should be on Jennifer. It made perfect sense to me. Still, I remembered how as a child I persisted in imagining that my parents were going to give me that one gift I really wanted each Christmas. One year it was a bike. One year it was a BB gun. And when I was sixteen, I really thought my folks were going to give me a little red sports car. Christmas proved to be one disappointment after another. No bike, no BB gun and certainly no little red sports car.

"And I heard him exclaim as he rode out of sight, merry Christmas to all, and to all a good night." I snapped the book closed and looked at my beaming child. The embers in our fireplace cast a warm glow about the room, and the sparkling white lights on our tree reflected in my little girl's eyes. The kitchen door pushed open and Hattie emerged carrying a tray of cookies and two glasses of milk.

"Here's one for our girl, and one for Santa," she said. I feigned a frown of disapproval. I knew that at heart, Hattie loved Christmas—decorating the tree, making cookies, putting up the stockings. Like me, she was just a grown-up kid.

"Daddy, don't you think we should put out the fire so Santa doesn't burn his bum?"

I nodded thoughtfully, and snatched a cookie from the tray. Then I promised that I'd take care of everything and gathered her up in my arms.

"You know," I said. "Santa won't come until you're fast asleep."

Hattie and I tucked Jennifer in, and pulled her bedroom door closed. Standing in the hall I gave my wife a long kiss.

"You know, dear," I said. "Santa really won't come until we're fast asleep."

She looked at me enticingly.

"That's right, babe. So Santa better get to work on that bike. And don't forget the tassels and training wheels."

It was a chilly morning and I stepped spritely across our hardwood floor to the thermostat and cranked up the heat. I inspected the scab forming over my raw knuckle— a mark which I undoubtedly shared with thousands of bicycle-assembling fathers. Then I looked in on Jennifer. She was snoozing peacefully, so I brewed some coffee and roused Hattie. At last, when our little girl came careening dreamily into the living room, one hand brushing the sleepy-dust from her eyes, Hattie and I were sitting together on the sofa, spectators to the best show in town.

At that moment, seeing the teary eyes of my child as she pranced on tip-toes with delight, I was reminded of the real meaning of Christmas. In Christmas we find hope, coming first to us out of a mystical story about a babe born in a lowly manger, and then upon a gilded sleigh drawn by eight wondrous reindeer through a cold and quiet eve. And in that hope we hear an endless prayer that all the children of the world might share in the joy of a new and brighter age. A child was born, and after all, Christmas is really about the children.

It was a beautiful argyle vest, and I knew Hattie had paid more than our agreed-upon limit. I was very happy with it. In fact, I wore it to the club the next Saturday. And there on the driving range I saw my friend Carl. I guessed that he had an early tee-time because he was just finishing his warm-up session when I arrived. I watched as he hit a few 3-wood shots.

"Hey, Carl. How ya hittin' 'em?"

"Don't ask, Jacky. Don't ask."

I could see my friend was under a gray cloud. I watched quietly as he hit a few more shots. Then he tucked his 3-wood back in his bag.

"Hey, aren't you gonna hit that big stick?" I asked.

"What big stick?"

"Carl? You know, that ERV driver of yours. Your big stick."

"Oh that. I busted it."

"You what?"

"Yeah. On the 10th tee yesterday, I hit one right on the screws, but the face caved in. I guess they haven't perfected it yet. You can only hit it a few dozen times before it caves in. Wish I'd known that before I bought it."

I watched with an open mouth as Carl picked up his bag and started walking glumly off the practice tee. But then he turned and, looking me up and down, said, "Hey Jacky, that's a nice lookin' argyle."

J. G. Nursall

More Chicken Soup?

Many of the stories and poems you have read in this book were submitted by readers like you who had read earlier *Chicken Soup for the Soul* books. We publish at least five or six *Chicken Soup for the Soul* books every year. We invite you to contribute a story to one of these future volumes.

Stories may be up to twelve hundred words and must uplift or inspire. You may submit an original piece, something you have read or your favorite quotation on your refrigerator door.

To obtain a copy of our submission guidelines and a listing of upcoming *Chicken Soup* books, please write, fax or check one of our Web sites.

Please send your submissions to:

Chicken Soup for the Soul
P.O. Box 30880
Santa Barbara, CA 93130
fax: 805-563-2945
Web sites: *www.chickensoup.com*
www.clubchickensoup.com

We will be sure that both you and the author are credited for your submission.

For information about speaking engagements, other books, audiotapes, workshops and training programs, please contact any of our authors directly.

In Support of Others

We hope that the stories in this book have shown readers the positive impact they can make on the lives of others. To that end, a portion of the proceeds from every *Chicken Soup for the Soul* book, go to a worthy charity.

A portion of the proceeds from *Chicken Soup for the Golfer's Soul: The 2nd Round,* will go to the Payne Stewart Family Foundation. Established in 1988, the purpose of the foundation is to primarily assist with programs that allow children and youth to have new opportunities to experience the joy of the Christian life.

The Payne Stewart Family Foundation
1900 Summit Tower Boulevard
Suite 770
Orlando, FL 32810

Who Is Jack Canfield?

Jack Canfield is one of America's leading experts in the development of human potential and personal effectiveness. He is both a dynamic, entertaining speaker and a highly sought-after trainer. Jack has a wonderful ability to inform and inspire audiences toward increased levels of self-esteem and peak performance.

He is the author and narrator of several bestselling audio- and videocassette programs, including *Self-Esteem and Peak Performance, How to Build High Self-Esteem, Self-Esteem in the Classroom* and *Chicken Soup for the Soul—Live.* He is regularly seen on television shows such as *Good Morning America, 20/20* and *NBC Nightly News.* Jack has co-authored numerous books, including the *Chicken Soup for the Soul* series, *Dare to Win, The Aladdin Factor, 100 Ways to Build Self-Concept in the Classroom, Heart at Work* and *The Power of Focus.*

Jack is a regularly featured speaker for professional associations, school districts, government agencies, churches, hospitals, sales organizations and corporations. His clients have included the American Dental Association, the American Management Association, AT&T, Campbell's Soup, Clairol, Domino's Pizza, GE, ITT, Hartford Insurance, Johnson & Johnson, the Million Dollar Roundtable, NCR, New England Telephone, Re/Max, Scott Paper, TRW and Virgin Records.

Jack conducts an annual eight-day Training of Trainers program in the areas of self-esteem and peak performance. It attracts educators, counselors, parenting trainers, corporate trainers, professional speakers, ministers and others interested in developing their speaking and seminar-leading skills.

For further information about Jack's books, tapes and training programs, or to schedule him for a presentation, please contact:

Self-Esteem Seminars
P.O. Box 30880
Santa Barbara, CA 93130
phone: 805-563-2935 • fax: 805-563-2945
Web site: *www.chickensoup.com*

Who Is Mark Victor Hansen?

Mark Victor Hansen is a professional speaker who in the last twenty years has made over 4,000 presentations to more than 2 million people in thirty-two countries. His presentations cover sales excellence and strategies; personal empowerment and development; and how to triple your income and double your time off.

Mark has spent a lifetime dedicated to his mission of making a profound and positive difference in people's lives. Throughout his career, he has inspired hundreds of thousands of people to create a more powerful and purposeful future for themselves while stimulating the sale of billions of dollars worth of goods and services.

Mark is a prolific writer and has authored *Future Diary, How to Achieve Total Prosperity* and *The Miracle of Tithing*. He is coauthor of the *Chicken Soup for the Soul* series, *Dare to Win* and *The Aladdin Factor* (all with Jack Canfield), and *The Master Motivator* (with Joe Batten).

Mark has also produced a complete library of personal-empowerment audio- and videocassette programs that have enabled his listeners to recognize and use their innate abilities in their business and personal lives. His message has made him a popular television and radio personality, with appearances on ABC, NBC, CBS, HBO, PBS and CNN. He has also appeared on the cover of numerous magazines, including *Success, Entrepreneur* and *Changes*.

Mark is a big man with a heart and spirit to match—an inspiration to all who seek to better themselves.

For further information about Mark, write:

MVH & Associates
P.O. Box 7665
Newport Beach, CA 92658
phone: 714-759-9304 or 800-433-2314
fax: 714-722-6912
Web site: *www.chickensoup.com*

Who Is Jeff Aubery?

Introduced to the golf industry at an early age, Jeff was mentored personally and professionally by Nat C. Rosasco, owner of Northwestern Golf Co. Now an entrepreneur in his own right, Jeff founded and is the president of Golf Sales West, Inc./Tornado Golf, the world's largest original equipment golf bag manufacturer.

Jeff has been committed to golf as a lifetime passion and has traveled the world extensively in pursuit of the game and the industry that surrounds it. Jeff is most proud of his tireless work to help bring millions of people to the game of golf by developing programs and products that are accessible and affordable for everyone.

Jeff is an active sponsor of junior golf programs and charity golf tournaments all over the world. Jeff makes time for a round of golf whenever possible and has enjoyed playing with some of the greatest names in the sport at many of the world's most famous courses.

Jeff is a two-time *New York Times* #1 bestselling author in addition to a *USA Today* and *Publishers Weekly* bestselling author. Jeff's books have sold millions of copies worldwide, and he is a veteran of hundreds of radio and television interviews.

Coauthor of *Chicken Soup for the Golfer's Soul, Chicken Soup for the Father's Soul* and *Chicken Soup for the Golfer's Soul: The Second Round,* Jeff is no stranger to the *Chicken Soup* phenomenon. Jeff is married to Patty Aubery, coauthor of *Chicken Soup for the Christian Soul, Chicken Soup for the Christian Family Soul, Chicken Soup for the Surviving Soul* and *Chicken Soup for the Expectant Mother's Soul.*

The couple and their two sons, Jeffrey Terrance and Chandler Scott, make their home in Santa Barbara, California. Jeff is a dynamic and enthusiastic speaker and is available for personal appearances. He can be reached at:

Golf Sales West, Inc./Tornado Golf
2100 Eastman Ave., Suite A
Oxnard, CA 93030
phone: 800-GOLF-BAG
E-mail: *SoupStory@aol.com*

Who Are Mark and Chrissy Donnelly?

Avid golfers Mark and Chrissy Donnelly are a dynamic married couple working closely together as coauthors, marketers and speakers.

They are the coauthors of the #1 *New York Times* bestsellers *Chicken Soup for the Couple's Soul, Chicken Soup for the Golfer's Soul, Chicken Soup for the Sports Fan's Soul, Chicken Soup for the Father's Soul* and *Chicken Soup for the Baseball Fan's Soul.* They are also at work on several other upcoming books, among them *Chicken Soup for the Romantic Soul* and *Chicken Soup for the Friend's Soul.*

As cofounders of the Donnelly Marketing Group, they develop and implement innovative marketing and promotional strategies that help elevate and expand the *Chicken Soup for the Soul* message to millions of people around the world.

Mark was introduced to golf at the age of three. He remembers following his father to the golf course and finding a four-leaf clover that he believes enabled his father to win a prominent local amateur tournament. As a result of this and other golfing experiences with his father, Mark developed an appreciation for the game, along with a respectable golf game. Mark grew up in Portland, Oregon, and unbeknownst to him, attended the same high school as Chrissy. He went on to graduate from the University of Arizona, where he was president of his fraternity, Alpha Tau Omega. He served as vice president of marketing for his family's business, Contact Lumber, and after eleven years resigned from day-to-day responsibilities to focus on his current endeavors.

Chrissy, COO of the Donnelly Marketing Group, also grew up in Portland, Oregon, and graduated from Portland State University. As a CPA, she embarked on a six-year career with Price Waterhouse.

Mark and Chrissy enjoy many hobbies together, including golf, hiking, skiing, traveling, hip-hop aerobics and spending time with friends. Mark and Chrissy live in Paradise Valley, Arizona, and can be reached at:

Donnelly Marketing Group, LLC
2425 E. Camelback Road, Suite 515
Phoenix, AZ 85016
phone: 602-508-8956 fax: 602-508-8912
E-mail: *chickensoup@cox.net*

What Is Golf Digest?

Golf Digest is America's oldest and most widely read golf monthly with a circulation of 1.55 million and six million readers. Since 1950, *Golf Digest* has advised golfers on how to play, what to play and where to play. It has won every major golf-writing award and twice in the last decade has been named finalist in the prestigious National Magazine Awards.

Its contributing editors include the best writers and teachers in the country, including writers Dan Jenkins, Dave Kindred, Nick Seitz and Tom Callahan and teachers David Leadbetter, Jack Lumkin, Hank Haney, Butch Harmon and Jim McLean, among many others. *Golf Digest* Schools, which serve as a laboratory to the magazine's highly respected instruction content, are recognized as the leading golf schools in the country. *Golf Digest* has twenty-five affiliated publications around the world, offering the magazine's editorial content to some one million golfers in more than fifty-one countries in fifteen languages.

Golf Digest assisted *Chicken Soup for the Golfer's Soul* in the solicitation and the selection of stories and cartoons for this book. Several of the stories will be excerpted in the magazine and its writers are well represented in these pages.

Contributors

Several of the stories in this book were taken from previously published sources, such as books, magazines and
newspapers. These sources are acknowledged in the permissions section. If you would like to contact any of the
contributors for information about their writing, or would
like to invite them to speak in your community, look for
their contact information included in their biography.
The remainder of the stories were submitted by readers of our previous *Chicken Soup for the Soul* books who
responded to our requests for stories. We have also
included information about them.

Ken Abraham is the author of over forty books, including collaborations with
professional golfer Paul Azinger on *Zinger!* as well as baseball All-Star catcher
Gary Carter on *The Gamer*. Abraham currently resides in Franklin, Tennessee.

Matt Adams is a veteran of the golf industry and a regular contributor to business reports on The Golf Channel. Matt is also a writer and coauthor of *Chicken
Soup for the Soul of America*. Matt can be reached at *mattadams422@aol.com*.

Ahmed Tharwat Abdelaal is married to a Minnesota native, Caren, who
teaches at the University of Minnesota. Together they came up with a lovely
daughter whose name is Sara. Ahmed runs a marketing consulting firm in the
Twin Cities that develops customer satisfaction programs for small business.
He has been teaching business and marketing at the University of St. Thomas
and abroad for the last twenty years. Another sidelight of his career is his
involvement in producing and hosting the only local Arab-American TV program in the Midwest as an alternative medium for the Arab-American community. This weekly TV program offers the audience a new perspective on
current events and a vehicle to strengthen the relationships among the many
cultures in the community.

Michael Arkush is an associate editor for *Golf World* magazine. He has also
worked for the *Los Angeles Times* and *People* magazine. Arkush has written three
books: *Rush!*, a *New York Times* bestselling biography of Rush Limbaugh; *Tim
Allen Laid Bare*; and *60 Years of USC-UCLA Football*, cowritten with Steve
Springer. Arkush lives in Connecticut with his wife, actress Pauletta Walsh,
and daughter Jade.

Paul Azinger won his first professional golf tournament in Phoenix, Arizona, in
1987. An eleven-time PGA Tournament winner, he was the 1993 PGA

Champion and cocaptain of the U.S. golf team's entry for the 1994 President's Cup. He lives in Bradenton, Florida, with his wife, Toni, and two daughters.

Aaron Bacall has worked as a research chemist, college instructor and teacher. All the while he created cartoons on a freelance basis in the evenings and out they went to magazines. As sales started to come in he built up his business, adding advertising and illustration work. He is a full-time cartoonist now, specializing in magazine cartoons, spot art and advertising illustration. His work has appeared in *The New Yorker, Barron's, Reader's Digest, Wall Street Journal* and corporate projects. A book of his cartoons will be published in 2002. He can be reached at *abacall@msn.com.*

Dave Barry is a humor columnist for the *Miami Herald.* His column appears in more than five hundred newspapers in the United States and abroad. In 1988 he won the Pulitzer Prize for commentary. Many people are still trying to figure out how this happened. Dave lives in Miami, Florida, with his wife, Michelle, a sportswriter. He has a son, Rob, and a daughter, Sophie, neither of whom thinks he's funny.

Dan Bickely is currently a sports columnist for *The Arizona Republic* and is the author of *No Bull: The Unauthorized Biography of Dennis Rodman.* He was a syndicated columnist for the Copley News Service from 1997 to 98 and worked at the *Chicago Sun-Times* from 1987 to 1997.

Ann Birmingham, the mother of three children, resides in her hometown of Bangor, Maine. Ann is a full-time student pursuing her bachelor of arts degree in business administration at Husson College. She enjoys making wooden crafts and hopes to open a small shop in the near future. Please reach her at *craftsbyME@aol.com.*

Alan Broderick is a freelance writer living in Alberton, Prince Edward Island, Canada. His story originally appeared in *Golf Journal,* a publication of the United States Golf Association. Proceeds from the reprinting of this story will be donated to the USGA Foundation.

Andy Brumer is a freelance writer who writes on golf, art, literature and other subjects. He is a published poet and a 2-handicap golfer. Andy holds a bachelor of arts degree in English literature from the University of Wisconsin-Madison and a masters degree from San Francisco State University, where he studied creative writing. He lives in the Los Angeles area. Please reach him at: *abrumer@aol.com.*

Bob Brust, a native of Montana, worked as an engineer for Chevron U.S.A. for thirty-two years. After retiring, he pursued two of his greatest passions, writing and golf. His works have appeared in *Golf Journal, Chicken Soup for the Golfer's Soul,* several magazines and periodicals. He has also authored two books, *Idaho in June* and *I Thought I Heard a Rooster Crow.* The latter is about his life and his family on a ranch in Montana and is in the process of being published. Bob passed away in June 1999. Further information concerning his writing is available from Harriett Brust, *hebrust@iowatelecom.net.*

Jack Cavanaugh covers sports and writes feature stories for the *New York Times.* He has also written for *Sports Illustrated, Reader's Digest* and a number of other national magazines. Cavanaugh is also an adjunct writing professor at Fairfield and Quinnipiac Universities in Connecticut. He has contributed several previous stories for *Chicken Soup for the Soul* books. He is also the author of *Damn the Disabilities: Full Speed Ahead!,* which recounts the stories of athletes who have overcome handicaps to excel in sports. He lives in Wilton, Connecticut.

Reid Champagne has been playing golf with no noticeable improvement for over forty years. He not only believes in gadgetry, but also magic, sorcery, incantations, smoke, mirrors and a rare Asian ointment as the ultimate solutions to his swing problems. Reach him at *reid4bar@aol.com.*

Mike Corcoran is a writer and former editor of *Golf Illustrated* based in Pennsylvania. His story originally appeared in *Golf Journal,* a publication of the United States Golf Association. Proceeds from the reprinting of this story will be donated to the USGA Foundation.

Gary D'Amato is an award-winning sportswriter for the *Milwaukee Journal Sentinel.* He has written two books—*Mudbaths and Bloodbaths: The Inside Story of the Bears-Packers Rivalry* and *The Packer Tapes: My 32 Years with the Green Bay Packers*—with Domenic Gentile. D'Amato's work has also appeared in *Chicken Soup for the Golfer's Soul* and *Chicken Soup for the Sports Fan's Soul.* Contact him at *gdamato@onwis.com.*

Paula DiPerna is a freelance writer based in Chicago. Her story originally appeared in *Golf Journal,* a publication of the United States Golf Association. Proceeds from the reprinting of this story will be donated to the USGA Foundation.

James Dodson is an award-winning golf writer and author of the bestselling book *Final Rounds.* James always felt closest to his father while they were on the links. So it seemed only appropriate when his father learned he had two months to live that they would set off on the golf journey of their dreams to play the most famous courses in the world. *Final Rounds* is a book never to be forgotten, a book about fathers and sons, long-held secrets, and the lessons a middle-age man can still learn from his dad about life, love and family.

Darlene Daniels Eisenhuth lives in rural South Newfane, Vermont, with her husband and their two teenage sons. She is a firm believer that the finer things in life are the simple ones. Most of her inspirations for her writing come from her family and their experiences together.

Jolee Edmondson writes about golf and many other subjects for national magazines. She is the only woman ever to have won a first-place award from the Golf Writers Association of America. A resident of Savannah, Georgia, she can be reached at *wordworx1@aol.com.*

Leonard Finkel, together with artist Gary Max Collins, produced *The Secrets to the Game of Golf & Life*. He is a freelance writer and regular contributor to *Orlando Golflife* and *Atlanta Golflife* and writes for and appears on the TV show *Links Illustrated*. Licensed products are being developed featuring the art and themes of the book. Information on books and products may be obtained from Leonard at 888-355-5179 or 800-621-1423, ext. 5631. Visit the Web site at *www.golfandlife.com*.

Deisy Flood is originally from Cuba. She is married and has a son. She has contributed to *Golf Journal*. She resides in Lakeland, Florida, with her three dogs and owns a business. She loves golf, reading and writing. She is sorry her father didn't live to see her work, although not exactly professional, published. She can be reached at: *deisy_f@hotmail.com*.

Dan Galbraith is a forty-second-time state and forty-second-time national award-winner in sports journalism. The sports editor for *The Holton Recorder* and *The Sabetha Herald* newspapers, his first book *Sports Column Writing Is Life* is expected soon at bookstores. His e-mail address is *baberuthfan@hotmail.com*.

Rhonda Glenn, a freelance writer living in Atlantis, Florida, is the author of *The Illustrated History of Women's Golf* and a contributor to *The Junior Golf Book* and *Golf for Women*. Her story originally appeared in *Golf Journal*, a publication of the United States Golf Association. Proceeds from the reprinting of this story will be donated to the USGA Foundation.

Ellen Goodman has been with the *Boston Globe*, where she is an associate editor as well as a columnist, since 1967. In 1980, she won the Pulitzer Prize for distinguished commentary. Her book on social change, *Turning Points*, was published in 1979. Five collections of her columns have also been published. *Close to Home, At Large, Keeping in Touch, Making Sense* and *Value Judgments*. Born in 1941, she lives with her husband in Brookline.

Melanie Hauser serves as Secretary-Treasurer of the Golf Writers Association of America based in Houston. Her story originally appeared in *Golf Journal*, a publication of the United States Golf Association. Proceeds from the reprinting of this story will be donated to the USGA Foundation.

Johnny Hawkins's cartoons have appeared in over 250 publications, including *Reader's Digest, Woman's World, Barron's, Saturday Evening Post* and many others. His nationally syndicated comic, "Hi and Jinx," runs in newspapers around the country. He can be reached at P.O. Box 188, Sherwood, MI 49089, (616) 432-8071 or at *cartoonist@anthill.com*.

Bob Hope is an avid golfer and is one of the foremost proponents of the game and has contributed immensely to the popularity of golf as a participant, a spectator and as an author. His book, *Confessions of a Hooker*, spotlights the memorable moments of his more than fifty years of golfing. Probably his greatest achievement in golf is the development and hosting of the Bob Hope/Chrysler Desert Classic, a pro-am tournament held annually in Palm

Springs, California. Now in its forty-second year, the Classic draws the most famous pros and celebrity amateurs. A total charity effort, the Classic has raised over 35 million dollars for the Eisenhower Medical Center and seventy other deserving desert charities.

John L. Hulteng (April 1, 1921 to March 9, 1996). In his twenty-two years with the School of Journalism at the University of Oregon (1955 to 1977), he achieved a reputation as a superb teacher, a nationally known author and able administrator. He was twice dean and a devoted citizen of the university.

Bob Hurt, a sportswriter for more than a half century, served as lead sports columnist on the leading newspapers in Topeka, Kansas, Oklahoma City and Phoenix. He is the author of a recently published book, *Return of the Football Fossils.*

Dan Jenkins, *Golf Digest* writer-at-large, is the author of seventeen novels and works of nonfiction, including two classic golf books, *The Dogged Victims of Inexorable Fate* and *Dead Solid Perfect.* He lives in his hometown of Fort Worth, Texas.

Bil Keane created "The Family Circus," based on his own family, in 1960. It now appears in well over 1,500 newspapers and is read daily by 188 million people. The award-winning feature is the most widely spread syndicated cartoon in America. Check out The Family Circus website: *www.familycircus.com.*

Dave Kindred has eaten breakfast with Julie Krone, lunch with Muhammad Ali and dinner with Robert Redford. Between meals, he has written six thousand columns and six books. The 1997 National Sportswriter of the Year, he is a winner of sport's journalism's highest prize, the Red Smith Award. He lives in Virginia with his wife, Cheryl.

Jim King received his bachelor of science from Purdue University. He currently works in the information technology field. Although he aspires to do more golfing and writing, most of his time is spent with wife Peg and their children, Tyler, Sydney, Ryleigh and Mykaela. He can be reached at *jimking_x4@yahoo.com.*

Michael Konik is well-known to frequent fliers as the west coast editor of Delta Air Lines' *Sky* magazine, where his monthly column "Tee Time" has been honored by the Golf Writers Association of America. Michael is also the gambling columnist for *Cigar Aficionado* and has been published in over 100 magazines and newspapers. He is the author of *The Man with $100,000 Breasts and Other Gambling Stories* (Huntington Press). Currently, he is working on his next book, *Good Shot, Mr. Nicklaus: Stories About the Game of Golf.*

Robert Lalonde retired from sales at the end of October 1999 and has spent most of his time traveling and playing golf. The adjustment came very easily and what little spare time he has left he enjoys visiting his two boys, Brendon in Toronto and Jeffrey in Montreal. "An author I am not and will never be, but playing a bit of golf with the guys in this story is very entertaining and adds a little laughter to my life."

Avid golfer **Henry Lawrence** is a freelance writer living in Davidson, North Carolina. Proceeds from the reprinting of this article will be donated to the USGA Foundation.

Dr. Jerry P. Lightner served eighteen years as executive director of the National Association of Biology Teachers followed by sixteen years as senior consultant with Xerox Corporation. Author of several books, his most recent is *I Remember Jack*, a biography of his fighter pilot brother killed in the Korean War. He now resides in Spain and the United States.

Kyle MacLachlan is currently guest starring on HBO's "Sex and the City" as Trey, Charlotte's (Kristin Davis) husband. He is perhaps best known for his performance in David Lynch's 1986 hit "Blue Velvet" and for his starring role as FBI Agent Dale Cooper in Lynch's television series "Twin Peaks," for which MacLachlan received two Emmy nominations and a Golden Globe Award.

Del Madzay teaches art at Centerburg High School. He runs a mini-golf and driving range in the summer. He collects antique golf memorabilia, photographs it and sells state-of-the-art golf prints, 22x28 available for purchase @ $5.00 each. (View at E-bay store, Sycamore golf prints). 740 393-0017. E-mail him at *sycamoregolf@axom.com*.

Marci Martin has been published in magazines and newspapers, winning many awards. Published books: *Go to Hell and Make A U-Turn, Muse on My Shoulder*, two series mysteries. *Secrets and Lies* and *License to Steal*. Her fourth mystery is a work in progress. She is coordinator for Arizona Mystery Writers.

Kate Meyers is a freelance writer whose work has appeared in *Entertainment Weekly, T & L Golf, Links, Fortune* and *Sports Illustrated Women*. She lives in Colorado with her husband and two daughters.

E. J. Montini has been asking annoying questions since his days at St. Titus Roman Catholic grade school outside of Pittsburgh, Pennsylvania, where the sisters of St. Joseph declared him a hopeless sinner whose persistent inquiries caused his guardian angel to weep constantly and who therefore would do little in life but disrupt the natural order of things. Naturally, the nuns were correct. Montini was born on Thanksgiving Day, 1954, the fortieth birthday of the great Joe DiMaggio. He grew up in the same steel town as Mike Ditka and Henry Mancini. After graduating from Penn State, he worked for newspapers in the East before going to *The Arizona Republic* in 1980. He saw the Doors perform when he was thirteen years old and when not quite six was taken by his mother to a speech by John F. Kennedy. He remembers that Kennedy's microphone didn't work correctly, and it didn't bother his mother a bit. Montini is married and the father of two children. From the moment they could talk, the children have been asking annoying questions. This pleases him very much.

More of . . . The Best of Bits & Pieces is a monthly publication that has been motivating people for more than thirty years. Every issue is filled with inspiration and insights to help readers reach beyond the stress of daily life and improve any situation. Visit *www.ragan.com* to see a sample copy or call 800-878-5331.

Bruce Nash of Studio City, California, produces reality-based television shows for the major networks.

J. G. Nursall is a forty-nine-year-old attorney/teacher living and working in Southern California. Formerly an avid golfer, he writes to relax and to record some of the valuable lessons he learned while playing the game. Mr. Nursall anticipates publishing a collection of short stories in the near future and invites your further inquiry. Please contact him at: *JGNursall@yahoo.com.*

Hugh O'Neill has been writing and performing commentary on fatherhood for several years, including work for National Public Radio's *Morning Edition.* He is the author of *Daddy Cool* and *Here's Looking at You, Kids.* He has also written for several magazines as well as for television's *The Cosby Show, Thirtysomething* and *Sisters.* He lives in Princeton, New Jersey.

Dennis Oricchio is a member of the United States Professional Tennis Association and is a full-time tennis teaching professional for twenty-five years.

David Owen is a contributing editor of *Golf Digest* and a staff writer for *The New Yorker.* His books about golf are *My Usual Game, Lure of the Links* and *The Making of the Masters.* Contact him at *david.owen@sent.net.*

Rod Patterson has worked at *The Oregonian* for thirty years, covering news and features and is presently a features copyeditor. He was raised in Hawaii, graduated from Portland State University with a degree in English literature.

Bill Pelham played on the PGA Tour from 1976 to 1980. Today, he owns a golf marketing company, specializing in promoting corporate golf events nationwide. He can be reached at Doubleagle, 8702 Stone Village Ln., Houston, TX 77040, or by phone at 713-937-3866.

Mike Pennella is a runner, freelance writer and very occasional golfer residing in Maplewood, New Jersey. This story first appeared in *Golf Journal,* a magazine of the United States Golf Association. Proceeds from the reprinting of this story will be donated to the USGA Foundation.

George Peper is the editor-in-chief of *Golf* magazine. He is the author of a dozen books on golf, and his script for the PBS documentary *The Story of Golf* was nominated for an Emmy. His story was the impetus for his current book *Playing Partners,* about golf with his son, which will be published by Warner Books for Father's Day in 2003.

Carol McAdoo Rehme, a frequent contributor to *Chicken Soup for the Soul* and other inspirational books, is a full-time storyteller, speaker and author. Her latest passion is a pilot program, "Silver Linings for Golden Agers." It is the recipient of several grants and provides highly interactive, multisensory presentations at eldercare facilities. Contact her at: *carol@rehme.com* or *www.rehme.com*.

Rick Reilly has been named Sportswriter of the Year seven times, including for the year 2001. He is the first signed weekly columnist in *Sports Illustrated*'s forty-eight-year history. He lives in Denver with his wife, three kids, rabbit, birds, eel and too many fish. His 6-handicap keeps him from concentrating on anything very important.

Bob Robinson a 1956 graduate of the University of Oregon, retired in 1999 after thirty-seven-and-a-half years as a sportswriter at *The Oregonian* in Portland, Oregon. He continues to do freelance writing, mostly on golf. He was named Oregon's Sportswriter of the Year in 1977 after covering the Portland Trail Blazers in their NBA championship season.

Steve Schokett's story originally appeared in *Golf Journal*, a publication of the United States Golf Association. Proceeds from the reprinting of this story will be donated to the USGA Foundation.

Bruce Selcraig, an Austin-based journalist, is a former U.S. Senate investigator and *Sports Illustrated* staff writer whose work has appeared in the *New York Times Magazine, Harper's* and *Sierra*, among others. He writes on topics as varied as corporate crime and baseball gloves, worships Irish golf and New Mexican food, and can be reached at *selcraig@swbell.net*.

Bob Shyrock has been a newspaper columnist for fifty-two years, writing about ten thousand columns, some of them golf humor. He also works for Pitman Golf Course as assistant manager/starter, and has been director of numerous golf tournaments, including the Gloucester County (New Jersey) Amateur for twenty years. A lefthander, he is a frustrated 14-handicapper.

John Spielbergs was born and raised in Toronto, Ontario. He currently is a custom homebuilder in Muskoka, a tourist area north of Toronto. He lives with his wife and two daughters and, in addition to golf, likes to play hockey. His story was written as a way of coming to terms with the loss of a life-long friend.

John St. Augustine is the creator/host of Power!Talk Radio and the author of "All Are Chosen." He also speaks to public and private groups on the essentials of success and opportunity through adversity. You can find out more about Power!Talk Radio and John's speaking availability at *www.powertalkradio.com* or call (906) 233-TALK (8255).

Payne Stewart was at the top of his game on every level when his life came to a sudden and tragic end on October 25, 1999. In June of 1999, he enjoyed the signature triumph of his career and solidified himself as one of the exemplary personalities in his profession with a victory at the U.S. Open and a place on the coveted winning U.S. Ryder Cup team. However, satisfying his professional accomplishments were, it was his personal triumphs that made him stand out.

Tracey Stewart was born in Queensland, Australia, where she also attended school. She met Payne Stewart in March 1980 during the Malaysian Open, in a meeting she describes as love at first sight. After romancing each other around the world, Payne and Tracey were engaged one year later in Singapore and married November 10, 1981, in Southport, on Australia's Gold Coast. As Payne's PGA career took off, the Stewarts moved to Orlando, Florida, where Tracey lives with their two children, Chelsea and Aaron.

Kay B. Tucker counts on her family and friends for inspiration for anecdotes and stories. She has been published in *Writer's Digest, Reader's Digest, Catholic Digest* and several upstate New York publications. Her e-mail is *Kaytuckerb@aol.com.*

Don Wade is a columnist and feature writer for the *Memphis Commercial Appeal.* His work has been published on *ESPN.com* and in many newspapers across the country. Don and his wife Deb have three sons: Stephen, Matthew and Jonathon. You can reach Don at *dwadeinMemmphis@aol.com.*

Bob Welch is a columnist at *The Register-Guard* newspaper in Eugene, Oregon, and author of six books, including *The Things That Matter Most* and the Gold Medallion award-winning *A Father for All Seasons.* He can be contacted at *bwelch1@concentric.net.*

Gordon Wells is a freelance writer based in St. Louis, Missouri. His story originally appeared in *Golf Journal,* a publication of the United States Golf Association. Proceeds from the reprinting of this story will be donated to the USGA Foundation.

Bob West has been sports editor of the *Port Arthur* (Texas) *News* since 1972. A single-digit handicapper, West is a past president of the Texas Golf Writers Association. His most memorable golfing experience was playing Cypress Point for the first time. He can be reached at *rdwest@usa.net.*

Ernie Witham writes a humor column called "Ernie's World" for the *Montecito Journal* in Montecito, California. His humor has also been published in the *Los Angeles Times,* the *Santa Barbara News-Press* and five *Chicken Soup* analogies. You can read his column at *www.ernieswebsite.com.* He is available to lead humor workshops for any age group and can be reached at *ernie@ernieswebsite.com.*

Ben Wright broadcast golf and other sports for CBS-TV for twenty-three years.

Allan Zullo of Fairview, North Carolina, has written over seventy nonfiction books on a variety of subjects.

Snakes Alive! Reprinted by permission of *Golf Journal.* From *Golf Journal* issue October, 1991.

More Trash Talk than the NBA. Reprinted by permission of Dan Galbraith. ©1995 Dan Galbraith.

Your Cheatin' Heart. Reprinted by permission of Golf Journal. From *Golf Journal* issue September, 1998.

Check Your Bag! Reprinted by permission of Robert Lalonde. ©2001 Robert Lalonde.

Play it As it Lays. The Boston Globe, Issue October 8, 1998 by Ellen Goodman. ©1998 by *The Boston Globe.* Reprinted by permission of *The Boston Globe* via the Copyright Clearance Center.

The Best Golfer Tantrum of All Time. The Oregonian ©1981, Oregonian Publishing Co. All rights reserved. Reprinted with permission.

Character Building. Reprinted by permission of James M. King. ©2000 James M. King.

Perfect Stroke—for the Car? Reprinted by permission of Marci Martin. ©1998 Marci Martin.

Old Jake's Shrewdest Trick. Reprinted with permission of Dan Jenkins. ©1999 Dan Jenkins. Appeared in *Golf Digest,* August 1999.

The Accidental Purist: Diary of a Beginning Golf Junkie. Reprinted by permission of Kate K. Meyers. ©2001 Kate K. Meyers.

Remembering My Father. From *Fairways and Dreams,* ©1998 by Michael Arkush and published by Rutledge Hill Press, Nashville, Tennessee.

Fear of the Father-Son Tournament. Reprinted by permission of *Golf Journal.* From *Golf Journal* issue June, 2000.

Corky's Wedge. Reprinted by permission of *Golf Journal.* From *Golf Journal* issue June, 1996.

A Matter of Course. Reprinted by permission of Carol McAdoo Rehme. ©1999 Carol McAdoo Rehme.

The Miracle Ball. Reprinted by permission of Bob West. ©2001 Bob West.

I Was in My Wife's Gallery. Reprinted by permission of *The Providence Journal*

The Y2K Crisis. Reprinted by permission of George Peper. ©1999 George Peper. Appeared in *Golf Magazine,* March 1999.

A Little Slice of Heaven. Reprinted by permission of *Golf Journal.* From *Golf Journal* issue October, 2000.

Charging Back. Taken from ZINGER by Paul Azinger and Ken Abraham. ©1995 by Paul Azinger. Used by permission of Zondervan.

The Luckiest Golfer Alive. Reprinted by permission of Robert B. Hurt. ©1999 Robert B. Hurt.

The Power of Charity Golf. Reprinted with permission from *Golf Digest®*, August 2001. ©2001 The Golf Digest Companies, which is a subsidiary of Advance Magazine Publishers, Inc. All Rights Reserved. *Golf Digest* is a Registered Trademark of The Golf Digest Companies, which is a subsidiary of Advance Magazine Publishers, Inc.

A Profile in Courage. Reprinted with permission from *Golf World®*, July 2001. ©2001 The Golf World Companies, which is a subsidiary of Advance Magazine Publishers, Inc. All Rights Reserved. *Golf World* is a Registered Trademark of The Golf World Companies, which is a subsidiary of Advance Magazine Publishers, Inc.

Making Contact. Reprinted by permission of Jack Cavanaugh. ©2001 Jack Cavanaugh.

A Thoughtful Gift. Reprinted by permission of Kay B. Tucker. ©1988 Kay B. Tucker.

A Childhood Memory Strikes a Chord. Reprinted by permission of Andy Brumer. ©1995 Andy Brumer.

Laboring to Fulfill a Dream. Reprinted with permission from *Golf Digest®*, July 2001. The Golf Digest Companies, which is a subsidiary of Advance Magazine Publishers, Inc. All Rights Reserved. *Golf Digest* is a Registered Trademark of The Golf Digest Companies, which is a subsidiary of Advance Magazine Publishers, Inc.

Start of a Love-Hate Relationship. Excerpted from *The Arizona Republic,* August 8, 1999 by Dan Bickley. Reprinted by permission of *The Arizona Republic.* ©1999 *The Arizona Republic.*

The Thrill of the Hunt. Reprinted by permission of *Golf Journal.* From *Golf Journal* issue January/February, 2002.

Fore! From DAVE BARRY IS NOT TAKING THIS SITTING DOWN by Dave Barry. ©2000 by Dave Barry. Used by permission of Crown Publishers, a division of Random House, Inc.

Thank God I Have a Day Job. Reprinted by permission of Kyle MacLachlan ©2002 Kyle MacLachlan.

Thursday Is Men's Day. Reprinted with permission of Dan Jenkins. ©2000 Dan Jenkins. Appeared in *Golf Digest,* July 2000.

Also Available

Chicken Soup for the Baseball Fan's Soul
Chicken Soup for the Canadian Soul
Chicken Soup for the Cat & Dog Lover's Soul
Chicken Soup for the Christian Family Soul
Chicken Soup for the Christian Soul
Chicken Soup for the Christian Woman's Soul
Chicken Soup for the College Soul
Chicken Soup for the Country Soul
Chicken Soup for the Couple's Soul
Chicken Soup for the Expectant Mother's Soul
Chicken Soup for the Father's Soul
Chicken Soup for the Gardener's Soul
Chicken Soup for the Golden Soul
Chicken Soup for the Golfer's Soul, Vol. I, II
Chicken Soup for the Grandparent's Soul
Chicken Soup for the Jewish Soul
Chicken Soup for the Kid's Soul
Chicken Soup for the Little Souls
Chicken Soup for the Mother's Soul, Vol. I, II
Chicken Soup for the Nurse's Soul
Chicken Soup for the Parent's Soul
Chicken Soup for the Pet Lover's Soul
Chicken Soup for the Preteen Soul
Chicken Soup for the Prisoner's Soul
Chicken Soup for the Single's Soul
Chicken Soup for the Sister's Soul
Chicken Soup for the Soul, Vol. I-VI
Chicken Soup for the Soul at Work
Chicken Soup for the Soul of America
Chicken Soup for the Soul Christmas Treasury, hardcover only
Chicken Soup for the Soul Christmas Treasury for Kids, hardcover only
Chicken Soup for the Soul Cookbook
Chicken Soup for the Soul Personal Journal
Chicken Soup for the Sports Fan's Soul
Chicken Soup for the Surviving Soul
Chicken Soup for the Teacher's Soul
Chicken Soup for the Teenage Soul, Vol. I, II, III
Chicken Soup for the Teenage Soul Journal
Chicken Soup for the Teenage Soul Letters
Chicken Soup for the Teenage Soul on Love & Friendship
Chicken Soup for the Teenage Soul on Tough Stuff
Chicken Soup for the Traveler's Soul
Chicken Soup for the Unsinkable Soul
Chicken Soup for the Veteran's Soul
Chicken Soup for the Volunteer's Soul
Chicken Soup for the Woman's Soul, Vol. I, II
Chicken Soup for the Writer's Soul
Condensed Chicken Soup for the Soul
Cup of Chicken Soup for the Soul

Selected titles available in Spanish, hardcover and audio format.

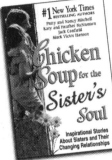